"Dave Jensen knows leadership — what it is a
everything every written on the topic, distil
relevant, coherent guidance. If you're new t
act, and feel like a leader. If you are a leader, captured in this book, providing practical tools not just for business, but for life. We live in an age that cries out for effective leadership. We'd all be better off if our 'leaders' steeped themselves in Dave Jensen's book."

MARK SIMON, *Executive Officer for Public Affairs, San Mateo County Transit District*

"After reading *The Executive's Paradox* and following Dave's approach, I now understand my leadership strengths and weaknesses. I also no longer guess what to do when I'm pulled in opposite directions by conflicting issues. Give yourself a decisive advantage by reading this book and you'll be making reasoned decisions that let you take advantage of contradictory demands—the same ones that used to cause chaos in your work world."

DAVID BRUFFY, *General Manager, Mountain Line Transit Authority*

"Eye-opening.... The possibilities of personal and professional growth are endless. Dave challenges individuals, teams, and organizations to achieve their strategic priorities using his highly researched and 'user friendly' EXPANSIVE LEADERSHIP MODEL™ (XLM). I am a much more effective executive because this book showed me how to apply the XLM to unleash the energy of my team toward our worthy goals."

LYNDA BARRY, *Vice President of Claims, AmTrust North America*

"Dave Jensen has combined his knowledge and experience as a leader with scientific data to provide a clear plan for current, as well as aspiring, executives to become more effective. He simplifies the otherwise overwhelming task of managing the tensions we all face on a daily basis."

ROBERT A. GUNNING, *Director (retired), Principal Financial Group*

"Much more than another 'how to' management book, this is the definitive executive handbook. I have profited personally and professionally from learning how to stretch when I'm torn by the competing goals of our diverse stakeholders. Jensen's ability to present compelling, scientific data in such a clear and entertaining manner will hook you from the start...just as it did me!"

JIM MONTGOMERY, *President, Diagnostic Specialties*

"I have benefited from Dave Jensen's leadership expertise for over twenty years. His latest book *The Executive's Paradox* is full of insights, applications, and real-life examples. Dave's recommendations are based on a thorough review of the empirical research on what predicts leadership success in today's environment. He is a relentless researcher and effective communicator. I highly recommend you get to know Dave and this groundbreaking book."

T. Jon Williams, *President, South Avenue Investment Partners*

"This book convinced me that anecdotes by business leaders do not predict business success. Dave Jensen showed me why only when we apply leadership skills that are grounded in both practice and research do we have the highest probability of reaching our goals. I've learned to celebrate my strong visionary and empowering leadership competencies while stretching to grow my 'developmental opportunities.' I now know how to stretch when I'm pulled by conflicting demands. When you read this book, you will too."

Jodi Walker, *President, Success Alliances*

"The principles delineated in this book have been essential to the growth of our medical group. Physicians, nurses, and administrators in leadership positions are all struggling to navigate the many contradictory demands in our chaotic environment. *The Executive's Paradox* provided evidence-based techniques that helped us manage the ambiguity and paradox inherent in our healthcare system. Instead of trying to solve unsolvable problems, we learned how to manage their tensions."

Michael Sullivan MD, *President, San Diego Hospital Based Physician Group*

"Put this book on your must-read list now! Don't make the mistake of thinking that this book is limited to the business sector. As an educational administrator I can tell you that this book has far-reaching implications for anyone, in any field, who is interested in expanding their leadership skills. This book takes you on an introspective journey that will continually challenge your thinking and force you to take a strategic look at how you can be transformed into someone who leads with passion, inspiration, and a strong ethical compass, without compromising the bottom line. This book is about building relationships that in turn will build capacity in whatever organization you're working for."

Dr. David J. Anderson, *Dean of Students, Maria Sanchez School*

THE EXECUTIVE'S PARADOX

How to **Stretch** When You're **Pulled** by Opposing Demands

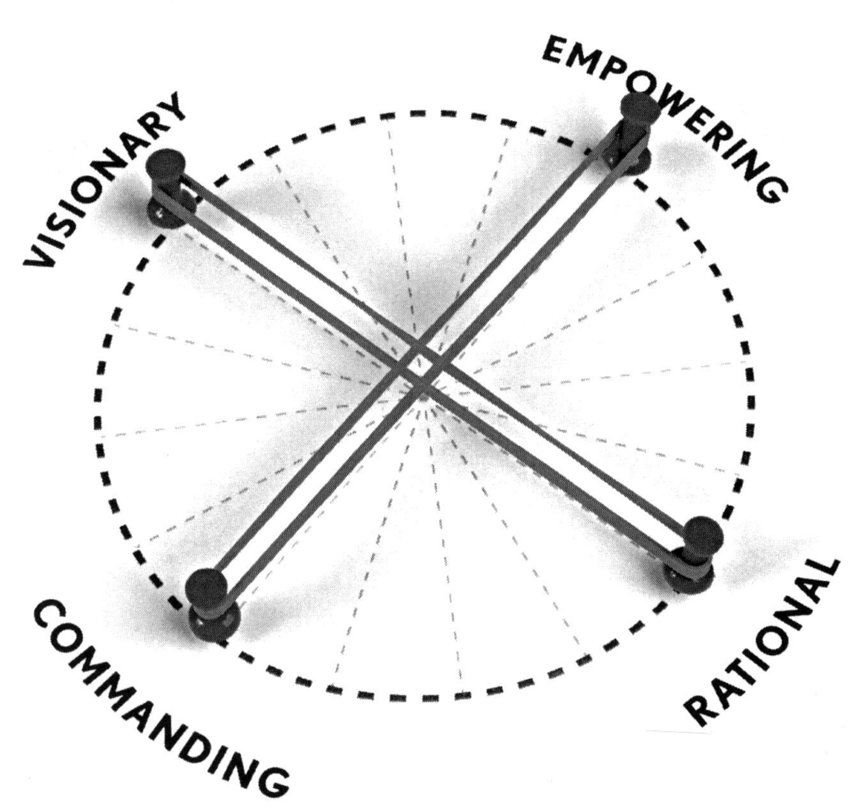

VISIONARY
EMPOWERING
COMMANDING
RATIONAL

THE EXECUTIVE'S PARADOX

How to **Stretch** When You're **Pulled** by Opposing Demands

Sherri,
Wishing you the very best in the coming year.

Dave

David G. Jensen

P.S. Keep stretching when you're pulled

WORLD
BUSINESS
PUBLISHING

This book is dedicated to...

Executives who are strong enough to doubt,
Leaders who are not deceived by what they believe,
And to all those who pursue what is true.

The Executive's Paradox
How to Stretch When You're Pulled by Opposing Demands
by David G. Jensen

World Business Publishing
3518 Barry Ave.
Los Angeles, CA 90066

Unattributed quotations are by David G. Jensen

Design & Text Composition by Steve Rachwal

Manufactured in the United States of America
Publishers Cataloging-in-Publication Data

Jensen, David.
The Executive's Paradox
How to Stretch When You're Pulled by Opposing Demands / David G. Jensen.
p. cm.
Includes bibliographical references and index .
1. Leadership 2. Management I. Title

Library of Congress Control Number: 2013949304

ISBN 978-0-9740577-1-2

Table of Contents

Section II

How Rational Executives Focus on the Task at Hand

Section III

How Visionary Executives Imagine the Future

Section IV

How Empowering Executives Take Care

Section V

How Commanding Executives Take Charge

Section VI

Use It, Don't Lose It—How to Apply What You Learn

Appendices

INTRODUCTION AND ACKNOWLEDGMENTS

A Leader's Journey

Life can only be understood backwards;
but it must be lived forwards.

Søren Kierkegaard

Leadership lessons at the Y

"Dave, we need to talk about your responsibilities around here."

It was Fred, addressing me shortly after he had replaced Bob as the youth director at our local YMCA.

"Okay—what should I be doing?" My teenage voice cracked as I rubbed my sweating palms.

"I know that Bob gave you a lot of responsibilities," Fred said. "I heard he even called you the assistant youth director. All that stops as of today—consider yourself demoted back to working the front desk."

I was stunned.

Two years earlier, Bob had hired me to work in the youth department. I worked hard for him and eagerly took on every new responsibility he tossed my way. By the time I turned 19, Bob had coached me to lead the YMCA's youth leadership program, junior high school teen center, and three extended camping trips.

Now, it seemed that my leadership responsibilities and opportunities for development at the Y had come to a crashing halt because Bob was gone and replaced by a lousy leader named Fred.

After a few weeks of wallowing in my own pity party, I met with Don, another director at the Y. Don arranged for me to escape Fred's drill-sergeant leadership style and work for him and his successor, Bill.

I'm forever grateful for the early mentoring from Bob, Don, and Bill. They nurtured my leadership development and inspired me to stretch beyond our local YMCA and college. Thanks to them, my leadership journey hadn't hit a dead-end—it merely took a detour. My journey continued in graduate school.

The question this book answers

My interest in research took root in the fertile soil of graduate school. At the University of Wisconsin, all our professors demanded a written review of the literature. They taught us that a quality review meant asking a great question and summarizing how the world's top scientists answered it. This book answers this question:

> *How can the latest leadership research help executives reach their goals when they're pulled by so many conflicting demands?*

I am deeply indebted to Professors Moss, Butts, Jones, and others for cultivating my passion to use the tools and rules of science to address this essential question. They were also instrumental in helping me integrate academic research with practical leadership experience.

The marriage of a researcher and leader

My passions for leadership and research were married when I interned at the University of California at San Diego after graduate school. This internship placed my early career in the caring hands of a world-renowned scientist, Dr. Victor Froelicher.

Dr. Froelicher molded my Wisconsin lessons into research experience by hiring me after the internship. My responsibilities included leading various research projects and supervising numerous students. I'm very grateful to Vic and my UC San Diego colleagues, including Eddie, Mike, Jon, Julie, Diane, and Martha. Their patience, counsel, and friendship were invaluable as I learned how to lead a team to collect, analyze, and publish research. Their support and guidance also paved the way for my next leadership adventure—this one in private industry.

The impact of executives

As our research projects neared completion, I decided that private industry might provide more financial security than academia. So, when the opportunity to work for global giant Siemens presented itself, I transitioned from my academic cocoon to the harsh realities of the competitive marketplace.

My exposure to leaders – the good, the bad, and the horrendous – allowed me to experience the enormous impact executives have on their teams. I learned that employees don't quit jobs—they quit bosses. A special thanks to all these leaders, especially Tom, John, Doug, Jerry, Jim, Debbie, and Jenny. Experiencing what works and what doesn't was the trampoline I needed to make the big leap to the executive suite.

An effective executive?

In the late 1980s, I was recruited from Siemens by Professor Michael Phelps, another world-renowned scientist. He'd been one of my customers at Siemens and needed a leader for an institute he was building at UCLA. Dr. Phelps wanted an executive with academic and industry experience. I took the job—and my executive education began.

My experience as an executive is one of the reasons this book targets executives — those individuals who lead managers. I wish I could claim that I was an effective executive, but leaders don't learn from experience unless they reflect on those experiences. I was successful in some areas, and less so in others. My scrape-the-knees lessons are now scattered throughout this book. I hope they cushion your fall. I'm thankful to my colleagues at UCLA (Mike, John, Saty, Jorge, Heines, Ed, Henry, Joyce, Debbie, and Wendy) for all they taught me.

I left UCLA in the mid-1990s because I fell in love... with teaching.

An effective executive educator!

Throughout my work at UC San Diego, Siemens, and UCLA, I continued to do what I first went to college to do: teach. Of course, teaching wasn't my primary responsibility in any of these positions, but it was a consistent theme in all of them. From presenting scientific studies at UCSD and national sales meetings at Siemens, to speaking at association and industry meetings while at UCLA, I kept finding myself sharing my research and experience with others.

When I realized that I loved teaching, I left UCLA and started my own leadership coaching/training business.

I'm not sure I would have survived the early bumps of my entrepreneurial journey without the leadership expertise and guidance from my friends at Quantum Leadership Solutions. Ahmed and Laurie introduced me to the extraordinary work of philosopher Peter Koestenbaum (and his Leadership Diamond) and Barry Johnson (and the concept of polarity management). These leaders molded my leadership experiences into executive teaching skills. It was under their tutelage that I realized "for this purpose I was born." I'm deeply indebted to them and all the executives with whom we worked (at Xerox, Boeing, PeaceHealth, Qualcomm, and elsewhere).

Working with Quantum Leadership Solutions also led me to university teaching appointments, including one with Emory University, where I was appointed senior lecturer in executive education for several years. Teaching with the extraordinary executive educators at Emory, especially Dennis, Peter, and Rick, was most illuminating. When I wasn't teaching with them, I was sitting in the back of the class learning from them. I'm very thankful for this privilege.

I'm also obliged to the thousands of executives I have taught and coached at Emory and at Rockhurst University (where I also had a teaching appointment) during the last two decades. I learned a great deal from those I taught, including the one who prompted me to write this book.

A prescription is a prediction

Rob marched into our five-day leadership class early. He sat in front and asked me a simple question with infectious enthusiasm as I was setting up my material in front of the room:

"Dave, what's your favorite book on leadership?"

I pointed out that there were a couple of good ones in the back of the room and mentioned a few others that were perhaps a bit too academic for most senior executives. Then I began class as I usually do—with a discussion of executive challenges and goals. As I scribbled yet another list of challenges on a flipchart, it dawned on me that I didn't really have a "favorite" leadership book, especially one that addressed top challenges.

In my hotel room that night, I decided that if I didn't have a favorite, I needed to write one.

Writing this book would have been easier had I chosen to write only about my lessons as an executive. Many leaders write leadership books about their experiences. Although their stories may be interesting, research and life have taught me that an author's personal success seldom translates into a reader's triumph. That's because each leader's genes, personality, upbringing, schooling, competencies, business environment, etc., are so unique that it's impossible to predict that one executive's experience can morph into another's success. You can read about Steve Jobs' leadership style, but science says you probably can't emulate it successfully.

In fact, research tells us that another leader's prescription could be your poison.

Imagine for a moment that your boss invites you into her office and asks you to find a great book on leadership. She tells you that she is going to use ideas from the book during an upcoming executive retreat that will focus on "leading by conquering today's leadership challenges." She explains that just as a physician must find the best treatment to cure a critically ill patient, you need to find the best resource to help her executives.

Back in your office, a quick Google search of the word "leadership" yields 502 million results in 0.18 seconds. You narrow your search in the book section of Amazon and find 84,289 results. Yikes! How would you decide which book to recommend to your boss? What criteria should you use to select a great leadership book?

If you reflect on your boss's medical analogy, it might be useful to ask, How do physicians decide which treatment is best?

The best physicians combine their experience with a heavy dose of evidence—what science says really works. Why?

Because the essence of science is *prediction.*

When physicians write prescriptions, they are predicting the patient will *probably* improve. The best physicians base their predictions on research filtered by their experiences.

Similarly, leadership authors are really saying that if you follow their prescriptions, they predict you *probably* will achieve a desired outcome. Unfortunately, they usually base their predictions only on their experiences—seldom on the research. If they needed to prove their case in a court of law, the judge would throw it out for lack of evidence.

Spending your limited resources on ideas grounded in one leader's perspective is like going to a doctor who prescribes medications that have only been used on himself.

I've tried to make the best use of your investment in this book by combining my analysis of thousands of leadership studies with the practical lessons I've learned as an executive, educator, and coach. You will learn only those ideas studied under a microscope of science *and* confirmed in the corridors of organizations.

If you follow the prescription described in this book, the evidence predicts that there is a high probability you will achieve your leadership outcomes.

How to use this book to improve your leadership

As a busy executive with numerous competing demands, you may find it tempting to complete the 360-leadership assessment discussed in Chapter 3 (and available online) and dive into the chapter that discusses the competency you want to improve. At its core, the book follows a consistent structure that makes it easy to use as a reference for enhancing your weaker competencies. Chapters 5 through 20 explain the 16 competencies needed to conquer today's challenges and achieve difficult goals. In each case, the chapter title indicates the topic or challenge, while the first subtitle of each of these chapters identifies the specific competency discussed.

However, because this book is a synthesis of the world's best thinking on executive leadership, and because the science says that all 16 of the core competencies are important, it's worth reading straight through. After you've read the book in its entirety, I encourage you to share your insights with your team and then use the book as a reference.

You may also find the Appendices useful in helping you apply what you learn. Appendix A discusses how to employ several competencies to interview and hire top talent. Appendix B reviews how to utilize other competencies to counsel underperformers. Appendix C substantiates the use of THE EXPANSIVE LEADERSHIP MODEL (XLM) for executive development by reporting what we discovered in our study of 77 transit executives, who were rated by 376 leaders on all 16 competencies and their overall leadership effectiveness.

Our journey begins, much like my executive classes, by discussing today's leadership challenges in Chapter 1.

Speaking of journeys, one last word of thanks to my family and friends, especially my wife Irene, who has been on this leadership trip with me for a long time. She has put up with my endless conversations about leadership and countless hours writing about it. I'm very thankful for all her love and support.

There are in fact two things, science and opinion;
the former begets knowledge, the latter ignorance.

Hippocrates

Section I

Why Executives Need to Stretch When They're Pulled

CHAPTER 1

The Executive's Paradox

The most difficult challenges facing leaders... present themselves as dilemmas, paradoxes, or tensions.

PATRICK DUIGNAN[1]

PULLED BY OPPOSING DEMANDS

"When I find a short seller, I want to tear his heart out and eat it before his eyes while he's still alive."[2] That's Dick Fuld, the high-commanding former CEO of the now-defunct Lehman Brothers (founded in 1850). Before the Great Recession, Madelyn Antoncic, chief risk officer at Lehman Brothers, issued a warning at a banking conference in Geneva about the "sense of complacency" regarding risk. Less than two months later, the bull-in-the-china-shop Fuld gored his own well-respected risk officer.

Fuld sacked Antoncic because he was unable or unwilling to stretch when pulled by two distinct paradoxes—one leadership and the other strategic. Instead of managing the tension between his commanding leadership style (take-charge drill sergeant) *and* his empowering style (take-care servant leader), his drill sergeant always won the tug-of-war with his servant leader (as Fuld's comment illustrates). In addition to snapping when he felt pulled by opposing leadership styles, Fuld also failed to manage a strategic paradox—the one most responsible for the Great Recession: increasing profits *and* mitigating risk.

Fuld is not the great exception in mismanaging the profit and risk paradox; he's the great example. In its special report on financial risk, *The Economist* concluded that the bankers who suffered the most during the Great Recession managed this tension most poorly.[3] Because bad loans were at the heart of the greatest financial disaster since the Great Depression, it's reasonable to conclude that millions of people suffered the loss of trillions of dollars because leaders (bankers, politicians, and borrowers) failed to stretch when pulled in opposite directions by profit *and* risk.

Of course, Wall Street is not the only place where leaders fail to manage opposing demands well. The negative consequences of mismanaging paradoxes pile up like trash on streets across the globe.

Consider Toyota, long the high-flyer in the auto industry, which crashed and lost $2.5 billion more than General Motors during the Great Recession. Toyota leaders over-focused on growth at the expense of quality when they should have been managing the tension between the two.[4]

Boeing's innovative 787 aircraft, the Dreamliner, was more than three years late and billions of dollars over budget because executives introduced a radically new aircraft using novel frame technology and an innovative manufacturing collaboration process.[5] Their overemphasis on change had created a nightmare of instability resulting from the mismanagement of the stability *and* change paradox.

High-tech guru Geoffrey Moore points out that many former technology giants, such as Digital Equipment Corporation, Silicon Graphics, and Wang, lost their way because they failed to develop effective strategies between today's realities and tomorrow's dreams. He admonishes executives to manage the short-term *and* long-term strategic paradox by "focusing on the middle term."[6]

These anecdotes are merely the tip of the iceberg. Although we can see what's above the surface (the story that makes the news), there is a mass of evidence below the surface demonstrating that executives who fail to manage paradoxes fail to lead effectively. One study of 1,000 organizations during a 20-year period reported that executives mismanaged paradoxes between 38% and 45% of the time, and suffered sinking profits because of it.[7]

So, why are there so many opposing demands these days, and why do smart executives fail to manage them well? The answers begin by understanding what keeps executives up at night.

What keeps executives up at night?

The 21st century executive must confront a range of challenges that would be unimaginable to executives of the *Mad Men* or *Pan Am* era. Historical research indicates that during the late 1950s and early 1960s, corporate executives were challenged by five or six performance goals annually. In today's complex workplace, top leaders are measured against an average of 20 or more goals. Table 1.1[8] captures the goal inflation that executives routinely confront.[9]

TABLE 1.1

Today's Top 20 Executive Goals

1. Control costs.
2. Grow the business.
3. Motivate employees.
4. Hold employees accountable for results.
5. Meet short-term objectives.
6. Innovate for long-term growth.
7. Get more done with less.
8. Take time to coach/mentor employees.
9. Increase cross-functional teamwork/collaboration.
10. Achieve your own performance goals.
11. Be a global company in a competitive world.
12. Address local, fragmented customer needs.
13. Explore the pervasive advances of technologies.
14. Stick to our core competencies.
15. Manage generational/cultural diversity.
16. Adhere to uniform policies/procedures.
17. Gain buy-in to the accelerated pace of change.
18. Provide stability to keep employees from being overwhelmed.
19. Meet the increasing demands of work.
20. Have a fulfilling home life.

What should keep you up at night!

How many of these goals are you expected to achieve? Most executives admit that they are pulled by at least a dozen or more on a regular basis. In fact, many executives admit that these goals feel more like ongoing challenges or demands—requirements of the job that seem omnipresent.

And did you notice anything unusual about the list? Don't worry—most leaders don't see the pattern at first glance. Read Table 1.1 again. This time, however, read the list in pairs, adding the words "and at the same time" after every odd-numbered challenge. In other words, read number one and number two together with the words "and at the same time" between them. Do this with numbers three *and* four, five *and* six, *and* so forth.

What did you observe as you read the list in pairs? Did the pairs seem to be at odds with each other? Good. That's because they are.

Many of the goals/demands/challenges executives face in our dynamic, hypercompetitive, and rapidly changing workplace are paradoxes — they pull in opposite directions simultaneously.

If we reformat the top challenges into paradoxes, we create a list of the top ten paradoxical challenges (Table 1.2). While these strategic and leadership challenges may not be new, arranging them as paradoxes illustrates the increased tension many executives feel in their current whitewater workplace. It's as if you are paddling down a raging river and your organization's numerous stakeholders are on opposite riverbanks and yelling for you to paddle to their side...at the same time.

TABLE 1.2

Top 10 Paradoxical Challenges

1. Control costs *and* Grow the business.
2. Motivate employees *and* Hold employees accountable for results.
3. Meet short-term objectives *and* Innovate for long-term growth.
4. Get more done with less *and* Take time to coach/mentor employees.
5. Increase cross-functional teamwork/collaboration *and* Achieve your own performance goals.
6. Be a global company in a competitive world *and* Address local, fragmented customer needs.
7. Explore the pervasive advances of technologies *and* Stick to our core competencies.
8. Manage generational/cultural diversity *and* Adhere to uniform policies/procedures.
9. Gain buy-in to the accelerated pace of change *and* Provide stability.
10. Meet the increasing demands of work *and* Have a fulfilling home life.

From balance scale to rubber band

Trying to meet conflicting demands is not new.[10] Executives have been balancing competing goals for years. But that's the point—it used to be all about balancing competing goals.

Now, it's more about stretching to achieve opposing demands. Do you feel as if you're balancing issues *or* being pulled by opposing demands? Our metaphor must morph from a balance scale to a rubber band because, as researchers continue to confirm, a perfect paradoxical storm is at work.

In a comprehensive review of 360 studies, Professors Wendy Smith and Marianne Lewis assert that paradoxical tensions are more prevalent and persistent in today's workplace because of three powerful environmental forces: pluralism, scarcity, and change.[11]

Pluralism

Executives are confronted by an increasing number of diverse stakeholders with competing agendas (thereby contributing to goal inflation). Leaders feel pulled to meet the demands of vocal shareholders, intrusive regulators, divergent employee groups, sustainability advocates, boards of directors, suppliers, myopic Wall Street analysts, local customers in the global economy—all at the same time.

Scarcity

Many executives have fewer resources to accomplish more goals. The carnage of the Great Recession and ongoing global turmoil create a foggy future. Senior executives are hesitant to rehire permanent employees and restore budgets, despite increasing workloads. In addition, many organizations are increasingly horizontal, matrix and virtual. This evolution of the organization decreases the executives' direct control over resources and increases their dependence on others. Commanding executives who once barked orders in their silos must now motivate teamwork and collaboration across the enterprise.

Change

Change is the new normal. Rapid advances in technology, information overload (62% of employees claim that "data smog" hinders job performance), demographic shifts, global markets, and a litany of other challenges that crowd our front pages create an avalanche of continuous change.[12]

While balance is possible some of the time, pluralism, scarcity, and change conspire to create an increasingly tension-filled, paradoxical workplace. Yet, as indicated by Fuld's story and considerable research, executives seldom stretch when pulled. They snap, especially under stress.

Why executives don't stretch when pulled

A paradox is a statement that seems self-contradictory but in reality expresses a possible truth. The word derives from the Latin *paradoxum,* meaning "beyond belief." An executive paradox seems beyond belief because, unlike a simple black/white, either/or choice, it involves contradictory yet interrelated elements that exist simultaneously.[13]

Most executives earned their promotions because of their skill at solving problems. They never learned how to address the two opposing elements (often referred to as issues, sides, goals, or demands) of a paradox at the same time.[14] And because the challenges of pluralism, scarcity, and change weren't as prevalent in days gone by, there was less pressure to manage opposing issues simultaneously.

It's no surprise that in our analysis of 77 executives rated by 376 leaders in the transit industry, the lowest-ranking leadership competency was "embrace ambiguity and paradox." (See Appendix C.)

But if managing paradoxes is so important these days, why haven't executives quickly learned to stretch when pulled by opposing demands? The curious case of Supreme Court Justice William O. Douglas provides a clue.

Narrow-mindedness begins in the brain

On New Year's Eve 1974, while vacationing in the Bahamas, Douglas suffered a debilitating stroke that left his left leg paralyzed. Despite being confined to a wheelchair, Douglas insisted that he was not paralyzed and that he could even kick field goals.[15] Disturbed by his delusional conduct, his fellow justices put off cases in which Douglas's vote might make a difference. Douglas continued to proclaim that he was fine and pressed the Court to be included in everything. Eventually, the other sitting justices signed a formal letter informing Douglas that after 36 years of service, his official duties on the Court were over.

Douglas's behavior emerged from a condition called anosognosia, which causes patients to remain unaware of their disability. His brain actually believed he was physically and intellectually fit. Even his experience in the wheelchair did not contradict his belief.

How could he actually think he was fine when there was so much opposing evidence surrounding him? His stroke damaged a small structure in his brain, the anterior cingulate cortex (ACC), whose primary purpose is to detect conflict and resolve it.[16] Think of it as the region in the brain that tells us that there is a fork in the road (conflict) and that we should take either path A or B (resolve the conflict by making a choice).

Like most judges, Douglas held the belief that he was a competent judge (path A). Unlike most judges, his damaged brain couldn't "see" any of the evidence (path B) that conflicted with his belief. He couldn't perceive the fork in the road. His vision became tunnel vision — as it does for many executives, especially when they experience stress.

FIGURE 1.1

The Human Brain

with ACC highlighted in dark gray

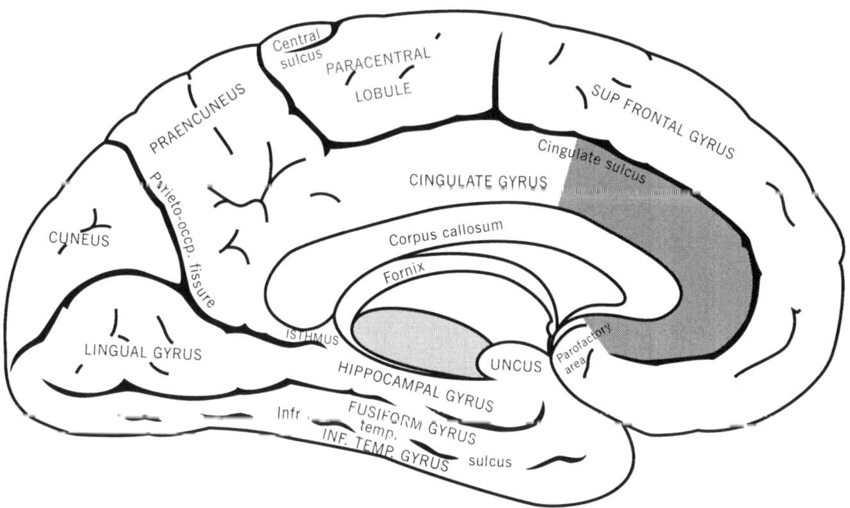

Douglas's story and an understanding of the ACC helps explain why executives with no brain damage (that would be you) have difficulty embracing new information that contradicts a strongly held belief. Leaders frequently *do* see the fork in the road (both paths) because the first job of the ACC is to detect conflict. Their healthy ACC then sends signals to resolve the conflict, which is its second job.

Your ACC wants to *settle* the conflict by picking path A or path B. Your ACC is not designed to *manage* the conflict between path A and path B.

One executive I've coached, Mark, believes he and his team must focus on fixing his organization's short-term financial problems (path A). Of course, he is correct. At the same time, I have also coached Mark to keep an eye on the importance of the long-term implications of his decisions (path B). Mark's healthy ACC "sees" both paths — he knows there is a conflict between the short and long-term. Nevertheless, he struggles because his ACC also tells him to resolve the "cognitive dissonance" between paths A and B — that is, between today and the future.

Mark's myopic brain — just like all healthy, high-functioning brains — wants to relieve the tension between paths A and B by discounting, diminishing, and devaluing conflicting information so that he can justify his choice.

Sound familiar?

Tell me what a leader believes and
I'll tell you what he sees.

Thus, a healthy ACC tells us why many executives have a hard time stretching when they feel pulled by opposing demands. Their brains see the fork in the road (conflict), but their brains are wired to solve problems ("pick path A *or* B") instead of manage tensions ("should I consider A *and* B?").

From an evolutionary standpoint, the ACC's purpose makes perfect sense. Mother Nature programmed us to make quick decisions when conflicts arise. You don't want to sit around the campfire debating the merits of fight or flight when a saber-toothed tiger is ravaging the camp or another tribe is attacking. For thousands of years, our ancestors who survived their brutal environments were those best at detecting and resolving conflict fast. Quick—pick A *or* B...or die.

Today, if A *or* B is our only response to our paradoxical challenges... we die.

To make matters worse, our brain's conflict-reducing nature is nurtured by an environment that celebrates either/or thinking. Students learn to solve problems by finding *the* correct answer. Business schools and corporate cultures condition executives to make black-or-white choices—decisions that *relieve* tensions, not *relive* tensions, as is required to manage a paradox. Time management experts urge leaders to check items off the daily to-do list instead of managing the ongoing tension between two opposing issues.

With our narrow mind conspiring with a problem-solving culture, what's a leader to do?

"The problem, of course, is that plain old management is complicated and confusing," write Jonathan Gosling and Henry Mintzberg. "Be global *and* be local. Collaborate *and* compete. Change perpetually *and* maintain order. Make the numbers *while* nurturing your people. How is anyone supposed to reconcile all this?"[17]

While Professors Gosling and Mintzberg have correctly identified management (and, by implication, leadership) as complicated and confusing, their healthy ACC has focused them on asking the wrong question. To reconcile means "to restore to harmony or to resolve." Yet the evidence suggests that we cannot "reconcile all this" because:

- Goal inflation has created numerous paradoxical tensions.
- Environmental forces (pluralism, scarcity, and change) amplify these tensions.

- Executives suffer negative consequences when they try to resolve the paradox. by focusing only on one side (i.e., fail to stretch when pulled).
- Executives have not yet learned how to manage paradox at work.

Instead of asking,

How is anyone supposed to reconcile all this?

we need to ask,

If paradox is the essence of today's leadership challenge, shouldn't paradox be essential to our leadership development?

THE DEFINITION OF LEADERSHIP AND YOUR ROLE AS AN EXECUTIVE

To answer that question, we must first define leadership and your role as an executive leader. There are many definitions of leadership. After years of researching, teaching, and coaching leaders, I've concluded that leadership is best defined as *"the process of unleashing the energy of others toward worthy goals."* If you reflect on this definition for a moment, it becomes evident that:

1. Leadership is a process.
2. Leadership requires tapping into internal motivation.
3. Leadership is about others, not just those who report to you.
4. Leadership is not a title or a position.
5. Leadership demands credible direction.

As an executive leader, your role is to use a process that inspires others to achieve valuable goals in today's environment.

The problem is, you can't conquer today's leadership challenges with yesterday's management thinking (i.e., processes). What got you here won't get you where you want to go because your environment and challenges have changed. Of course, making either/or choices is still critical. The intent of this book is to supplement your black-and-white thinking with paradoxical tools that increase your effectiveness today. Because as a golf pro once told me, "You can't hit the shot if you don't have the club."

By the way, while I may at times use the terms *leader* and *executive* interchangeably, this book targets executives and those who aspire to be executives. My simple definition of an executive is "one who leads other managers."

The next chapter introduces THE EXPANSIVE LEADERSHIP MODEL™ (XLM)—a simple yet powerful paradoxical tool that identifies the four fundamental styles and their four corresponding core competencies needed to conquer competing demands. The XLM integrates thousands of research studies with the practical lessons I've learned as an educator (teaching/coaching more than 10,000 leaders during the last two decades) and an executive (former chief administrative officer of an institute at UCLA). It is a process that will help you unleash the energy of others toward worthy goals.

The greatest danger in times of turbulence
is not the turbulence;
it is to act with yesterday's logic.
PETER DRUCKER

CHAPTER 2

The Power of Paradoxical Thinking

The test of a first-rate intelligence is the ability to hold two opposed ideas in the mind at the same time, and still retain the ability to function.

F. Scott Fitzgerald

There are two ways to become a better leader. First, you can improve the quality and consistency of your day-to-day decisions. This may seem obvious — after all, making daily decisions is the very heart of leadership. Second, you can develop the specific competencies that research says you need to conquer your challenges and achieve your goals.

This chapter introduces THE EXPANSIVE LEADERSHIP MODEL™ (XLM), which helps you accomplish both.

The primary dimensions of leadership

As complicated and difficult as executives' responsibilities are, the job has only two primary dimensions: *what to do* (task-oriented behaviors) and *how to interact with others* (relationship-oriented behaviors). We can subdivide each of these dimensions into two sides (examples in parentheses):

1. *What to do: task-oriented behaviors*

Major tasks	Minor tasks
(Contemplate strategic issues)	(Focus on project details)

2. *How to interact with others: relationship-oriented behaviors*

Direct others	Support others
(Confront a poor performer)	(Celebrate team accomplishments)

Defining the leader's job in this manner is not new. Researchers at Ohio State University and the University of Michigan identified the importance of task-oriented and relationship-oriented behaviors back in the 1950s and 1960s.[1] Since then, various researchers (identified in parentheses) have assigned different labels, competencies, and behaviors to these dimensions:

1. *What to do: task-oriented behaviors*
   Innovate and Coordinate (Quinn)
   Vision and Reality (Koestenbaum)
   Strategic and Operational (Kaplan and Kaiser)
   Create and Control (Lawrence, Lenk, and Quinn)

2. *How to interact with others: relationship-oriented behaviors*
   Director and Facilitator (Quinn)
   Courage and Ethics (Koestenbaum)
   Forceful and Enabling (Kaplan and Kaiser)
   Compete and Collaborate (Lawrence, Lenk, and Quinn)

The Four Fundamental Styles of the Executive

How wonderful that we have met with a paradox.
Now we have some hope of making progress.
Niels Bohr

Professor Richard Farson writes, "There's nothing as invisible as the obvious."[2] Although researchers have identified both leadership dimensions and each of their two sides, they have rarely placed all four sides in the interdependent model of opposing elements—the paradoxes of leadership—illustrated in Figure 2.1.

FIGURE 2.1

The Four Sides of Leadership

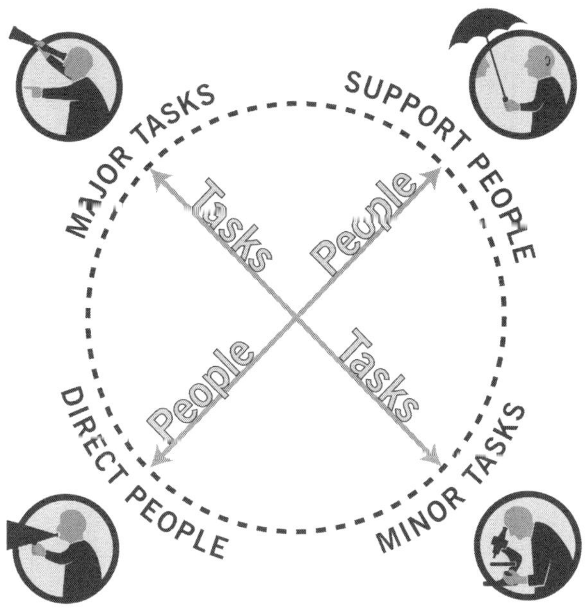

If we consider these four sides as four fundamental leadership styles (relabeled rational, visionary, commanding, and empowering in Figure 2.2), we have a model that helps executives think about what to do and how to interact with others throughout the day in a paradoxical manner.

FIGURE 2.2

The Four Interdependent and Opposing Leadership Styles

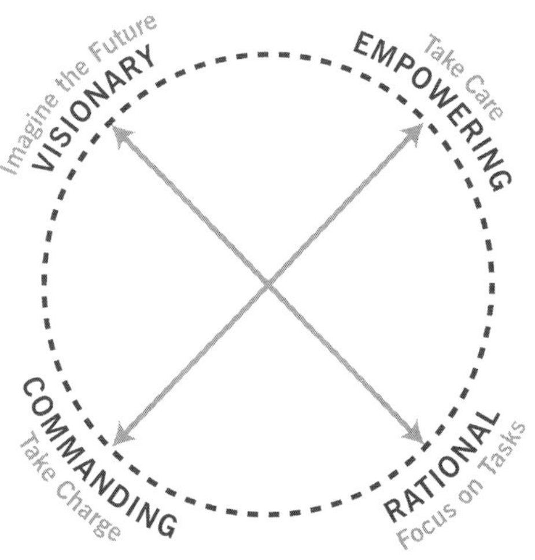

A leadership style is a general and philosophical way of thinking. How well you think about daily tasks and interactions is crucial because the quality of thinking dictates the effectiveness of decisions, which determines actions, thereby delivering results. This concept is illustrated as a pyramid:

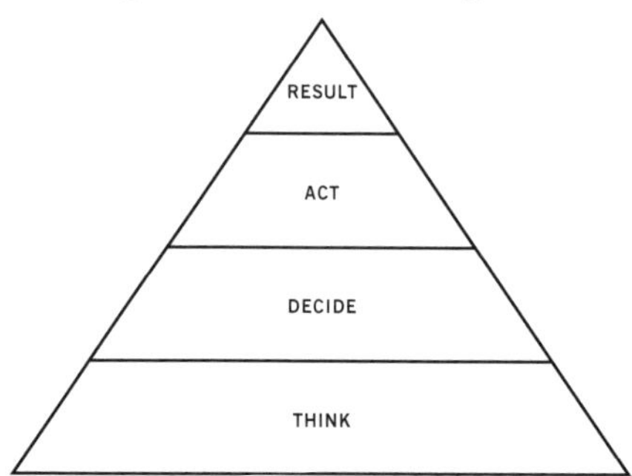

Better leadership results require better thinking.

We have already concluded that many executive challenges are paradoxical —they require thinking about opposing demands at the same time. This is why the four styles are placed in an interdependent and opposing relationship in this model. The arrows in Figure 2.2 represent the tension executives often feel as they try to stretch when pulled by conflicting demands.

For example, do you ever feel the tension between empowering others ("I care about engaging the team members") and commanding them ("I need you to be accountable for these results")? Do you ever feel pulled between being a visionary thinker ("Let's explore the future as we brainstorm strategic options") and a rational thinker ("Let's exploit the present by focusing on these objectives today")?

Of course, you already deal with these competing tensions every day. Yet how consistently do you consider all four styles, and how well do you stretch—especially when making decisions under pressure?

Answering this question requires a better understanding of each style.

The rational style: Focus on facts

Rational leaders demonstrate the left-brain, logical thinking side of leadership. Executives who are highly skilled in this style clearly define their and their team members' roles. They excel at setting short-term objectives and generating detailed plans with milestones. They spell out performance expectations plainly. Because they actively seek feedback, effective rational leaders understand their strengths and weaknesses, as well as the strengths and weaknesses of those around them. They stay in touch with their team members and peers, their boss, and their customers.

The visionary style: Imagine the future

Visionary leaders excel at the creative, dreamer aspect of leadership. Those highly skilled in this leadership style create flexible approaches to solve problems, make decisions, and achieve strategic goals. They bring new products, services, or processes to fruition because they are effective in launching cross-functional experiments. Visionary leaders also inspire others to question the status quo by embracing change, creativity, and open mindedness. They enjoy reflecting on global issues, thinking about long-term consequences, and pondering future possibilities.

The empowering style: Take care

The empowering leader represents the servant or healer side of leadership. Those highly skilled in this style enable others to do their best every day by delegating well, coaching, and involving team members in decisions. They are masters at orchestrating diverse individuals into high-performing, energized teams that work well across the enterprise. Empowering leaders build trust and empathy by patiently listening to other perspectives and beliefs without prejudgment. They also demonstrate fairness, honesty, integrity, and humility in all their interactions.

The commanding style: Take charge

Leadership also has a strong, forceful side. Those highly skilled in this leadership style work extremely hard to fulfill commitments. They push to accomplish tasks, projects, and goals on time. They are not afraid to solicit opposing views when making important decisions. They are also comfortable with ambiguity; they don't need all the data to move forward. Commanding leaders control their emotions and moods under pressure. In addition, they refuse to allow themselves or their team to play the victim during adversity. They take personal responsibility for their choices and consequences.

These four fundamental styles, when placed in an interdependent and opposing model, provide a reproducible process to help executives think effectively and efficiently about the avalanche of paradoxical issues assaulting them every day. Remember, leadership is the *process* of unleashing the energy of people toward worthy goals. Most leaders don't even have a process. The XLM fills this void.

We will discuss how to use this model as a decision-making tool in later chapters, after we advance our discussion from general leadership styles to specific leadership competencies. This is important because leaders don't just sit around thinking about tasks and people. They also engage in specific behaviors. As discussed at the beginning of this chapter, the second way executives can improve their capacity to lead is by developing specific competencies—the skills and behaviors—that help meet their challenges.

From general styles to specific competencies

I have been studying how exceptional executives achieve extraordinary results for decades. Like a crime scene investigator (for you CSI fans), I've scoured the leadership literature, listened to leaders in the classroom, and coached them in the boardroom as I searched for clues to the most powerful leadership competencies. At one time, I papered my office walls with spreadsheets to examine all the evidence that addressed the central question:

> *What core competencies have the highest probability of increasing executive effectiveness in a paradoxical environment?*

Unfortunately, the sheer number of leadership competencies presented a problem: How many and which competencies should one use to create a practical and predictive model that you can apply usefully? Pick too many, and the model is not practical; pick too few or the wrong ones, and the probability of success is low. Einstein reminded us to strive to balance simplicity and complexity when he said, "Make things as simple as possible, but not simpler."

To identify the core competencies to include, I clarified the criteria I would use to make the selections by asking five questions.

1. Is there compelling evidence that executives who use this competency achieve better results?
2. Does this competency link to current, evidence-based leadership models?
3. Is this competency relatively hard to find?
4. Does it apply to international leadership issues?
5. Does improving this competency h elp executives stretch?

Answering these questions, helped me filter the data and create THE EXPANSIVE LEADERSHIP MODEL,™ or XLM, which is represented visually in Figure 2.3. Within each of the four fundamental styles are the four core competencies that best meet these criteria. Dashed lines separate the styles and competencies; this is my way of saying that, despite its good looks (if I do say so myself), the XLM is not so clean-cut. The competencies don't always fit so nicely into their respective styles. They influence each other. I'm confident that as more research is done, the XLM will evolve. Nevertheless, I think you'll find that it is a useful and adaptable tool.

FIGURE 2.3

The Four Styles and Competencies of THE EXPANSIVE LEADERSHIP MODEL™

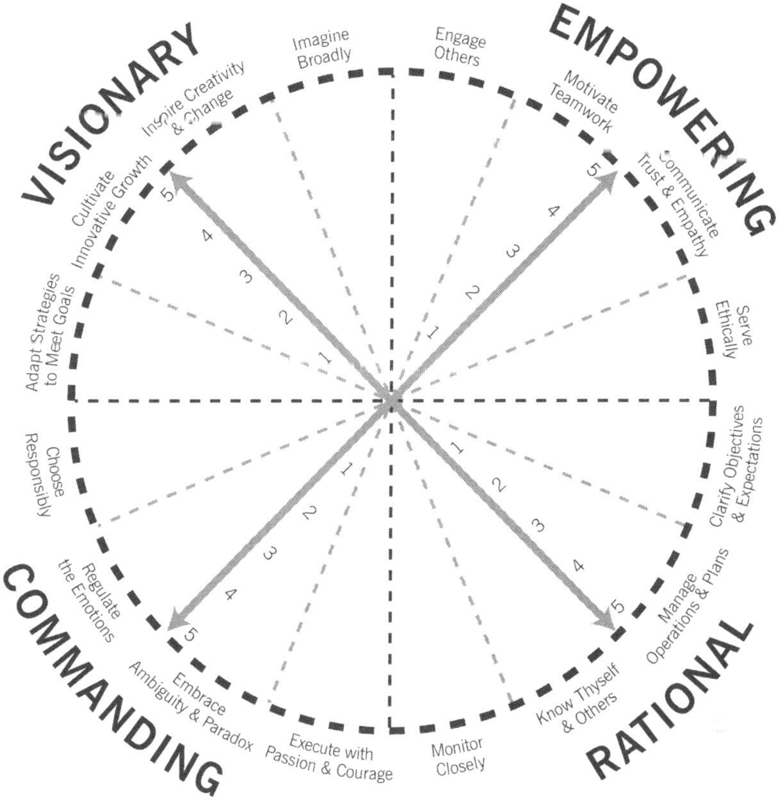

The XLM is my closing argument, summarizing the best evidence in the case of the elusive core competencies. It is a highly researched model that provides a practical, predictive process to help you improve your leadership skills in two ways. First, as you discover which core competencies are your strongest and weakest, you will learn how to lead with your strengths and manage your weaknesses. Second, as you learn how to apply the XLM's four fundamental leadership styles in a paradoxical workplace, you will be able to make better and more consistent daily decisions.

By improving both your weaker competencies and your decision-making, you will learn how to stretch when you are pulled by your opposing demands. You will become a more effective executive because you know how to manage the executive's paradox.

To understand further how the four styles and their four competencies can help you conquer your challenges and achieve your desired outcomes, complete the XLM assessment, as discussed in the next chapter.

A theory is the more impressive...
the more different the kinds of things it relates
and the more extended the range of its applicability.

ALBERT EINSTEIN

CHAPTER 3

Who You Are Is How You Lead

There are three things extremely hard:
steel, a diamond, and to know oneself.

Benjamin Franklin

Who are you?

The temple of the ancient Oracle of Delphi had only three inscriptions: "Know thyself," "Nothing in excess," and "Make a pledge and mischief is nigh." The XLM embraces these concepts. This chapter is about learning who you are as a leader. Subsequent chapters will help you apply the XLM in moderation and to commit to a developmental action plan.

Knowing who you are is critical because it forms the basis of how you make decisions. The decisions you make every day are based on your impressions of your skills, knowledge, talents, values, and leadership styles. For example, if you volunteer to take on a difficult project, you would do so because you believe you have the right skills to accomplish the mission. You assess your ability and then decide. If your assessment is accurate, you make a good decision. If your self-assessment is flawed, your project may be in trouble. Thus, your evaluation of yourself (and others) is essential to your leadership decision-making.

Of course, as a leader, you need to unleash the energy of *others* toward worthy goals. These others will respond to your leadership based on their perspective, not yours. Therefore, knowing yourself is not enough. To lead well you need to know yourself well and understand how others see you.

Benjamin Franklin was right: It is hard to know oneself, especially when you consider that knowing yourself includes understanding how others perceive yourself. It's hard, but not impossible.

We don't see things as they are, we see things as we are.

Anaïs Nin

Your XLM 360 assessment

One of the best ways to know yourself is to take a 360-leadership assessment. The XLM 360 assessment is available to you online at http://xlmassessment.com/?book. It's free for those who purchased this book. The XLM assessment allows you to invite others (your boss, peers, direct reports, others) to rate you after you have rated yourself. Their anonymous feedback provides a 360 perspective of your leadership strengths and relative weaknesses.

No one but you will see the responses unless you choose to share them. The objective is to leverage your strengths and manage your weaknesses, so you can conquer your paradoxical challenges and achieve your contradictory goals.

Remember, their feedback is not the truth about you; it's their opinion of your leadership behaviors. Yet, because their opinion forms their reality, knowing where they are coming from will help you lead them where you need to go.

After you and your raters complete the 15-minute assessment, you will be able to download your personalized, 25-page XLM report. This comprehensive pdf is divided into seven sections:

I. THE EXPANSIVE LEADERSHIP MODEL™ (XLM) Summary

The XLM summary provides a chart of your overall leadership effectiveness. The chart plots your scores for each of the four fundamental leadership styles, as well as the four competencies that comprise each style. The average scores of all your Raters are plotted on the same diagram so that you can compare your self-assessment to your Raters' assessment.

II. XLM Core Competencies

The XLM core competency section provides your overall score for each leadership style and a graphical representation of the four competencies that constitute that style. Scores for each Rater category are also displayed.

III. 4/4/4 Section

The "4/4/4" section shows you the scores for your four highest-scoring competencies and the four lowest-scoring competencies out of the 16. It also identifies the four competencies that have the largest discrepancy between your Raters' scores and your scores (i.e., blind spots).

IV. The Great Eight Leadership Skills
This section contains the description and scores of the great eight leadership skills (e.g., agility, systems thinking, emotional intelligence). These eight skills are "meta-competencies" that provide another way to understand and expand your leadership effectiveness.

V. Open Questions Section
This section shows the answers from the assessment's open-ended questions.

VI. Development Plan
The development plan aggregates the four lowest-scoring competencies and puts them into a one-page template. You can use this template to record the specific actions you plan to take as a result of this feedback.

VII. Individual Questions Section
This section shows your scores from the individual survey questions. The questions are divided into the four fundamental leadership styles and subdivided into the four core competencies. The tables provide your scores, as well as the number of Raters and the average of each Rater category that had at least three responses.

If you want to get the most out of the book, I urge you to take the XLM assessment. It's not mandatory. You'll still get a lot out of reading the book and using the highly researched and extensively tested ideas. However, you'll be able to get the biggest bang from this book by knowing yourself well—after all, who you are is how you lead.

How expansive are you?

As your review your XLM report, you might ask yourself how expansive a leader you are at this point. Our research indicates that most executives have scores of 4.0 or higher in several of the 16 competencies. (The average score is about 3.5.) However, fewer than 5% of leaders score higher than 4.0 in all the competencies.

So, don't feel bad if you have opportunities to grow. That's what the rest of the book is about.

The four fundamental leadership styles

Research tells us that a challenging workplace requires leaders to juggle the opposing sides of both dimensions *simultaneously* throughout the day. The XLM expresses these four "requirements" as four fundamental leadership styles. The rational and visionary leadership styles represent the task dimension (what to do) as discussed in Chapter 2. The empowering and commanding leadership styles represent the relationship dimension (how to interact with others).

The four core competencies of each style

As you look at your XLM assessment, notice that each of the four fundamental styles is comprised of four core competencies. Taken together, these competencies describe the essential behaviors leaders must develop to master each style.

The XLM blends all four styles, and their competencies, into a holistic leadership model. As illustrated in Figure 2.3, the four interdependent styles are separated by dotted lines because, although they represent different dimensions and sides of leadership, there is overlap among the styles and competencies.

An avalanche of evidence confirms that one leadership style is not enough if you want to conquer the daunting challenges confronting most leaders. By developing your lower-scoring competencies, you will increase the size and improve the shape of your XLM (i.e., it will grow larger and more circular). Becoming a more well-rounded executive, especially under pressure, grows your leadership agility—your ability to respond rapidly to a changing environment.

How surprised will you be when you discover that expanding your leadership agility, as explained in the next chapter, is the key to managing the executive's paradox because it teaches you to stretch when you feel pulled?

CHAPTER 4

How the Most Agile Executives Stretch

It is not the strongest of the species that survive,
nor the most intelligent,
but the one most responsive to change.

ATTRIBUTED TO CHARLES DARWIN

VISIONARY OR RATIONAL LEADERSHIP?

The CEO felt Debbie was a good senior executive in their financial service firm. Debbie clearly defined her expectations, assigned roles and responsibilities well, and required detailed project plans from her direct reports. She managed by walking around (MBWA) and earned loyalty from her team and respect from her peers.

Under pressure, however, Debbie overused her rational competencies. Her direct reports felt the M in MBWA stood for micromanaging and that her walk-arounds were sometimes drive-bys loaded with machine-gun, dictated tasks. Stress, the CEO knew, turned a well-rounded leader into a lopsided one.

As part of her XLM feedback session before an executive team retreat, Debbie and I had the following conversation about stretching—instead of snapping—when she felt pulled.

DEBBIE: I guess I need to learn how to back off my high rational skills when I'm feeling tense.

ME: That's not a bad idea, but it's not the only way to avoid overusing your strengths. How might strengthening the opposite side also help?

DEBBIE: You mean work on my weaker visionary competencies?

ME: Exactly. When the heat is on, we all tend to gravitate toward our strengths because that's our comfort zone. It's hard to throttle back on that strength. Most leaders find it easier and more effective to spend a little time managing their relative weakness, which is often on the opposite side of their strength. In essence, you fix lopsided leadership like you're fixing a flat tire with a patch.

DEBBIE: That is going to be a stretch for me. I'm not that good at that big-picture stuff.

ME: You're not alone. Most leaders say it's stretching to work on a relative weakness. But if your weakness is hurting you, you need to deal with it while holding onto your strength. You shouldn't over-focus on the weakness—but if you are shooting yourself in the foot, shouldn't you stop?

Managing tension is the essence of growth.

After our conversation (and the retreat), Debbie decided to improve her overall leadership effectiveness by expanding her visionary competencies. She created a plan to stretch. Her development plan included asking more questions during MBWA, brainstorming more in meetings, and launching small cross-functional experiments with colleagues to improve business processes.

When she returned to work, she reviewed her implementation plan with her CEO and a few colleagues to align her goals with their strategies. The following week she met with her direct reports and shared her key learnings and development plan. She then asked them to help her grow her visionary competencies, especially when she felt stressed. She also invited them to identify their own opportunities to grow.

For the next six months, Debbie and her team met every other week to discuss their progress and problems in achieving their leadership goals.

When I met with Debbie and her CEO again, to review her progress, we discussed how well she stretched and discussed ideas for a customized leadership retreat as she transitions to her new position as the CEO of another subsidiary in her organization.

Debbie and her CEO believed that investing a little time every day to develop her visionary competencies that were relatively weak and opposite her strengths helped her expand from good to great. Debbie did not over-focus on her weak skills. She stretched to work on a weakness that was holding her back, especially when stressed. She earned her promotion because she learned to lead with her strengths and manage her weaknesses. In other words, Debbie improved her agility—her ability to respond flexibly to a rapidly changing environment. You could say she added another club to her golf bag.

You can do the same.

TABLE 4.1

Visionary or Rational Leadership?

Visionary	Rational
Strategy	Operations
Future	Today
Creative	Organize
Flexible	Stable
Change	Order
Enterprise	Division
Innovate	Imitate

How often do you feel the tension between the opposing, interdependent imperatives of a visionary and rational executive? More important, how well do you manage the tension between these two forces when you are under stress? How often do you become a lopsided leader when you feel pulled?

Figure 4.1 illustrates the tension, or stretch, many leaders feel when accomplishing tasks—the "what to do" aspect of leadership. Leaders who score low in both rational and visionary competencies will underperform. They have a lot of stretching to do if they want to become effective leaders.

Leaders who score low in rational, but high in visionary competencies often allow their vision to blind them. Think of entrepreneurs who don't develop detailed plans to achieve their big-picture goals. They tend to get carried away by their dreams. Like the mythological Icarus, they fly too close to the sun, melting the wax on their wings. They need to be tethered to the ground.

A leader who scores high in rational, but low in visionary thinking will tend to micromanage under pressure. This was Debbie's challenge. When the heat was on, she managed operations and plans well, but failed to think about the big picture, didn't inspire others, and rarely collaborated across the enterprise.

FIGURE 4.1

Tasks That Stretch Leaders

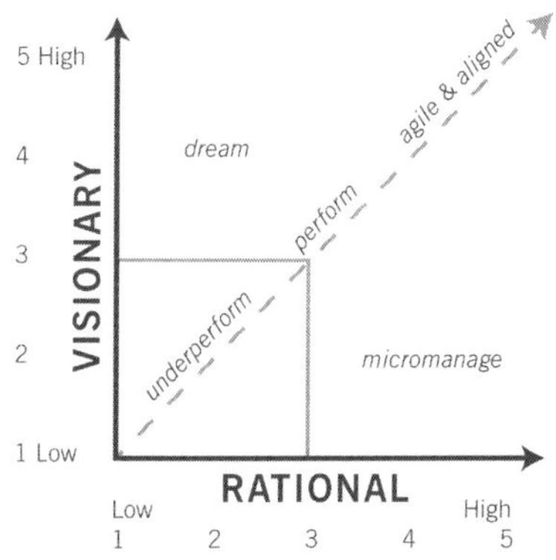

I once had the good fortune of having lunch with Peter Drucker, considered the father of management, according to *Harvard Business Review*. We met to discuss the overall strategy of the new organization we were building at UCLA. With my head soaring with Professor Drucker's ideas and insights about the future, I later drove back to UCLA—only to find myself in my office, reviewing budget numbers for a project.

This experience summarized my responsibilities as a chief administrative officer. One minute I was thinking big picture and creating long-term strategies, and the next I was clarifying objectives and managing operations. Was I leading or managing? My pragmatic answer is, I was doing both.

Agile executives have been answering "both" for years.

Consider Sam Walton, founder of retail giant Wal-Mart, who envisioned a chain of stores worldwide as he analyzed the weekly sales reports of his early stores. Roberto Goizueta, who led Coca-Cola to become the most recognizable trademark in the world, was an above-the-fray CEO and a hands-on detail man. Of course, Walt Disney would never have been able to build his castles in the air if his business-oriented, bottom-line brother Roy had not been at his side building their foundations.

In his analysis of industrial leaders, Professor Edwin Locke pointed out that "this constant movement between concrete (details) and the abstract (vision) is critical in business because one has to know not only where one is going but how to get there."[1]

After reviewing approximately 1,300 scientific studies on leadership in his comprehensive book, Professor Gary Yukl concluded that "most scholars seem to agree that success as a manager...in modern organizations necessarily involves leading."[2]

To which I add, success as a leader also involves managing.

If I spend all of my day in the details as a CEO of a company like Wal-Mart, it would be trouble, because I wouldn't be prepared to speak to the big issues that the country or the world should face. But...if you spend all of the time at 50,000 feet, [you] are not out talking to customers [as] real people.... Often the interaction directly with customers, in the details of their family and their issues, is what inspires me to want to help solve the big issues.

WAL-MART CEO MIKE DUKE[3]

In this chapter's opening story, Debbie stretched by investing a little time every day improving a few of her vision competencies. She expanded her XLM, which enabled her to become a more agile executive under pressure.

A journey begins with the end in mind
and *knowledge of the terrain.*

Where do you need to grow? Perhaps your visionary and rational competencies are both well developed. How about your people skills — the relationship aspect of leadership?

Commanding or Empowering Leadership?

Greg was an empowering leader who lacked some of the key competencies of the commanding style. He failed to address conflict and poor performance among his team members. Greg didn't manage the tension between the commanding and empowering leadership styles, especially when stressed. Under pressure, instead of agility, he demonstrated rigidity by over-focusing on empowering competencies at the expense of commanding competencies. He had yet to learn that in leadership, too much of a good thing can be a bad thing.

Table 4.2 asks whether you are a commanding or empowering leader. Of course, the answer is yes, you need to be both! Do these leadership styles ever pull you in opposite directions at the same time when stressed? How comfortable are you managing the tension between being both a commanding and empowering leader?

TABLE 4.2
Commanding or Empowering Leadership?

Commanding	**Empowering**
Take control of the situation	Take care of people
Increase accountability for results	Create meaningful work
Confront conflict	Comfort the afflicted
Use an iron fist	Apply the velvet glove
Advocate your position	Inquire about the other's position
Demand individual initiative	Encourage teamwork

Another executive who attended our leadership class was Roger. I encouraged Roger to stretch by accessing his empowering competencies (engaging others) to help offset his strong commanding competencies (executing with passion and courage). A few weeks later, I received an e-mail from him:

> I've taken your feedback to heart and have been working to increase the level of "personal touch" in my conversations. It's not as difficult as I imagined. And while I know I need to be patient to see results, I'm certain it will help me become better at building and maintaining relationships and polishing my interpersonal skills.

Roger began having more one-on-one meetings with his staff, occasionally taking them out for a social lunch, and sharing a little more of his personal life with them. In the e-mail, he mentioned that he needed to be patient for results. Six months after receiving his e-mail, I got a call from him, announcing that he'd earned a promotion. (He didn't have to be *too* patient, apparently.)

The tale of these two executives (Greg and Roger) is illustrated in Figure 4.2. The figure illustrates the dynamic tension between the commanding and empowering leadership styles by plotting the commanding competencies along the horizontal axis and the empowering competencies along the vertical axis.

FIGURE 4.2

Relationship Issues That Stretch Leaders

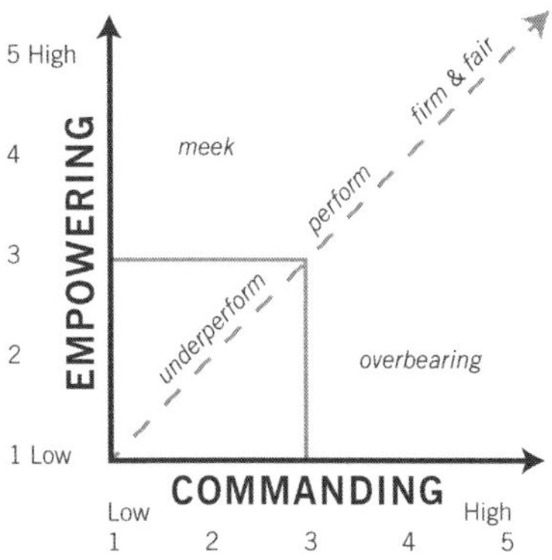

A leader who scores low in both the commanding and empowering styles when interacting with others will underperform. A leader who scores low in the commanding, but high in the empowering style often will be perceived as meek.

Greg's XLM score was 2.5 in the commanding skills and 4.25 in the empowering skills; he was operating in the meek zone. I encouraged him to spend a little time every day increasing one or two of his lower-scored commanding competencies, while holding onto his high empowering leadership style. This would have moved him closer to the firm and fair line. As we'll explore in more detail in Chapter 17, Greg chose not to stretch in that direction and paid the price.

A leader who scores high in the commanding, but low in the empowering styles often will be perceived as overbearing. Roger's XLM score was 4.5 in the commanding skills and 3.25 in the empowering skills; he was operating in the overbearing zone. I encouraged him to spend a few minutes every day increasing a few of his empowering competencies, while holding onto his high commanding leadership style. This moved him closer to the firm and fair line. He reaped the rewards by choosing to stretch, thereby becoming more agile.

Where do you usually operate? Under stress, where do you tend to migrate? What situations push you into certain zones? Do you choose rigidity or agility?

How to lead with your strengths and manage your weaknesses

When you took the XLM assessment, you discovered your leadership strengths and weaknesses. In the chapters that follow, you will learn more about each of the four leadership styles and their four core competencies, why research says they are important, and how to develop them. For now, though, we turn to the first method of expanding your leadership capacity —leading with your strengths while managing your weaknesses.

To lead with your strengths means to celebrate them and make sure that they are a big part of your job. For example, many of the finance executives I coach are strong in the rational competencies. They should be—their responsibilities demand it. They should celebrate their strengths, right?

Now, consider the CEO who told me that one of her finance executives becomes "too much of a bean counter under pressure." She said this executive needs to throttle back his strengths.

I reminded the CEO that in a paradoxical model , when you have an executive who is "strong to a fault," you shouldn't diminish his assets. Instead, you applaud his "bean counting" tendencies (i.e., clarifying objectives and expectations) *while at the same time* strengthening his opposing visionary competencies (i.e., cultivating innovative growth).

I explained to the CEO, that it's like the bodybuilder who has limited flexibility. He doesn't need to stop lifting weights—he needs to start stretching. Of course, a new stretching routine may impinge a bit on his weightlifting time. That's logical and okay. It's simply a matter of focus: Are you focusing on what you *don't* want (becoming too muscle-bound) or what you *do* want (increasing your flexibility)? To beware of your strengths in a paradoxical environment doesn't mean you have to dial back on your strengths, it means to be aware of them while stretching to strengthen the opposite side.

The bottom line is that stretching by developing a relatively weak competency allows you to become a more well-rounded leader; thereby increasing your agility under pressure.

Answer the following questions to gain further insight about where you need to grow to achieve your goals. Please do not skip this process. Insights will flow from your answers. Tap into your internal wisdom by responding to the following:

1. Your weakest leadership competency is ______________________.
2. How has this weakness hindered your overall leadership effectiveness?
3. Write a specific example illustrating when this relative weakness has hurt you.
4. What specific actions could you take to strengthen this weaker competency? (Review the chapter on your weakest leadership competency and adapt the ideas in that chapter to your development plan.)
5. If you did improve your weaker competency, how would you and your organization benefit?
6. Identify the person with whom you will discuss your improvement plan and get frequent feedback regarding your progress.

What did you learn from answering these questions? (You did answer them, didn't you?) Remember, things don't get better unless you do.

Here are a few comments from leaders who answered these questions and then acted on their insights:

- "People have often told me that I was too commanding and that I needed to throttle it back. My XLM assessment tells me that I don't have to give up my strength, I only need to access my empowering style a little more each day to avoid being strong to a fault."

- "I realize that being weak in this area is hurting my ability to advance in my organization."
- "I'm going to share my XLM with my team and invite them to help me grow in my relative weak style. I'm not going to over-focus on my weakness, but I am going to spend a little time every day working on it."
- "Now that I've been using the XLM for a while, I realize that although I still feel the tension of the opposing styles at times, I can manage this tension much better."

There is a dynamic interaction among all four of your leadership styles. We all have strengths and relative weaknesses. We need to spend most of our time celebrating and leading with our strengths. At the same time, we must be aware of overusing our strengths. Otherwise, we may end up like media mogul Rupert Murdoch, whose strong commanding skills (execute with passion and courage) lead him to ignore empowering skills (serve ethically). As a result, a phone hacking scandal caused the closing of one of Murdoch's British newspapers, *News of the World,* and severely damaged his legacy.

Consider also Henry Ford, who was so blinded by his vision of mass production that he couldn't see the value of giving consumers more choices (Instead he said, "You can have any color as long as it's black.") Or U.S. General Douglas MacArthur, who overused his commanding strengths during the Korean War and was relieved of command. Perhaps MacArthur would have been more effective near the end of his career had he added a little tenderness to his toughness, like effective generals such as Colin Powell and Norman Schwarzkopf.[4]

Many leadership experts admonish leaders to focus only on their strengths. Yet the above-mentioned examples, my research, and experience with thousands of leaders tell us that while emphasizing your strengths is imperative, overusing them is a problem. Too much of a good thing can be a bad thing. Strengths that are overused become weaknesses—they are double-edged swords. Lopsided leadership, especially when the heat is on, causes blowouts.

So spend a little time every day strengthening your relative weakness, but do not ignore your strengths. If you spend too much time working on weaker competencies, it will feel like a pebble in your shoe—annoying you as it raises a blister.

When my position as chief administrative officer of an institute at UCLA morphed into a high rational job, where my relative weaknesses are,

I didn't enjoy it anymore. That's when I started consulting, coaching, and speaking at conferences, eventually leaving UCLA. Today, I have strengthened my weaknesses where they are important and I use my strengths (empowering and visionary competencies) throughout the day.

Each of the four leadership styles in the XLM has benefits, as well as negative consequences if overused. In Figure 4.3, the competencies for each leadership style are above the line, while negative consequences associated with overusing those competencies are below the line.

FIGURE 4.3

Each Style Is a Double-Edged Sword if Overused

VISIONARY
Adapt strategies to meet goals
Cultivate innovative growth
Inspire creativity and change
Imagine broadly

Unclear direction
Too many initiatives
Unrealistic change
Dreamer

EMPOWERING
Engage others
Motivate teamwork
Communicate trust and empathy
Serve ethically

Abdicate responsibly
Pollyanna
Weak
Wishy-washy

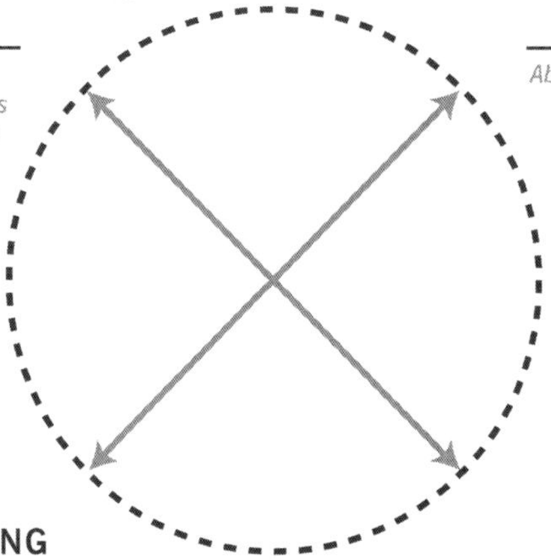

COMMANDING
Execute with passion and courage
Embrace ambiguity and paradox
Regulate the emotions
Choose responsibly

Willful
Indecisive
Remote
Heartless

RATIONAL
Clarify objectives and expectations
Manage operations and plans
Know thyself and others
Monitor closely

Rigid
Micro-manage
Intrusive
Info overload

Your leadership effectiveness improves as you expand the area of your leadership circle. Size and shape do matter, especially when you are under pressure. You can prove it to yourself by writing the names of three leaders you admire. They could be historical, political, or religious leaders. It doesn't matter—for now, just make the list.

The three leaders I admire are:

1. ______________________________

2. ______________________________

3. ______________________________

Next, think about their XLMs. I know you may not know these leaders intimately, so just give it your best shot. Score them on a 5-point scale (1 being never and 5 being always) in each of the four leadership styles.

I suspect that if the leaders you are thinking of unleashed the energy of others toward worthy goals, they have a large and well-rounded XLM. I say "worthy results" because someone like Hitler achieved extraordinary results, but only delusional skinheads claim that he achieved worthy results or that he was an extraordinary leader. (Hitler's empowering score on our scale would be negative.)

If we look at a few of my favorite historical leaders—Mother Teresa, Abraham Lincoln, Winston Churchill, Martin Luther King Jr., George Washington, and Mohandas Gandhi—I think it is clear that they often stretched when pulled by opposing demands.

If you turn to business leaders, you can do the same exercise. Make a list of three senior executives you admire who have unleashed the energy of others toward worthy goals. Then give them a score in the four leadership styles.

Three senior executives I admire are:

1. ______________________________

2. ______________________________

3. ______________________________

What did you learn from this simple exercise? Are they agile leaders? In his exhaustive studies of great companies, *Good to Great,*[5] Jim Collins warns us about the perils of celebrity leaders. He labeled the most successful executives as Level 5 executives—those who build enduring greatness through a paradoxical blend of personal humility (they serve ethically) and professional will (they execute with passion and courage).

An inflated ego is a
mismanagement of the me and *we paradox.*

Of course, we can always find isolated leaders who are the exception—the solitary geniuses poised at the top of the organizational pyramid commanding the troops with a compelling vision. These are the exceptions, not the examples of agile leaders. If you look behind the curtain of these heroic icons, you usually see a team empowered to develop a plan to execute the hero's vision.

To summarize, there are two ways to become a more agile leader:

1. Stretch a little every day by working on your relatively weak competency. The next four sections (one each on the rational, visionary, empowering, and commanding leadership styles) detail the four core competencies of each style and how to strengthen them.
2. Improve the quality and consistency of your decision-making and problem-solving. These topics are covered in Chapter 21. Appendices A and B also present specific examples of how to use the XLM to make better decisions when confronting specific business problems.

We begin by considering the competencies of the rational leadership style and the case of Randy and his unhappy promotion.

The universe is expanding.
How about you?

Section II

How Rational Executives Focus on the Task at Hand

Everyone was enthusiastic about Randy's leadership skills when he was promoted to head a new business unit within the $125 million medical device company. His task: Catapult sales of a new product using the existing distribution channels and sales organization.

Randy had been an excellent regional manager, successfully turning around a failing region and leading his team to market success. His team sold more of the company's traditional product line during his three years of leadership than they had in the previous ten years. Everybody in the organization admired his teamwork and collaborative skills.

Unfortunately, the signs of failure were apparent within Randy's first few months as head of the newly created business unit. When he requested resources to help his new sales team, the senior executives balked. At regional meetings, Randy was given limited time to discuss his vision for the new unit. Other sales managers discouraged their salespeople from working with Randy. As the pressure for Randy to perform increased, his frantic pace to accomplish more also increased. What should have been a dream job turned into his nightmare. The talk around the watercooler was that he was a good guy, but a dreamer.

The reality was that Randy's rational leadership skills were lacking. Within a year, he was gone.

The lesson behind this true story is that Randy had accepted a position that did not have clearly defined responsibilities. To be successful in the new business unit, Randy needed to work effectively with the current, "established" sales organization. However, his former colleagues were threatened by his new role because of the new dual reporting nature of "their" salespeople. And Randy didn't take the time to understand or monitor the problems his role caused the sales managers, nor did he develop a detailed plan endorsed by senior management to achieve his lofty vision.

Randy was not aware of his leadership weakness and it blindsided him. What happened to Randy can happen to any leader who does not develop the four critical competencies of a rational leader:

1. Clarify objectives and expectations.
2. Manage operations and plans.
3. Know thyself and others.
4. Monitor closely.

In the following four chapters in Section II, we'll explore each of these competencies, and how you can avoid Randy's fate by developing them.

CHAPTER 5

Knowing Where You're Going

Look and you will find it.
What is unsought will go undetected.

SOPHOCLES

Clarify objectives and expectations

Executives who are strong in rational thinking are clear about rules, roles, and expectations. They would never think of taking a job in which the organization did not spell out the objectives and expectations clearly, which is what Randy did.

Highly skilled rational leaders set realistic short-term objectives for themselves and each of their direct reports. They have well-defined standards of performance designed to meet or exceed internal/external customer requirements and expectations efficiently. They understand that measurement minimizes argument. Their mantra is: You can't manage it if you can't measure it.

Rational leaders also prioritize tasks based on how well they align with the overall goals and strategy of the organization. They ask Peter Drucker's focus question every day:

> *What specific contributions can my unit and I make that, if done really well, would make a substantial difference to the performance and results of my company?*[1]

Executives who expect the best tend to get it. In an article reviewing the relationship between expectations and performance, Professors John Humphreys and Walter Einstein recommended that leaders follow research-proven guidelines to maximize employee performance.[2] Their approach is outlined in Table 5.1. We can apply most of the guidelines to your direct reports' daily activities, as well as your overall job responsibilities.

TABLE 5.1

8 Guidelines to Clarify Objectives and Expectations

1. Articulate clear goals and performance outcomes.
2. Provide challenging work that the person values.
3. Verify that the individual understands the assigned duties and responsibilities.
4. Equip the person with the tools needed to do her or his best every day.
5. Frequently discuss how the individual's work aligns to the organization's strategy, especially as it relates to customer expectations.
6. Deliver clear, specific, and candid feedback frequently.
7. Provide appropriate and equitable rewards.
8. Recognize that the attractiveness of outcomes and rewards varies with cultures and individuals.

To follow these guidelines, leaders must stay in touch with their team members on a regular basis. Unfortunately, many leaders feel that this effort requires too much time. Yet it is achievable. Mary Kaye, a high-performing middle manager from Grapevine, Texas, reported in one of our leadership classes that she was able to follow the majority of these guidelines by conducting short meetings with each of her team members on a regular basis.

Mary Kaye sets up one five-minute meeting every day with one of her direct reports. Because she has five direct reports, this means all of her team members know they'll each get five minutes of uninterrupted one-on-one time with their manager every week. (If she needs more time, Mary Kaye schedules a separate meeting.) During these brief one-on-ones, she focuses on three issues:

1. Helping them with anything that is getting in their way of doing their job
2. Complimenting them for something she saw or heard them do well during the week
3. Asking if there were something else that they want to discuss

How might you adapt this idea to clarify objectives and expectations with your team?

Six keys to exceed your customer's expectations

Amid the impersonal busyness of the airport, I feel drawn to a warm oasis. *My shoes don't really need shining,* I think, as I take a seat to have my polished shoes shined at Nacho's shoeshine stand in Terminal 1 at LAX. Nacho (his real name) looks up and smiles. I rationalize my decision: *Well, my shoes can't be too polished to work with the Federal Reserve Bank.*

Why would I choose to spend money at Nacho's getting my shoes shined when they really didn't need it? Because Nacho delivers what scientists tell us are the keys to profitable repeat customers—he knows how to exceed his customers' expectations.

Do you?

Researcher Timothy Keiningham and collaborators followed 8,000 customers for two years to explore the relationships among survey responses, loyalty behavior, and company growth.[3] They concluded there were six strategies that leaders could adapt to keep their internal or external customers coming back. These strategies were what compelled me to have my polished shoes shined at Nacho's stand:

1. Reliability: Provide dependable and accurate service.
2. Assurance: Convey trust and confidence.
3. Responsiveness: Deliver prompt service, especially when customers need help.
4. Empathy: Offer personalized experience with a caring attitude.
5. Delight customers: Investigate and measure what "high level of satisfaction" means to your customers. Then, create systems to deliver that delightful experience—consistently.
6. Calculate your net promoter score (NPS).

Determine your NPS by measuring your customers' responses to this question:

> *How likely is it that you would recommend this company (or our service) to a friend or colleague?*

Those who rate you as a 9 or 10 (on a 10-point scale) are Promoters. Those who rate you 6 or lower are Detractors. Your NPS score is the difference: that is, the percentage of Promoters minus the percentage of Detractors.

Although some people have touted NPS as "the one number that you need to grow,"[4] Keiningham's follow-up study of 15,000 customers from 21 companies revealed that the connection is modest.[5]

In our search for simplicity, we sometimes see simplistic solutions to complex issues. Linking your customers' experiences or loyalties to growth is not easy. Nacho's secret recipe for success is a magical mix of all six of these strategies. In the past year, he has changed my shoelaces (without being asked) and given me a new canister of shoe polish (when I merely made a simple inquiry)—all without charging me. That's what keeps profitable customers like me coming back...even when our shoes don't need shinning.

One middle manager of a Silicon Valley high-tech company used these ideas to create an internal customer service survey. She discovered that her team's internal customers perceived her team as less than empathetic. She immediately embarked on an investigation to understand how her internal customers defined empathetic service. Then she created a brief workshop to teach her team this skill. She understood that when you clarify objectives and expectations, it is important to measure what matters.

How will you adapt these ideas to polish your customers' experiences?

Table 5.2 presents a series of 14 questions to help you clarify objectives and expectations. Answering them will help you grow this competency. You can also think of each question as a practical tool.

TABLE 5.2

14 Tools to Clarify Objectives and Expectations

1. How can you better understand your organization's vision and strategy?
2. How well are your group's goals aligned with the strategic goals of your organization?
3. Are you prioritizing your goals with your manager's on a regular basis?
4. Which few priorities have the biggest impact on your organization's success?
5. Have you matched the roles and responsibilities of each team member to these priorities?
6. How often do you communicate the priorities to your team?
7. Do you invite team members to identify obstacles to, and methods of achieving, your goals?
8. Have you developed methods to easily measure and visualize progress on your priorities?
9. How well do you inform others about what needs to get done, but let them decide *how* to do it?
10. Are your meetings action-oriented, and do they end with specific objectives and timelines?
11. How well do you use feedback to stay on track toward your goals?
12. Do you ensure that there are positive consequences for progress toward your goals and negative consequences for lack of progress?
13. How frequently do you ask questions to increase clarity before giving your opinion?
14. Who is highly skilled in this core competency from whom can you learn?

Use the ideas in this chapter to become a better leader by clarifying your objectives and expectations. Randy, who we met at the beginning of this section, failed in this area. He neither developed this competency nor adapted his leadership style to accommodate the fact that what he saw didn't match his expectations. Although he dreamed of the contributions he and his new unit could make, he didn't translate his big-picture thinking into reality.

In the next chapter, we'll consider how to create plans that do just that.

CHAPTER 6

Knowing Where You're Going Doesn't Get You There

To achieve great things, two things are needed: a plan, and not quite enough time.
LEONARD BERNSTEIN

MANAGE OPERATIONS AND PLANS

After leaving my position as chief administrative officer of the institute at UCLA, I started my own company and developed our first product – an interactive CD-ROM called *Strategy*. This innovative product automated marketing for medical imaging centers. It even led users through a step-by-step process of creating an individualized marketing plan. My conservative goal was to realize $100,000 in profit after the first year.

Unfortunately, the product did not sell well. (I'm still convinced it would have been a bestseller...if more people had bought it!) At the end of one year, I was $50,000 in debt. Two years later, I had doubled the debt and come within a whisker of losing my home.

Research tells us that the proverb is correct: I had planned to fail because I had failed to plan.

You probably know how to set goals. You may even know that Professors Edwin Locke and Gary Latham wrote the definitive book on the topic, *A Theory of Goal Setting and Task Performance,* in which they reviewed 393 separate research studies on goal-setting involving more than 40,000 subjects.[1] Their comprehensive review proved that setting goals can improve performance for you, your team, and your organization.

However, they also discovered that as goals *increase* in difficulty, the predictive value of having goals *decreases*. In fact, they report that "[a]cross the range of goal-setting studies using different tasks, the magnitude of goal effects on performance decreases as the complexity of the goal increases."

Think of the relationship between goal difficulty and achievement as an inverted U-shaped curve (∩). Goal difficulty increases across the bottom (the x-axis). Goal achievement runs up the left side (the y-axis). As goals become increasingly difficult, the probability of achieving goals starts to fall as you pass the mid-point (i.e., along the right half of the curve). Because you probably pursue challenging goals on a regular basis, the question becomes, How can I increase the probability that I will actually reach my most difficult—and rewarding—goals?

Our research with Professor Locke and the late Zig Ziglar has shown that the number-one method for reaching any difficult goal is to create an effective plan.[2] Ironically, I had created a product that automated marketing plans, but I failed to create a plan for my very own business.

As goals become harder to achieve, the plan to reach them becomes increasingly important. Think of it this way: If you had a desire to venture forth to a land far, far away, your chances of reaching this destination would be remote unless you had a map or a Global Positioning System (GPS) to show you the way.

The 3Ds of Effective and Efficient Plans

There are three simple tools, referred to as the 3Ds, for creating an effective and efficient map to reach your destination. Rational executives coach their managers to:

1. Define the deliverable.
2. Determine who should be on the team.
3. Decide on the tasks and time frames.

Define the deliverable

Achieving a goal begins by describing exactly what the result should look like. Whether you are managing an operation or planning a project, you and your managers must describe the scope of your goals, including:

- What the output is
- Why the project is important
- How it relates to the overall strategy of your organization

This scope must also include critical success factors. Critical success factors are the three to seven deliverables your key stakeholders consider essential before calling your project a success. They describe the general characteristics of your project. For example, if your goal is to install a new information system by a particular date, the critical success factors could include security features, compatibility requirements, or timing of the installation.

The scope also must encompass the assumptions associated with the project. Assumptions are those things that you believe to be true but have not been proved true. Assumptions ignored become risks. My favorite way to ferret out the assumptions is to brainstorm with people who are familiar with what I'm trying to achieve. For example, you could stand at a flipchart and write these two words across the top: *I assume*...Then, ask people to complete the sentence. You write down whatever they say. This is not the time to process what they say—just write it down. Discuss the assumptions and how to deal with them after brainstorming. Separate idea generation from idea evaluation to maximize contribution.

Not all risks are created equal. Therefore, once you have identified the risks, categorize them using the two major dimensions of probability and impact. Ask your team to help you place each risk in one of the nine boxes in Figure 6.1.

FIGURE 6.1

Plot Probability Against Impact to Categorize Risk

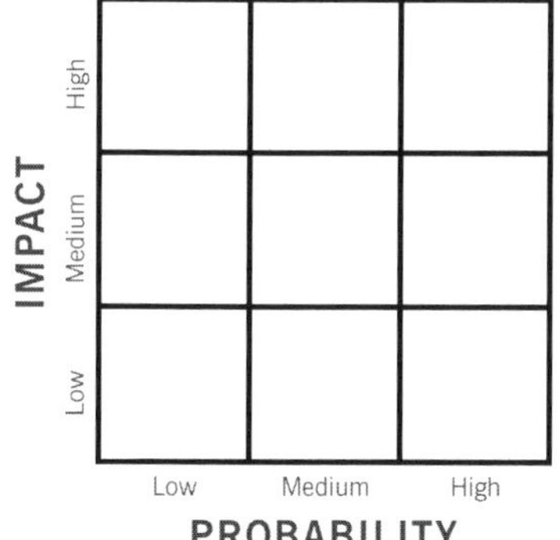

Determine who should be on the team

Most goals can't be achieved alone. After you've defined the deliverables, rational executives consider the personnel required to execute the plan. The primary criteria in selecting team members should be the skills and the subject matter expertise necessary to implement the plan. Work with your management team and obtain the people required to deliver on the scope.

Also, make sure the people you've selected have time allocated to do the work required by the project. I've seen many executives assign managers to projects without considering their time constraints. That's a prescription for burnout and turnover.

Decide on the tasks and time frames

An effective plan must include a list of the tasks the team must complete. One way to generate a task list is to first schedule a task-creation meeting. A few days before the meeting, ask team members to e-mail you a list of the tasks necessary to complete their portion of the project. Organize these tasks in a spreadsheet. For larger projects, use project management software.

At the meeting, brainstorm the tasks that people might have missed when they were working on their own.

The last step is to fill in the time frames necessary to complete the tasks. Figure 6.2 shows an example of a major task spreadsheet. These are tasks at the 10,000-foot level. Most task lists contain many smaller tasks. Feel free to adapt this spreadsheet to suit your project plan.

FIGURE 6.2

Major Task Spreadsheet

Action Item List	Revised						
	Time	Owner	Support	Start Date	Due Date	%Complete	Comments
1. Concept–Identity potential products							
2. Planning–Detailed definition of project							
3. Development–Detailed specs							
4. Prototype–Build prototype to prove design							
5. Validation–Alpha, Beta, Compliance tests							
6. Transition–Manuf. & support doc.							
7. Pilot–Test manuf. process							
8. Production–Sustain production							
9. End-of-Life–Manage end of production							
TOTAL							
Our team will begin manufacturing a fully integrated system by…							

When I left UCLA, I sailed the seas without a map and almost wrecked my ship. Don't let that happen to your team. Whenever you set a goal, create a plan to reach your goal using the 3Ds.

Here are several other tips to grow your executive planning skills:

1. Identify co-workers who have excellent plans. Ask to take them to lunch in exchange for sharing the process they use to develop their plans.
2. Invite your direct reports to comment on your preliminary plans during one-on-one or offsite meetings.
3. Share your preliminary plans with your managers.

4. Create a chart (such as the one seen in Figure 6.3) that allows you to view all your projects simultaneously.
5. Find a balance between long-range plans and day-to-day activities. At least once a week, spend time reflecting on the big picture and overall strategic direction. This perspective will help you focus on what is most important.
6. Apply the Pareto principle—what most people call the 80/20 rule. As it relates to time management and planning, this rule states that 80% of the value is in 20% of your tasks. Thus, if you have ten items on your project to-do list, focusing on two of them will probably get you 80% of the results desired. Many executives confuse activity for accomplishment. They work on the meaningless many instead of focusing on the fundamental few. Don't let that happen to you.
7. Collaborate cross-functionally. Whenever you create a plan, consider the impact on other units in your organization. How is what you are planning going to affect other people or processes? The world of work is becoming increasingly interdependent. Involve those affected by your plan in the process as early as possible.

FIGURE 6.3

Project Tracker

Revised								
Project List	Priority	Time	Project Manager	Start Date	Milestone	Due Date	%Completed	Comments
1. Project 1								
2. Project 2								
3. Project 3								

TABLE 6.1

Manage Operations and Plans with These 17 Questions

1. How closely aligned is your operation to your management's strategy?
2. Do you dedicate half of your project time to planning?
3. Is there adequate detail in your approach to your job?
4. How well do you consider the impact of your operation and projects on others?
5. How often do you involve your peers and direct reports to improve your operation?
6. How well do you mitigate risk to your operation or projects?
7. Do you set deadlines and milestones with your team and boss?
8. Do you solicit feedback from others regarding your plans and planning skills?
9. What assignments could you take on that would improve your ability to plan?
10. How well do you hold team members responsible for delivering on their due dates?
11. Do you obtain status reports from your direct reports on an ongoing basis?
12. Do you use scheduling tools to create and manage your plan?
13. How often do you compare your plan to reality?
14. How well do you coordinate efforts to improve your operation with other work units?
15. What could you do to build continuous improvement into your environment?
16. Do you assign your best people to the most important tasks?
17. What can you learn from great planners at work?

One of the major reasons that my *Strategy* CD-ROM product failed is that I failed to develop a plan. Like Randy, I built castles in the air, but did not build foundations under them. There are lots of excuses for my mistakes and Randy's—inexperience, ignorance, overconfidence—but, honestly, most of these excuses boil down to not knowing ourselves well enough to see where our blind spots are. Neither Randy nor I knew how important it was to manage operations and plans, or how poorly we executed this core competency.

In the next chapter, we'll explore how to know yourself and others so well that you avoid similar missteps on your leadership journey.

CHAPTER 7

Getting to Know All About You

Nothing is easier than self-deceit;
for what each of us wishes, we also believe to be true.
DEMOSTHENES

KNOW THYSELF AND OTHERS

"Well, I guess everybody in class believes that the typed manuscript for my new book is worth purchasing...except Mr. Jensen!" The executive director of our graduate program scowled at me as class started.

"Professor Wallace, my roommate and I have agreed to share your manuscript during the semester. He already bought it. Then, we'll both buy your book when it comes out in book form," I replied calmly, despite thinking, *Why are you calling me out in front of all my classmates?*

"I guess that makes you smarter than everybody else." He glared at me, turned his back to class, marched to the front of the room, and started writing on the blackboard.

He is influential in our profession, I thought. *I had better not get on his bad side.* Right then, I pulled out my checkbook and wrote a check to purchase his manuscript, then walked on eggshells to the front of the room. "Maybe it *is* better that I get my own copy." I offered my olive branch.

Professor Wallace turned to face me. "Too late!" He grabbed my check and ripped it in half. The pieces floated to the floor in slow motion.

I scooped them up, made my way back to my seat in front of a stunned classroom, and thought, *You've just made an ass of yourself in front of the entire class, Professor Wallace. How did you ever become a leader?*

Although this episode happened many years ago, I use it as a lesson even today. Professor Wallace's deficiency was in the third competency of a rational leader: Know thyself and others. This competency requires leaders to assess accurately their strengths and weaknesses, as well as the strengths and weaknesses of those around them. It includes the ability to perceive correctly the subtle cues, emotions, and feelings that they and others experience. Understanding why people feel the way they do and how to generate the appropriate mood to fit the occasion are other key components of knowing thyself and others.

Years later, it became clear to me that Professor Wallace's poor skills in this area hurt him professionally. For example, a famous scientist I met while at UC San Diego once told me that he informed a publisher that he would not co-author a book with Professor Wallace because Wallace was "a pain in the [anatomical reference] to work with." On another occasion, the head of an important association divulged that he wouldn't invite Wallace to speak at his meetings because he had seen Wallace "squirm like a worm at the end of a hook" during the question-and-answer session following a presentation; in his assessment, Wallace "did not have the expertise to deliver...."

Professor Wallace is not the only leader to have suffered from a flawed self-assessment. The inability to see who we are clearly and how well we perform objectively is an epidemic among executives.

Can I see the real me?

Not very well.

That's the conclusion of Professor David Dunning and his colleagues after reviewing 293 research papers on flawed self-assessment.[1] When they reviewed studies comparing self-assessment with objective performance measures, they found a low correlation — usually around 0.25, where 0 is no correlation and 1.0 is a perfect correlation. This makes many self-report assessments very suspect. In addition, there was only a 0.2 correlation between how well employees expected to perform on a complex task and how well they actually performed it.

The bottom line from this meta-analysis of the research: Most of us do not assess our strengths or weaknesses accurately, often because of flaws in our thinking. Let's address four flaws in particular.

We all think we are above average

Did you know that 94% of college professors say they do above-average work? Among high school students, 70% of them believe they have above-average leadership skills. And at one high-tech company, 42% of engineers rated their own performance in the top 5% of all engineers.

Compounding matters, this tendency to think we are better than we actually are is greatest among the lowest performers.[2] So it seems the team members who need to improve their performance the most are the very individuals who tend to believe they are doing the best.

We overestimate the likelihood of desirable events

In one large university lecture class, 83% of the students predicted that they would buy flowers in an annual charity drive for the American Cancer Society. Yet, they guessed only 55% of their fellow students would do the same. Four weeks later, the actual percentage of those buying flowers was a mere 43%.

Let me share a more personal example: Two months before embarking on a biking trip I estimated I would lose seven pounds by modifying my diet. I lost only three.

Where do you need to increase the accuracy of your predictions?

We underestimate the amount of time to complete tasks

This phenomenon is known as the planning fallacy. In one classic study, scientists asked students working on an assignment to indicate when they were 50% certain they could finish the project, as well as when they were 99% certain they could finish.

If the students' assessments were accurate, about half of them would have finished by the 50% deadline and 99% would have finished by their very conservative 99% deadline. In actuality, only 13% of the students finished by their 50% deadline and only 45% finished their assignment by their 99% deadline. The planning fallacy is why Microsoft builds a 30% to 50% time buffer into most of its projects.

What kind of buffer might you need?

We are overconfident in our predictions

We tend to place too much confidence in our ability to make accurate predictions. This phenomenon is known as the overconfidence effect. For example, among doctors diagnosing patients as having pneumonia, doctors who made predictions with an 80% certainty turned out to be right only 20% of the time. It's also why traders on Wall Street remind each other, "Don't confuse brains with a bull market."

Overconfident executives or so-called experts who base their strategy on their ability to predict future events should take heed.

Like a warped circus mirror, these four common causes of self-delusion distorted Professor Wallace's perception of who he was, his strengths and weaknesses, and his ability to see those around him accurately. These distortions clouded his decision-making and problem-solving. Here are three practical tactics to help you overcome the same tendency.

Get the facts

Executives seldom have the all knowledge required to assess their competence in a given area, which often contributes to poor problem-solving and decision-making.

To address this limitation, it's usually best to assume you do not have adequate expertise and ask those who do. One study that compared successful and unsuccessful microbiology labs found that the best labs had more group meetings at which researchers had to answer difficult questions from skeptical peers.[3] When I was a researcher at UC San Diego, our team employed this strategy during weekly research meetings. It worked. We knew our colleagues had our best interests at heart when we challenged each other's perceptions, assumptions, and conclusions.

Although actively seeking candid or negative comments is rare among executives, it has many positive outcomes. If you do it more often, science says you will improve your self-awareness and performance, as well as increase positive perceptions of your leadership by direct reports and peers.[4]

Learn from frequent and candid feedback

If you receive incomplete or inaccurate feedback following a decision that is subsequently implemented, it creates an erroneous sense of accomplishment, thereby hindering your efforts to know yourself and others. Performing rapid after-action reviews (AARs) following your important decisions can help.

After you or your team complete a project or important activity, discuss these fundamental questions with those individuals who will tell you the truth:

- What was the desired outcome?
- What was the actual outcome?
- Why the difference?
- What are the lessons learned?
- What will we do differently next time?

- Do we need to adjust our goals?
- With whom should we share our lessons?

The truth—not your opinion—sets you free.

Select the right standard

A senior executive once complained to me that the ratings he received from his CEO during his annual review were not as high as the ratings his peers were given. When I asked how he knew so much about his peers' evaluations, he confessed that he actually had no data.

I suggested that he compare himself to an objective performance standard and invited him to take the XLM 360-leadership assessment. When he did, he was able to compare his self-evaluation to the perceptions of his boss, peers, and employees. These additional data points were enough to convince him that he had a few "development opportunities" to work on to become a more effective executive.

Make sure you select the right standard when you evaluate your strengths and weaknesses, as well as those around you. (Incidentally, six months later, this executive's XLM assessment follow-up showed significant improvement in two competencies. His delighted CEO has promoted him.)

The three practical tactics discussed above will help you understand your strengths and weaknesses, as well as those of the people around you. However, knowing thyself and others is not merely about your cognitive strengths and weaknesses. Achieving extraordinary results requires that you know and apply the four skills of emotional intelligence as well.[5]

The Four Skills of Emotionally Intelligent Executives

The story about Professor Wallace that opened this chapter not only illustrates the importance of accurate self-assessment, it highlights the power of emotions at work (and school). Although my professor seemed to have a high IQ, his leadership suffered because of his low Emotional Intelligence (EI).

Like Professor Wallace, executives have long assumed the workplace is a logical environment. Set goals, pay people to do a job, monitor their work, and watch the organization grow.

We now know this simplistic generalization is not the way work really gets done. Humans are rational *and* emotional beings. To lead effectively, one must be logically and emotionally intelligent. Effective executives are beginning to understand that emotions are always at work. The only question is, are they working for or against you?[6]

So what is EI? It's "the ability to carry out accurate reasoning about emotions and the ability to use the emotions and emotional knowledge to enhance thought."[7] This definition informs us that EI is much more than keeping calm under pressure or hiding our anger. Emotionally intelligent executives know themselves and others so well that they actually use their emotions to create better outcomes. In their review of 178 EI studies, Professor John Mayer and his colleagues concluded that high EI is linked to better social relations, decision-making at work, negotiation results, and long-term leadership success.[8]

Similarly, Professors Sigal Barsade and Donald Gibson summarized EI research by asserting that employee emotions "influence critical organizational outcomes such as job performance, decision-making, creativity, turnover, pro-social behavior, teamwork, negotiation, and leadership."[9]

These findings should encourage you to marry reason and emotion—to lead with your head as you listen to your heart. To know yourself and others emotionally is to apply four specific EI abilities:[10]

1. Perceive emotions: Are you in touch?
2. Use emotions: Do you have emotions or do they have you?
3. Understand emotions: Can you forecast the emotional future?
4. Regulate emotions: How's the marriage between your head and your heart?

The remainder of this chapter discusses the first three of these emotional abilities because they are critical to knowing thyself and others. The fourth skill, regulating emotions, is discussed in Chapter 19.

Perceive emotions

In an EI certification workshop I attended not long ago, Professor David Caruso from Yale University invited us to think of emotions as data. Emotions have useful information. Understanding yourself and others begins by accurately identifying what we and those around us feel. If we misperceive an emotion in ourselves or others, it is impossible to accurately use emotion, understand the emotional future, or regulate the emotion appropriately. The old saying "garbage in, garbage out" applies because a mislabeled emotion leads to an inappropriate response.

But perceiving emotions is more than awareness—it is *accurate* awareness. Executives who are highly skilled in this area have the ability to read subtle signals in themselves and others, label feelings appropriately, and express correct emotional signals. One of my colleagues at Siemens paid the price for missing these cues.

I recall a meeting at which passions were running high and hot regarding a new software release. Bill, the product manager for this software, sat there like a totem pole, seemingly oblivious to the intensity of people's feelings about the flaws in the software. I didn't feel he was in tune with the frustration we (the sales teams) were experiencing. He came across like Commander Data (or, if you prefer, Spock) on *Star Trek*—indifferent and disconnected. It seemed that Bill was confusing managing emotions with masking them.

Bill, like Professor Wallace, failed to perceive what was going on because he missed the emotional smoke signals sent by others. I am convinced this contributed to Bill's firing a year later. Where do you see executives miss or misread emotions? When does it happen to you? What are the consequences of not developing this ability?

Contrast Bill's failure with the success of Procter & Gamble CEO A.G. Lafley, who has the ability to read the emotional tea leaves of his employees. Lafley demonstrated a major concern for what employees were feeling when he took the helm of a listing ship in the early 2000s. "Appraising the emotional landscape" was his critical first step in rescuing P&G.[11] The company conducted interviews, focus groups, and extensive surveys of employees. P&G's leaders used the brutally honest results to create a number of critical initiatives that led to long-term organizational success. During Lafley's decade of leadership, sales doubled, profits quadrupled, and P&G's portfolio of billion-dollar brands increased from 10 to 23.[12]

To improve your ability to perceive emotions accurately at work (and home), here are ten tools and techniques that you should consider employing.

1. Write Morning Pages: In her book *The Artist's Way,* Julia Cameron describes a powerful writing technique called Morning Pages.[13] She recommends that the first thing you do in the morning is write three pages by hand, fast and continuously. Write anything that comes to mind without editing. Don't think, don't hesitate, and don't stop. The key is to keep your hand moving, no matter what splats out onto the pages. If it takes you more than 20 minutes, you're thinking too much.

Morning Pages are not prose, poetry, or journaling. You shouldn't share them with anyone. You will be amazed at what you learn about your emotions through your writing.

2. Use an emotion scale: David Caruso and Peter Salovey suggest that you assess your emotions several times a day, using this 10-point scale:

	Definitely Don't Feel					Maybe				Definitely Feel
Happy	1	2	3	4	5	6	7	8	9	10
Sad	1	2	3	4	5	6	7	8	9	10
Angry	1	2	3	4	5	6	7	8	9	10
Anticipating	1	2	3	4	5	6	7	8	9	10
Fearful	1	2	3	4	5	6	7	8	9	10
Surprised	1	2	3	4	5	6	7	8	9	10
Accepting	1	2	3	4	5	6	7	8	9	10
Disgusted	1	2	3	4	5	6	7	8	9	10
Jealous	1	2	3	4	5	6	7	8	9	10
Ashamed	1	2	3	4	5	6	7	8	9	10

3. Pay attention: As you increase your awareness of your own emotional state, it is also important to understand others' feelings. The first step in becoming a people reader is to pay attention to what people are saying with their body language. Facial expressions can tell you a lot if you focus on the mouth, eyes, and nose. A smiling mouth with no eye crinkles is usually a fake smile. A smile that appears too quickly, or with the lips stretched horizontally instead of curled upward, is also not a real smile.

4. Catch a movie: Dr. Amy Van Buren recommends that you scan through a movie and stop at any point you see two people talking. Turn the sound off and watch the scene for about 30 seconds. Next, evaluate the emotion in this scene using the emotion scale above. You may want to compare notes with a partner. Then, watch the scene again with the sound on to assess your ability to evaluate emotions.

5. Find a model of EI at work: Identify a leader who demonstrates high emotional awareness. Find ways to work more closely with that leader. Volunteer for projects or committees on which he serves. Ask if you could shadow him occasionally. Then, observe how he interacts with others. Answer these questions:

- What kind of questions does he ask?
- How does he listen?
- When does he choose to speak in meetings?

6. Be more like others: What would you guess your heart rate is right now? Please write that number on a piece of paper. (Come on, this is an interactive book.) Now, take your pulse and measure your actual heart

rate. The closer you are to your guess, the higher your *interoception*—your ability to read and interpret sensations in your own body. Research shows that people who track their own heartbeat well are better at perceiving their emotions.[14]

Further investigations have revealed that our ability to perceive bodily sensations is linked to emotional awareness by an area of the brain called the right frontal insula. It is here, neuroscientists tell us, that we find the true mind-body connection, and where we can improve our ability to perceive the emotions in others.[15] Here's how.

At your next meeting, identify someone with whom you would like to better connect emotionally. We will call her your "customer." During the meeting, observe your customer's breathing and speaking pace, as well as her posture and gestures:

- How many breaths is she taking?
- How fast is she talking?
- How is she sitting?
- Is she moving her hands or crossing her legs?
- What are her eye movements?

As you observe her movements, begin duplicating them. In other words, follow her lead by doing what she does...subtly. The more you tune in with the other person physically and verbally, the more you will connect with her emotionally. Don't take my word for it—try it.

How surprised will you be when you discover that you feel what others feel when you are more like them?

7. Reflectively listen: During your next conversation with one of your direct reports, when he says something significant, reflect it back to him in your own words to confirm you heard him correctly. This forces you to listen carefully, which creates a higher emotional awareness.

8. Discover what emotion is talking: You may listen to what others say, but how well do you hear what emotion is talking? Do you hear what people say beneath the surface of their words? Where are they coming from—is fear, worry, or doubt doing the talking, or do confidence, certainty, and clarity describe their states of mind?

Too many executives are fond of listening to their own tune. They confuse broadcasting for communicating. The better you can tune into other people's communication stations, the more in tune you are with them. Write yourself a reminder to focus on where others are coming from (perhaps at the top of a notepad where you write notes during your conversations). Stop merely talking *to* your employees and start communicating *with* them.

9. Notice the details: When I worked in sales for Siemens, I once walked into a busy physician's office to discuss her computer needs. She would give me 5 minutes, she said, to tell her why she should purchase our medical computers. I thanked her for her time, pointed to a picture on her desk, and let her know that I would be happy to tell her about my computers if she would first tell me where on Cape Cod the picture was taken.

She smiled and asked how I knew it was the Cape. After I told her I grew up in Connecticut and visited the Cape frequently, she spent 10 minutes discussing her family experiences on Cape Cod. She then gave me 20 minutes to discuss computers. I met with her and her staff a few times during the next few months, and they purchased our computers. This sales success flowed from my observing and caring about what was important to her emotionally.

Can you accurately describe people and/or their office after you visit? What is the color of their clothes, eyes, hair? How do their voices sound? What's in the picture frames on their desks and walls? What colors are the carpets and doors? Practice the game of observation to improve your perception of what is important to others.

10. Work with a coach: A good coach will help you identify an ideal image that you have of yourself (which includes increasing your EI), provide feedback regarding your EI, assist in the development plan to bridge the gap, and coach you through the process of learning new behaviors.

Use emotions

Several years ago, I was helping a colleague set up for a very important presentation. As he welcomed guests into the meeting room, my initial excitement turned into frustration because I couldn't get the two projectors focused correctly on the two screens in the front of the room. Just before the presentation was about to begin, and as my frustration boiled into silent anger, one of the guests pointed out that the side-by-side projectors were focused on opposite screens.

I had been trying to focus one projector while looking at the other's screen. I felt like an idiot. I also realized that I did not have the emotion of anger—it had me!

How often do your emotions use you instead of the other way around?

Using emotions to get in the right mood, prioritize thinking, and improve decision-making is the second EI skill. How we feel affects how we think, which influences our decisions and outcomes. In the projector story, I was initially excited about helping a brilliant colleague with an important presentation. Unfortunately, I did not know there was a downside to being up.

That's right—research suggests that being upbeat may hinder the execution of specific tasks.[16] In my case, I allowed myself to become a prisoner of my feelings. If I had put myself in the right frame of mind (neutral or mildly sad), there's further evidence (from pioneering research by Professor Joseph Forgas of the University of New South Wales) that I might have enhanced my thinking and solved my problem.[17]

Let's conduct a quick little experiment. Imagine, just for a moment, that you are going for a walk in a beautiful environment with someone you really care about. Flood your imagination with the rich sights, sounds, and other physical sensations of this relaxing, leisurely stroll. Are you in the mountains, a valley, on a secluded beach? Do you smell mountain air or salt water? Can you hear your partner's conversation, the thundering surf of the ocean, whistling birds, or a babbling brook? Is the warmth of the sun on your shoulders or face?

Next, imagine that you and your strolling partner decide to brainstorm all the benefits you might experience if you improved your EI. Now that you have the picture, sensations, and feelings, please take a blank piece of paper and write down as many of these benefits as you can think of. Do it right now.

Go ahead. I'll wait.

How did your brainstorming session go? Whether you wrote a few ideas or a flood, research tells us that you brainstorm better when you are in a better mood.[18]

Being upbeat may hinder our efforts to focus on tasks (as my story illustrated), yet that same mood facilitates creative thinking. The rationale is that "people use their moods as indications of the state of their environment."[19] Thus, negative feelings signal that something is wrong, so our brains subconsciously pay close attention to the environment, then search for specific information to solve the problem or address the issue. Newscasters know that our reptilian brains are wired to focus on drama, which is why the news is so often negative. On the other hand, because positive emotions communicate that all is well, focus and analysis are not needed, liberating our attention to be open to creative ideas.

The bottom line is that using your emotions is about creating a specific feeling to generate a desired outcome.[20] Just as the best athletes channel their emotions to rally their teams to victory, effective leaders use their emotions to achieve their team's worthy goals.

Consider basic emotions like sadness or happiness that affect our thinking. When we are sad, we tend to notice details—this is the upside of being down. Positive moods, by contrast, yield ideas that are more creative—which is the upside of being up.

To use emotions well, we need to be able to generate the feelings we want when we want them. One way is to tell or write a story that evokes that emotion. Another way to create the desired feeling on demand is to learn from Hollywood. I've adapted the renowned method acting approach, pioneered by Russian director Constantin Stanislavski (and a technique recommended by Professors Caruso and Salovey), to help you use your emotions to make better decisions and create a desired outcome.

- Relax: Close your eyes. Find a quiet, peaceful place in your imagination. Create a rich mental representation of this serene scene by imagining it completely, with vivid and detailed objects, sounds, and smells. Use all your senses to relax into the scene.
- Recall an emotional event: Which emotion will help you create the thinking you need to make a better decision? Use the emotion descriptions to guide your imagination to an emotional scene that accesses this desired emotion. For example, if you are gathering information on a technical project, you might want to recall a memory that contains the emotion of surprise, because this feeling is associated with being open to new information. You could think of an unexpected award you received at work or that surprise party friends gave you. Create a sensory rich environment as you go back in time to experience the event fully. The more details the better. What did it look, feel, smell, taste, and sound like? What expressions did you have on your face? What emotions did you feel?
- Affirm the emotion: Use affirmations to anchor the emotion by repeating statements that are consistent with the feeling you're creating. As you affirm the emotion verbally, take on the emotion physically. Create the facial expressions, posture, body movements, breathing, etc., that you felt during the emotional event. How you act (your physiology) influences how you feel. Your motion affects your emotion.
- Connect the emotion to the task: Finally, maintain this physiology as you work on the task at hand. For example, if you are in your

office and want to stay open to new information by accessing the emotion of surprise, you can stand up and walk around your office, acting as if you are at the surprise party as you jot down a few notes on a notepad. On the other hand, if you're preparing for a meeting, take the first three steps of this process — relax, recall, affirm — *before* the meeting to create the emotion *for* the meeting. Then, act (take on the physiology) and affirm (repeat to yourself) the desired emotion as you discuss ideas at the meeting.

If you employ these techniques to use your emotions—instead of being used by them—science says you are likely to achieve your desired outcome.[21] I encourage you to try this technique—I think you'll find it a "moving experience."

Understand emotions

Traffic lights are called signals because they provide information that directs our action. Understanding the signals tells us to stop, go, turn, or — in the case of yellow — hit the gas and race through the intersection. (Just kidding about the yellow signal.)

Emotions are signals, too. They contain information that communicates direction. Just as with traffic lights, we can understand emotional signals only if we detect the signal accurately, assess its intensity (akin to how far you are from the light), and evaluate our options regarding taking action. Thus, the third EI ability—understanding emotions—helps us predict the future accurately so that we can take appropriate action.

You know a leader is *not* using this skill when you see him shuffle out of a meeting puzzled about his team's reaction to his latest news. Leaders who fail to understand emotions will also complain about interactions that seem to be going well and "all of a sudden" fall flat. They often say things that upset people, find it hard to explain their emotions, and seem to blow hot or cold...without much between the extremes.

These are all signs that the leader is clueless regarding how emotions progress through predictable intensities. If leaders miss the emotional signals, they limit their ability to conduct an effective emotional what-if analysis. Because they don't know where people are coming *from* emotionally, they can't predict where people are going *to*. For instance, an employee who is wary about a major change at work will usually become worried first, then fearful, and then finally panicked if she doesn't understand the cause of her fear (a perceived threat) properly.

Executives who are strong in this ability comprehend the causes of emotions, have a rich emotional vocabulary, and employ what-if analysis to predict and create the desired future. That's why they always seem to know the right thing to say. They know that truly understanding emotions requires knowing their causes. Executives skilled in this area monitor employees' emotions when they introduce any change. Their emotional radar detects employee wariness before it mushrooms into fear because they understand what causes our six basic human emotions — sadness, happiness, anger, fear, surprise, and disgust.

- Sadness: We usually feel sadness when we do not achieve a goal or lose something that we care about.
- Happiness: A feeling of well-being bubbles up when we experience something that we value. Happiness is often related to achieving a meaningful goal.
- Anger: This emotion boils up when we perceive someone has been wronged, offended, or denied justice. Anger targets our energy on specific threats. Although anger has its place, it is misplaced when it becomes destructive.
- Fear: Fear grabs us when a perceived threat is near. Because fear communicates that something undesirable is happening (or is about to), it frequently is accompanied by a feeling of uncertainty and/or a desire to take some action. Fear drives our "fight or flight" instinct. Anxiety is related to fear, but is usually more persistent and generalized.
- Surprise: Surprise springs out like a jack-in-the-box when events do not go according to plan. It catches our attention and signals us to figure out what's up—which helps us to gather new information quickly. Surprise is why we become "all ears" when we listen to shocking news. It can be perceived as positive, negative, or neutral.
- Disgust: Associated with things that are unclean, gory, or offensive, disgust is felt most acutely in relation to the sense (real or imagined) of taste. This emotion may help us to avoid things or situations that are distasteful, but it seldom creates the type of thinking we find useful.

Understanding the causes of these basic emotions leads to an expanded emotional vocabulary, thereby allowing us to fine-tune our understanding of emotional signals and make subtle distinctions that lead to better predictions.

Executives without a robust language don't express themselves accurately. They are like children who describe a destructive hurricane as a rainy day. For example, I could say that I was surprised when I received an executive coaching contract yesterday. But that would not be accurate because I actually was amazed. My amazement stemmed from having our agreement signed and delivered within a week of submitting it.

Each of the basic emotions, listed in Table 7.1, has related emotional terms adapted from Caruso and Salovey.[22]

TABLE 7.1

Emotional Vocabulary

SAD	ANGRY
• pensive	• annoyed
• down	• frustrated
• gloomy	• upset
• sad	• anger
• grief-stricken	• rage
HAPPY	**FEARFUL**
• serene	• attentive
• pleased	• wary
• happy	• worried
• joyous	• fearful
• ecstatic	• panicked
SURPRISED	**DISGUSTED**
• content	• bored
• distracted	• disinterested
• surprised	• dislike
• amazed	• disgusted
• shocked	• loath

Where emotions come from predict where you go

Once you understand that it's not just another rainy day, but a Category 5 hurricane heading your way, you know what's coming and how to think more clearly about possible actions. Understanding the causes of emotions and expanding your emotional vocabulary are preludes to predicting the emotional future. As you become more skilled in this competency, you comprehend where you and others are coming from emotionally, and you can also forecast where you and they are going.

Prediction in emotions is like prediction in any other discipline; you employ what-if analysis to generate a plan of action. The key ingredient in an emotional what-if analysis is recognizing the patterns that emotions follow. Please take another look at the basic emotions listed in Table 7.1 and their related emotional terms. Do you notice the pattern of progression in each emotion? By recognizing how emotions usually advance through predictable sequences, you can test certain assumptions about the various plans to deal with that emotion.

Imagine you are in a project meeting with two colleagues. Diane is one of your direct reports, while Don is one of your colleagues. As Don drones on about some of the stakeholders in the project, you notice that Diane seems to be getting annoyed. You therefore think there is a high probability that she may become frustrated, upset, and even angry if you don't manage the situation well.

By identifying the emotion of annoyance accurately and early, you can consider various actions to avoid an emotional escalator. Because you feel Don's excessive rambling annoys Diane, you decide to ask others for their opinion, thereby decreasing Don's domination of the meeting. It works. Congratulations! You have just used your understanding of emotions to create a desired outcome. But how well and how consistently are you applying your emotional vocabulary, in other situations, to create outcomes you want?

The most powerful way to develop your emotional forecasting skill is to reflect on your feelings frequently throughout the day. Keep Table 7.1 near you to improve your awareness of your precise feelings. As you increase your capacity to make emotional distinctions, expand your self-awareness to think about where your emotions lead (recalling Diane and Don's story). You might also find it helpful to exercise your emotional understanding at home and then extend your learning to work.

For example, I use to become angry (at the television) when my sports teams played poorly. As I learned that anger is often caused by feelings of being wronged or offended, I asked myself, why do I feel wronged or offended when the Lakers play poorly? That's when I realized my feelings came from my belief that these highly paid sports stars weren't trying hard enough. If I always played hard, even though I didn't possess half their talent, why couldn't they?

My team losing was not what angered me; it was my perception and judgment of their lack of effort. Knowing this, I now catch myself being annoyed by *my perception* before I jump on the emotional escalator toward anger. My lesson? When someone triggers my emotional button, it's *my* button. I need to accurately detect my emotion early, then quickly assess where this emotion will lead me, then choose how I want to deal with it. It's about me, not them.

I encourage you to refer to the emotion list throughout the day to expand your emotional vocabulary and experiment with what-if analysis. How surprised will you be when you become a better executive because you understand the emotional future?

Let's return to the story that opened this chapter: Professor Wallace did not demonstrate emotional intelligence when he ripped my check in half in front of the class. Yet, neither did I. If I could go back and apply the EI skills we're discussing in the chapter, here's what I would do differently:

- Identify that the professor was in a negative mood. (Identify emotions.)
- Recognize that his negativity would limit his receptivity to my explanation. (Use emotions.)
- Understand that his being upset with me might lead to anger toward me if I said or did anything in class. Also, understand that my annoyance at being called out in front of class might lead to anger, thereby causing me to become defensive. (Understand emotions.)
- Regulate my emotion by not responding to his initial statement during class. Then, visit him at his office another day to discuss the situation, apologize for any misunderstanding, and perhaps write a check that might not get ripped in half. Learn more about this fourth skill (regulating the emotions) in Chapter 19.

TABLE 7.2

15 Tools to Know Thyself and Others

1. How much effort do you exert to know yourself?
2. How often do you ask others (e.g., direct reports, peers, customers, bosses) for feedback?
3. How well do you know those around you?
4. Do you have one-on-one meetings with your direct reports at least once a week?
5. Do you receive confidential 360-feedback every few years?
6. How many of your strengths are so strong that, at times, they are perceived as weaknesses?
7. How well do you size up people?
8. Have you outlined the strengths and weaknesses of your direct reports?
9. How well have you aligned your direct reports' strengths and weaknesses to specific job duties?
10. How much time do you spend trying to read other people's emotions?
11. How often do you look below the surface to assess and predict other people's motivations or feelings?
12. How well do your expressions of emotions allow others to understand how you feel?
13. Do you understand that different moods affect thinking and decisions in different ways?
14. How much do you feel what others feel when they describe an emotional event?
15. What can you learn from those who know themselves and others well?

The tools listed in Table 7.2 complement the emotional vocabulary in Table 7.1.

Remember Randy and the story of his unhappy promotion that introduced Section II. As you ask and answer these essential questions, consider what Randy might have done differently to manage his challenges in selling the new product through his company's existing network.

If Randy knew himself and others well, he would have recognized his own strong visionary competencies and lower rational competencies. He could have managed the expectations of his colleagues if he knew where they were coming from. Additionally, had he developed his emotional intelligence, he might have recognized his colleagues' subtle reactions to his efforts early enough to do something about them. He could have devised a wiser strategy to earn their support for his new position.

If Randy had used the ideas in this chapter, he probably would have achieved his goals. Amazingly, even if he didn't apply these tools, he still could have succeeded if he had learned how to monitor closely, the fourth competency of rational leadership style, and the topic of the next chapter.

CHAPTER 8

Be Here Now

It isn't the mountain ahead that wears you out—
it's the grain of sand in your shoe.

ROBERT SERVICE

MONITOR CLOSELY

I heard the whining engine and screeching tires a split-second before the white Miata flew around the mountain's curve. I jumped off my bike and watched the petrified driver wrestle with the wheel. Unfortunately, the next curve came too fast. The car flew off the mountain.

I staggered downhill ten yards, to the spot where his tires last clawed the road. Praying for a miracle, I peered over the edge...and was shocked to see one.

Instead of plunging 300 feet down the ravine, Jeff Gordon (not his real name) had landed against several thick bushes 30 feet down. The car was banged up, but upright, and Jeff crawled up the embankment toward me.

As he reached the road, Jeff straightened up and assured me that he was fine (he had no visible bruises and he had been wearing his seatbelt). He asked to use my cell phone to call for a tow truck, and then encouraged me, numerous times, to continue my bike ride up the steep mountain road. So I did.

As I strained up the 15% grade, I thought about all the curves Jeff had negotiated as he came down this twisting road and wondered why he missed the one near me, and how his story was a metaphor for the monitor closely competency.

To monitor an environment closely means to pay attention to feedback. Webster's defines feedback as "the return to the point of origin of evaluative or corrective information." Feedback is everywhere. A market-based economy works because consumers give continuous feedback to producers. The human body incorporates thousands of feedback mechanisms that keep us alive. Failure to monitor feedback closely threatens our livelihoods and our health, and it's what almost killed Jeff on that mountain. It also hurts us our ability to stretch when pulled.

I counted 37 curves from the spot where he went over the edge to the top of that mountain. This means he had 37 opportunities to become aware of, learn from, and adjust to the feedback the mountain and his car were giving him as he raced down. He was getting feedback about the road conditions, his car's handling, his ability to negotiate hairpin curves. Unfortunately, he was — to paraphrase T. S. Eliot — getting the experience but missing the meaning.

How about you?

To keep from going off the road, rationally thinking executives must closely monitor their environment by actively seeking feedback from their business climate, customers, the organization, upper management, colleagues, and direct reports. This monitoring provides the accurate knowledge needed to adjust course on the mountain. Without such knowledge, leaders risk being labeled "out of touch." One study found that "denying reality" was responsible for 23% of CEO firings.[1]

Unfortunately, according to Professors Kathleen Sutcliffe and Klaus Weber, there is also a high cost to trying to gather too much knowledge.[2]

They surveyed 329 top management team (TMT) members in 85 diverse organizations. They found the relationship between accuracy of information and magnitude of positive organizational change followed an inverted U-shaped pattern (∩). Initial investments in improving the accuracy of perceptions (by monitoring closely) trigger more and better change, but as improvements in accuracy began to taper off, so did the magnitude of positive change. Eventually, spending more time obtaining information (i.e., obtaining feedback) became negatively associated with change.

By contrast, executives who worked with a moderate amount of information were able to make decisions and act in a timely manner while maintaining a consistent strategy.

This research tells us that it is possible to miss important information as we race down our daily mountains, thereby flying of the cliff like our Miata racer. The results also remind us that we can't monitor so closely that we crawl down the mountain, thereby missing our deadlines. We must manage the tension between accurate information and timely action.

When it comes to monitoring closely, the middle road seems to be the best road.

Do not allow the possibilities to blind you from the probabilities.

Eight tools to help you stay in touch

There are eight tools, described in this sub-section, to help you manage the tension between information and action by closely monitoring your challenging, paradoxical environment.

Monitor where the action is

I met with an executive who told me that her CEO had not visited her office in the four years she had been with the company. Granted, her boss reported to the CEO, not her. But executives must make time to visit those a few layers below them. I also encourage you to visit the front lines, where change happens first. One of Toyota's five basic principles is *genchi genbutsu,* which means "going to the source to find the facts to inform your decisions, build consensus, and achieve goals."[3]

Remove your environmental blinders

We all have filters that fog our view of the landscape. Professors Anthony Mayo and Nitin Nohria studied 1,000 successful executives and found that the best leaders have the ability to understand the context in which they live and seize the opportunities in the present.[4] Specifically, these leaders closely monitored six factors to help them accurately understand their environment:

1. The amount of government intervention
2. Global events
3. Demographics
4. Social mores
5. Technology
6. Labor issues

Knowledge of their environment, the context in which they operate the business, allowed these successful leaders to adapt their strategy and their style to match the opportunities presented to them.

How are you staying in touch with your environment?

Value variety

Management expert Gary Hamel points out that it takes a thousand ideas to produce a dozen promising products, thereby yielding a few genuine successes.[5] Yet many organizations suffer from the "big bet" fallacy. Their executives set audacious goals and scramble to cut costs when their big bets don't pay off. Big bets are fine once in a while, but nature teaches us that conducting small experiments and paying attention to the feedback leads to an agile, adaptable organization amenable to a changing climate. Effective leaders who monitor closely take small steps, observe the environmental response, and adjust to the feedback.

Be open to most things, attached to few

If the driver on the mountain had been open to what the hairpin turns were teaching him, he might not have plunged off the road. Do you ever find yourself going so fast that you fail to monitor your environment? It happens to me way too often. At times, I find myself so attached to my way of looking at things as I race to achieve my goal that I miss the corrective information someone or something is offering me.

Remember: Your team members don't care how much you know until they know how much you care about what they care about. Being open to their feedback (even if you don't agree with it) is one way you let others know you care about what's important to them.

Quit when your intuition says so

Previously, we discussed Julia Cameron's book *The Artist's Way*, and the powerful technique called Morning Pages. If you really want to be in touch with your intuition, write three pages in the morning. Anything that comes to mind, write it down, without editing. You might be surprised at what you learn by closely monitoring your internal environment. The insights gained from this self-awareness exercise can then be used to inform your decisions, especially when you are about to quit.

How often have you heard, "Never quit, never give up, or quitters never win"? What a bunch of crap. Reflective and effective executives may not like quitting, but they know it is almost always an option. Deciding when or how to quit is hard. Listening to the feedback you gain from your Morning Pages can help.

For example, when I chose to terminate my CD-ROM product (*Strategy*), I used the insights gleaned from my Morning Pages (they felt like "mourning" pages at the time) as well as market feedback to make that decision. The wisdom to "know when to hold 'em and when to fold 'em," as the song says, flows from monitoring your internal awareness and external environment.

Avoid multitasking

Yes, you read that right. We are living in an age of "continuous partial attention," according to Linda Stone, a former senior executive at both

Apple and Microsoft.[6] Walk into any cubicle or office and you see individuals texting, working on a document, reading an article, checking e-mail, scanning the latest news...all at the same time. Employees simply do not want to miss anything. Stone calls that complex multitasking because the tasks demand cognition. She also points out that a study commissioned by Hewlett-Packard (HP) found that people who attempt to deal with a barrage of messages while they work on other tasks experience a temporary 10-point drop in IQ.

You cannot monitor your environment well by trying to stay in touch with everything at once. Successfully monitoring your environment requires that you strategically select the most important information and focus on it... sequentially. Energy directed by a unifying force is close to genius.

Call and visit customers

Make it a habit to call and visit customers to solicit their perceptions of your services and the overall business environment. One transit CEO told me that he frequently rides his trains to stay in touch with his customers. He called it MBRA—management by riding around.

Stay in touch with your troops

Leadership is not possible without "followership." Research by Professor Stephen Reicher and his associates demonstrate that strong leadership flows from a symbiotic relationship between leaders and followers.[7] They point out that the most effective executives understand and monitor the values and the opinions of their followers, thereby enabling a productive dialogue about where the group is and what actions the group must take to reach a given destination.

The term *social identity* was coined in the 1970s to refer to the part of a person's sense of self that is defined by a group. Social identity allows people to feel connected to other group members. People long to belong to something larger than themselves, so they identify with their country, company, sales or sports team.

This social identity helps the group reach consensus on what is important and how to coordinate actions that are consistent with shared goals. Leaders are more effective when they can help followers see themselves as members of a particular group, as well as see the group's interests as the leaders' own interests.

This is what U.S. President George W. Bush did after 9/11, when he promised to "hunt down" and "find those folks who committed this act." Bush often portrayed himself as an everyday American who was able to speak for America. He used this folksy, Texas communication style to come across as a common man, rather than a member of the Association of Yale Alumni. We not only like people who are like us, we like to follow leaders who are like us.

Reicher also points out that the best leaders are symbolic representations of the group they seek to lead. They not only belong to the group, they exemplify what makes the group different from and superior to other groups. Think Bush's cowboy clothes and Palestinian leader Yasser Arafat's trademark keffiyeh. U.S. President Barack Obama's presidential victories stem partly from his ability to "sell" his story as a quintessential rags-to-riches American story.

Abraham Lincoln emphasized equality during his presidency and in his Gettysburg Address. He rallied people around this ideal to emancipate the slaves and save the union. The leadership lesson is clear: A journey begins on common ground. To lead others, you must first understand and monitor their norms, values, and beliefs.

A Case Study in Successful Rational Leadership

Who comes to mind when you think of leaders who are strong in rational thinking? Can you name any historical, military, or business leaders? In many of our leadership classes, the initial response is often silence because the rational style is not often associated with great leadership.

After a little prodding, names such as Alan Greenspan, Ben Bernanke, Colin Powell, and Jack Welch often pop up. Of course, these leaders have other strengths, but they all are highly skilled in most of the competencies of rational leaders:

1. Clarify objectives and expectations.
2. Manage operations and plans.
3. Know thyself and others.
4. Monitor closely.

Because this book is about you and not them, please think about your work responsibilities for a moment. When do you need to access your rational leadership competencies to conduct these responsibilities effectively? Where do you and your team need to grow?

Table 8.1 lists 14 questions to help you monitor closely. Each question is also a practical tactic that can help you develop the critical competencies of rational leadership. Which ones will help you and your team stay in touch?

TABLE 8.1

14 More Tools to Monitor Closely

1. How often do you check in with upper management, colleagues, peers, and direct reports?
2. How well do you stay in contact with the business environment, customers, and organizational culture?
3. How effective is your use of visuals in tracking progress toward your goals?
4. Have you created a detailed diagram of the flow of work in your operation?
5. What systems and tools are in place to help your teams monitor their own work?
6. How often do you require status reports on key projects?
7. How often do you review your priorities with your boss?
8. How do you and your team stay in close contact with your changing customer needs?
9. What performance metrics do you use to assess your internal or external quality?
10. How well do you and your team members track the use of your time?
11. Are you in touch with the changing emotions of your team members?
12. How well do you adjust your behaviors to fit changing environments?
13. How quickly do you learn when approaching new problems and challenges?
14. How sensitive are you to other cultures, attitudes, and values?

Walter Wriston, the former CEO of Citicorp, says that he has driven through his share of rainstorms while listening to some local radio announcer in a windowless room telling him that it's a sunny day. He says that the biggest mistake an executive can make is not recognizing the changing economic climate.

His advice: Never stop looking out the window.

My advice: Use the ideas presented in this section to help you see reality more clearly by becoming a more rational thinker and grounded executive.

In Section III, we'll soar with high-flying visionary executives who reach for the stars.

Section III

How Visionary Executives Imagine the Future

When people mention AOL today, it's most frequently with amused nostalgia about the ubiquitous CDs the company used to deliver to mailboxes across the U.S. when dial-up Internet access seemed as futuristic as Star Trek's phasers and tricorders.

That's probably because we'd all rather forget that AOL also drove what was, back in early 2000, the largest media deal in history — and ended up destroying more stock market value than almost any other deal in history.

The leaders of AOL and Time Warner — Steve Case and Gerald Levin, respectively — believed themselves to be visionary leaders. Many outside observers agreed. Case ran the company that most people considered to be the Internet back then, while Levin controlled such valuable brands as CNN and the Cartoon Network, *Time* and *Sports Illustrated,* and HBO and Warner Brothers. Together, they shocked business and government leaders when they announced that AOL (with revenues of only $4.8 billion) would acquire the much larger Time Warner (with revenues of $14.6 billion) in an all-stock deal valued at $164 billion, enabled by AOL's dot-com bubble-inflated stock price.

Shareholders saluted the deal. It seemed to make sense: AOL got Time Warner's diverse entertainment and information content and access to its cable systems to deliver high-speed Internet access, over which Time Warner could deliver that content in new and innovative ways and generate new advertising revenue in new markets. If Case and Levin seemed like an odd couple, their shared vision promised substantial rewards.

Then the dot-com turned into the dot-bomb. The Twin Towers came down in New York and the recession came down across the country. The first Iraq war had driven CNN to the top of the ratings; the new war increased costs and created competition — ironically enough — from Internet-enabled reporters with cheap technology who were delivering on-the-spot content that seemed more compelling for being unmediated.

Meanwhile, Case and Levin's visionary leadership apparently didn't do much to inspire the new company's other executives, who struggled to merge the diverse cultures of the dot-com and legacy media organizations. "Obstinate refusal" might be considered a polite description of the efforts to get the two sides to work together. AOL Time Warner's market value dropped by more than $100 billion by the middle of the decade, and then plummeted further, driving rumors of a divorce as big as the marriage.

In May 2009, when Time Warner's board of directors approved the dissolution of the merged companies, their market capitalization was less than $40 billion — down from $350 billion at the time the merger was announced. It's probably safe to say that a $310 billion loss was not exactly how Case and Levin imagined their futures. It's also safe to say that they failed to execute the four competencies of visionary leaders:

1. Adapt strategies to meet goals.
2. Cultivate innovative growth.
3. Inspire creativity and change.
4. Imagine broadly.

The next four chapters in Section III will describe each of these competencies for expanding visionary leadership and how to use them to unleash the energy of your team toward worthy goals.

CHAPTER 9

Follow Which Yellow Brick Road?

The future's already arrived. It's just not evenly distributed yet.

WILLIAM GIBSON

ADAPT STRATEGIES TO MEET GOALS

Dawn is the chief financial officer of a midsize technology firm in California. Several of the division managers in her organization have complained about the new financial reporting system Dawn's team was rolling out.

Dawn met with these managers and explained the rationale behind the new system. She told them that it was going to allow them to better monitor the performance of their team and efficiently execute the organization's strategy. Their jobs would be easier, she said, because they would be able to hold their people accountable for results and obtain timely financial reports.

At the end of the meeting, the managers thanked her for her time, shuffled into the corridor, and continued to complain about the "inflexible, bureaucratic system that was not meeting their needs." Dawn's boss, the CEO, knew this was not the first time other managers pushed back on her major projects. He felt he needed to do something.

Your choices as Dawn's CEO

If you were her boss, how might you unleash Dawn's energy toward worthy goals? Here are four options:

1. Do nothing. Don't mess with success. The project is needed. The managers are just resisting change. They'll get over it when they see the benefits.
2. Meet with Dawn. Discuss her strengths and how she might over-focus on them at times. Help her understand the needs to throttle back her strengths.
3. Ask Dawn to attend leadership development class. Encourage her to learn how to lead with her strengths and manage her weaknesses.
4. Transfer Dawn. Move her to a position where she doesn't need to involve or persuade other managers to buy into her projects.

What Dawn's CEO did

Dawn developed many skills on her path to the CFO position. She was detail-oriented, organized, and clear about expectations. However, the CEO believed that the resistance she experienced with the new system was a sign that she needed to grow her visionary leadership style. While choices 1, 2, and 4 might have worked, Dawn's CEO chose option 3. He invited her to attend a leadership course that he had attended a year ago. He hoped she would further develop the key competencies of a visionary executive—especially the ability to adapt strategies to meet goals.

And it worked. Dawn learned to stretch when she felt pulled. She expanded her skills, acquiring a few of visionary competencies while maintaining her strong rational style. A year later, Dawn earned a promotion to the presidency of another division in the same company.

This chapter discusses why adapting strategies to meet goals is critical to executive effectiveness and how to further develop this skill. (A disclaimer: Growing this skill will increase your leadership effectiveness, as it did for Dawn, but I can't guarantee that you'll be promoted to president.)

Strategic plans expand visionary leadership

The first priority of the visionary executive is to define and communicate strategy. That's because an effective strategic plan makes sense of the world in a manner that helps employees focus their energy on organizational priorities.

Unfortunately, most strategic plans, even if well crafted, gather dust on the bookshelf, seldom directing priorities on the shop floor or the front lines.[1] Like an old map in the trunk of a car, a strategic plan that doesn't inform today's actions can't help reach tomorrow's destination. Is it any surprise that "various studies done in the past 25 years indicate that 60% to 80% of companies fall short of the success predicted from their new strategies?"[2]

Before taking her leadership class, Dawn seldom talked with her team about the big picture or how it aligned with their daily work. She is not alone. Results from a Towers Perrin (now Towers Watson) survey of more than 60,000 employees tell us that only 51% of employees rated leaders favorably in communicating a clear vision for long-term success.[3]

This comes as no shock when you realize that only 48% of 763 global leaders surveyed by McKinsey and Company believe it is their job to provide inspiration and direction during stressful times.[4] Lopsided executives who are weak in their visionary competencies — especially when they are under pressure—fail to "unleash the energy of others toward worthy goals" precisely because they fail to communicate a vision. And, as Proverbs says (29:18), "where there is no vision, the people perish."

If you want to build a ship, don't drum up the crew
to gather wood, divide the work, and give orders.
Instead, teach them to yearn for the vast and endless sea.

ANTOINE DE SAINT-EXUPÉRY

Another one of Dawn's pre-leadership-class problems was that she didn't adapt her plans to meet the changing challenges of a dynamic work environment. Instead of having plans, her plans had her. Like many executives, she became a prisoner of her strategy instead of its owner. Her vision became tunnel vision.

Watching the Super Bowl reminded me of this lesson when the *Mad Men* of marketing at General Motors aired a commercial directly attacking Ford.[5] I would much rather GM's executives adapt their strategy and look beyond their cross-town, 50-year, petty rivalry with Ford, to their real competitors across the oceans.

Similarly, a colleague at Emory University once pointed out that when Xerox's market share was collapsing in the face of Japanese competition in the early 1970s, the competitors' names (Canon, Ricoh) were never even whispered by Xerox executives in the boardroom. During this same time, Xerox's share of worldwide copier revenues plummeted from 93% (1971) to 60% (1976).[6]

If you don't strategize about the competition, you can't adapt your plans to beat them. Ignoring reality is not strategy—it is what the Japanes call *seppuku:* suicide.

Research on 60 companies confirms that, unlike rigid executives w inflexible plans who do not stretch when pulled, expansive executives define and refine their strategic plans are much more successful in c ing their desired future.[7] These effective leaders know that the only s gic plan worth having is one that makes sense of the dynamic envir and thus informs daily priorities.

A flexible plan is like a GPS — it knows where you are, re when you are off course, and tells you how to get where you ne

It ain't what you don't know that gets you
It's what you know for sure tha

Before discussing how to create a strategic plan, let's dispel the common myths and confirm the compelling truths about strategy. Label the following 18 statements *True* or *False* to test your general knowledge about strategy and strategic planning.

1. Growth rate is determined largely by the industry the organization is in. T F
2. The larger the organization, the harder it is to sustain growth. T F
3. Companies located in high-growth, emerging economies perform better over the long haul. T F
4. Globalization is a major factor influencing growth. T F
5. Growth slows as companies age. T F
6. Companies started by entrepreneurs perform better than those formed as the result of mergers or spinoffs. T F
7. The most successful organizations conduct a lot of experiments. T F
8. Successful organizations make small bets early and diversify their portfolios. T F
9. Limiting the number of big, high-risk acquisitions predicts success over time. T F
10. Having a diverse portfolio that complements the core businesses [illegible]redicts long-term success. T F
[illegible]uiring companies builds new capabilities in new [illegible]ets quickly. T F
[illegible]jor strategic challenges should be centrally coordinated. T F
[illegible]organizations tend to favor adaptability over efficiency. T F
[illegible]hat is integrated throughout the organization [illegible]. T F
[illegible]zations highly value stability as well [illegible] T F
[illegible]mpanies pay close attention to values, [illegible] T F
[illegible]not change high-level [illegible] T F
[illegible]ave the most stable [illegible] T F

The first six statements are false and the last 12 statements are all true, according to Professor Rita McGrath's analysis of 4,793 companies.[8]

While most executives affirm the importance of revenue growth in their strategic plan, McGrath and her team at Columbia Business School discovered that only 8% of all companies actually grew their revenues by at least 5% for five consecutive years. When they compared the differences between the 8% who grew successfully and the 92% who did not, they were able to bust these six myths and confirm 12 truths.

If predictable and sustainable growth is important to your organization, consider these research findings as you proceed to the next section and the six steps of creating a strategic plan.*

How to create a strategic plan

The fundamental question to ask when planning strategy is, How do we know that our plan will produce these results? Where's the evidence or proof that our plan will take us where we want to go? It is a scientific question because the essence of science is prediction, as discussed previously. Science is a set of tools and rules to discover how things work. When we know how things really work, we can make predictions with a high degree of confidence (i.e., a high predictive value). Applying scientific research allows us to say that if we take this action or follow this plan, we can expect to produce these results.

If you want to increase the probability that you achieve your difficult, strategic goals, use the research (in this chapter and throughout this book) to create and execute your strategic plan.

---

*It is useful to think of any plan as a prediction. We make plans (a trip, party, strategy, etc.) because we predict the plan will probably get us from point A (where we are) to point B (where we want to be). In other words, every time we make a plan we are predicting—consciously or unconsciously—that we will achieve specific outcomes. As the desired outcomes become more difficult to achieve (such as sustainable organizational growth), the plan to achieve the outcomes becomes more complex due to the increased number of variables that influence those outcomes. Meteorologists need supercomputers to run complex algorithms to give us the probability of rain because so many factors affect the weather. This is also why the most effective executives use the latest scientific research to create strategic plans that increase the probability of success.

TABLE 9.1

Create and Adapt Strategic Plans in 6 Steps

1. Define the business/market.
2. Analyze the situation.
3. Identify assumptions.
4. Create strategic alternatives.
5. Commit to a flexible action plan.
6. Implement and adapt the plan.

In its most basic form, planning is an organized process for anticipating and dealing with the future. Competence in the strategic planning process enables executives to understand their environments and focus employees on actions relevant to the health of the businesses. In a five-year study of 1,850 companies, researchers reported that the most profitable organizations were those whose strategies expanded their boundaries.[9] Developing a strategy that grows beyond your core begins by answering fundamental questions about the business you are *really* in.

Define the business/market

In 1984, two Canadian street performers, Guy Laliberté and Daniel Gauthier, saw a blue ocean strategy and called it Cirque du Soleil (Circus of the Sun). A blue ocean strategy is that place in the market "untainted by competition." The red ocean is the current arena, where traditional competitors scrap for shrinking pieces of the pie.[10]

Since its maiden voyage, Cirque—a dramatic and luxurious mix of circus arts, street entertainment, extravagant costumes, and music—has expanded from one show to 19 unique shows, delighting more than 90 million people in 271 cities worldwide.[11]

Meanwhile, in the traditional three-ring circus, the clown cries an ocean of red tears.

The first step in the strategic planning process is to redefine your unit's mission and markets. To do so requires the Janus-like skill of looking forward and backward. Janus was an ancient Roman god who could look both ways at the same time. He was often associated with doorways, beginnings, and transitions.

Researchers W. Chan Kim and Renee Mauborgne, who studied 150 blue ocean creations in 30 industries during a 100-year period, found that Janus had it right.[12] From the first mass-produced car (Ford Model T) to the game-changing iPhone, it's the same old story, same old song and dance:

Creating new markets demands paradoxical thinking—exploiting red sea probabilities while exploring blue ocean possibilities.

Thus, a flexible strategic plan begins by reflecting about where you've been, where you are now, and where you might want to go. To explore these issues, invite a broad cross-section of your team to a strategic brainstorming session. E-mail them the following "super-strategic" questions ahead of time to stimulate thinking inside *and* outside the box. Tell them you want to exploit the red ocean *and* explore the ocean blue.

- What business are we *really* in?
- How could we profit from serving our best customers better?
- Who might be our most profitable *non*-customers?
- What is the profitability in our industry and why?
- What current trends might affect our future?
- What needs or wants do we satisfy and fail to satisfy, and which ones should we satisfy?
- What markets are at the borders/margins of what we do now?
- What products or services might deliver both lower cost and better differentiation?
- How might we extend our products and services into neighboring markets?
- What new distribution channels could we explore?
- What new geographies might offer new customers?
- How could we conduct quick experiments (rapid prototyping) to test these ideas?

Analyze the situation

Anheuser-Busch capitalized on the low-carb diet trend that emerged several years ago. They were pioneers in this segment when they launched their low-carb Michelob Ultra in September 2002 and captured a significant share of this market in a short period. Coors, on the other hand, entered the market 18 months late(r). Despite $30 million investment in the launch, the Coors low-carb competitor captured a meager 0.4% of the market.[13]

Anheuser-Busch's strategic planning process included a situational analysis—a series of questions that help determine the "condition" of an organization. The company's leaders identified the internal and external factors influencing their company:

- Internal factors included marketing, manufacturing, materials, labor, technology, finance, quality, equipment, service, distribution, and service.

- External forces included customers, suppliers, the economy, capital markets, regulatory climate, and—of course—the competition.

Obtaining the business intelligence needed for an excellent situational analysis depends on a network of individuals. Involving employees at all levels of the organization increases the probability that executives will detect weak signals that could have profound implications.

This is how Anheuser-Busch's radar picked up an important trend before Coors. The company's situational analysis identified potential customers at the edge of the market. When the low-carb craze captured the attention of millions of people, Anheuser-Busch's strategic plan had the agility to respond flexibly to the dynamic market.

The diverse cross-section of individuals from whom you can solicit input includes salespeople, service engineers, shipping personnel, accountants, and employees on the front lines. For example, highway maintenance personnel often claim they can tell when the economy is turning one direction or the other by the quality—or lack thereof—of beer cans tossed out by drivers. Pay special attention to what your employees say about local economies, early adopters, and nimble competitors. Listen to those who are sensitive to early, changing conditions at the boundaries. These are often your outliers—your Paul Reveres—warning the minority about what may lay ahead for the majority.

Professor Michael Porter of the Harvard Business School points out that one of the key roles of the strategist is to understand and cope with the competition.[14] Yet leaders often define the competition too narrowly. Porter reminds us that competition extends beyond traditional industry rivals and includes four other competitive forces: buyers, suppliers, new entrants, and substitute products.

Effective executives who created a boundary-expanding situational analysis enabled Pepsi to capture a much larger share of the bottled water market than Coca-Cola and blazed the trail for Apple to conquer the music distribution business.

Analyze your organization's situation by exploring answers to these questions:

- What are our organization's internal strengths and weaknesses?
- How can we increase and integrate innovation throughout the organization?
- How can we increase our adaptability by decreasing processes and procedures that impede our progress?

- What are the opportunities and threats facing our organization?
- What trends are affecting local and global economies, government regulations, capital markets, etc.?
- What can we learn from those areas/segments hardest hit by past economic downturns?
- What is changing for our customers, suppliers, distribution channels, and competitors?
- Where are there possible substitute products/services and potential new entrants?
- How can we use the mavericks, lunatic fringe, and early adopters to tell us about what is happening at the periphery or margins of our business?
- How well are we managing our strategic paradoxes?

Anheuser-Busch's leaders listened to a few customers near the margins of their business because they answered these types of questions in their strategic plan. Their peripheral vision provided the insight to capitalize on a low-carb trend and their situational analysis conditioned them to take immediate action. Unlike flatfooted leaders at Coors (and others like them at Kodak, Nokia, and Blockbuster in other industries), Anheuser-Busch executives understood that training for agility leads to rapid adaptability.

Identify assumptions and quantify risks

This step of the strategic planning process generates assumptions and quantifies risks. As discussed earlier, an assumption is something that is accepted as true, without proof. Understanding assumptions is critical to strategic planning because assumptions are the precursors of risk. When you bring assumptions to the surface, you can categorize and then mitigate risk. Precisely how is outlined here:

1. SEND team members the first two phases of your strategic plan prior to a 30-minute meeting.
2. START the meeting by asking them to complete this sentence in two minutes, on their own: I assume ____________________. Then compile all their assumptions.
3. CREATE a probability/impact risk matrix (see Figure 6.1 and the associated discussion in Chapter 6) to quantify the risks your team has surfaced.
4. DIVIDE the team into sub-groups and ask all the groups to rank all the assumptions. This ranking is done by assigning each assumption to one

of the nine squares in the matrix, from low impact/low probability to high impact/high probability.

5. CATEGORIZE the highest-risk assumptions (high impact/high probability) in one of two ways:
   - Relevant variables (the economy, inflation, consumer demand, manufacturing capacity, labor conditions, availability of material, transportation issues, changing demographics, etc.)
   - Your five competitors (traditional rivals, buyers, suppliers, new entrants, and substitute products)

   You and your team's goal is to identify the critical factors that might affect your operation positively or negatively.
6. DISCUSS steps needed to address the assumptions that have the greatest risk.

   Perhaps Mattel would not have lost 20% of its worldwide share in fashion dolls to smaller rival MGA Entertainment had Mattel used this process to generate assumptions and quantify risks for Barbie. MGA recognized that pre-teen girls were becoming more sophisticated and maturing more rapidly. These girls were outgrowing Barbie and increasingly preferred dolls that look like their teenage siblings and television/music pop stars. MGA's insight led to foresight, and the Bratz line of competing dolls.

Of course, Mattel responded—but not until it lost a fifth of Barbie's realm.

Create strategic alternatives

This step of the strategic planning process invites you to write three scenarios that depict the future of your organization. Scenario planning is critical because of the tendency of executives to be overconfident in their ability to predict the future, combined with their diminished capacity to think clearly during stress. The three scenarios should describe the most probable future, an optimistic future, and a pessimistic future.

- The most probable scenario is the one that will deliver your company to its desired future if successfully implemented.
- The second scenario outlines an optimistic view of what the future may bring. (Even excellent companies, such as Apple, have often *failed* to describe this scenario accurately, leading to shipping delays for new products.)
- The third scenario is the pessimistic one. It identifies the various options that would allow your organization to maintain profitability if your

projections are way off. This worst-case scenario ensures that executives carefully and calmly think through the actions needed to survive if a tsunami hits.

When creating the worst-case scenario, consider these questions:

- If a recession lasted more than a few years, how will our organization survive?
- What happens if a major customer or funding source goes away?
- How quickly can our company cut spending strategically?
- How do we think about layoffs in a compassionate way?
- What is our plan to retain top talent during tough times?
- Do we know how to manage the tension in our strategic paradox?

Each scenario should summarize the basic strategy for the company, including how the strategy might affect distribution channels, geographies, customer segments, product development, facilities, equipment purchases, acquisitions, and suppliers.

Another important component of each scenario involves competition. Although the situational analysis discusses competitors, consider a response for each strategic alternative. Answer these questions to craft your approach:

- What are our competitors' strengths and weaknesses?
- What is the financial condition of our major competitors?
- What might be our competitors' strategies?
- How would our competitors' products sell under these different scenarios?
- How quickly and effectively could we respond if a competitor stumbles?
- How would our competitors respond to our market success?
- What are the negative consequences of mismanaging our strategic paradox?

Commit to a flexible action plan

Nike's considerable success can be attributed to its perimeter-expanding, flexible action plans.[15] Nike enters a race by ensuring that it is number one or number two in athletic shoes in a target market. It then unveils a new clothing line endorsed by a top athlete in that target market (e.g., Tiger Woods' $100 million golf contract in the mid-1990s). As it stretches into the new market, Nike grows its distribution channels and suppliers. It then employs these channels and suppliers to win the race for higher-margin products in this market. Nike eventually begins competing in the global market.

As it takes each incremental step, Nike learns lessons that it uses to set new goals and adapt the plan. Its plans also pass the three fundamentals tests of great strategies:

1. Create superior value for customers.
2. Be difficult for competitors to imitate.
3. Increase the organization's capacity to adapt to change.

Your plans should, too.

This fifth step of a strategic plan involves writing an action plan that summarizes how you will create your future. The plan should summarize what you learned about your organization, your unit, the environment, the competition, and the future. Base the plan on the most probable scenario.

The essence of the plan is the goals that clarify where you want to go. Professors Edwin Locke and Gary Latham summarized 393 separate scientific studies on the predictive power of goal setting.[16] According to their research, the probability of reaching any goal increases when you:

- Set specific and difficult goals.
- Limit the number of goals.
- Create short-term and long-term goals.

The most profitable growth is often found "when a company pushes out the boundaries of its core business into an adjacent space," where the tides of your familiar red ocean meet the unexplored blue ocean.[17] Thus, the goals should explore the frontiers of existing distribution channels, geographies, customer segments, and product development. Many of the goals should be within reach (attainable) *and* a stretch, as if you are hiking a new trail, yet in a familiar forest.

Identify the tactics needed to achieve each stretch goal. Executing the tactics results in achieving that goal. Hence, if your goal is to "increase profits in that market by this date," the tactics might include increasing sales and/or decreasing expenses by a specific date.

Create a method to measure the progress of these goals and report on them quarterly. If you can't measure it, you won't manage it. For example, if the boundary-pushing goal is to increase sales, measurements could include reaching new customers, breaking into adjacent market segments, or learning from experiments with distributors.

The time frame to achieve goals depends on how quickly things change in your industry. The rule of thumb in strategic planning has been a five-year plan. However, if you are an industry in which the rate of change is accelerating (which includes most industries), consider a three-year time horizon.

Implement and adapt the plan

Peter Drucker reminds us that "the best plan is only good intentions unless it degenerates into work." The biggest mistake executives make in strategic planning is putting the strategic plan on the shelf instead of on their monthly agendas.

To work the plan, set regular meetings to follow up and adapt the plan as the environment changes. In tough times, conduct monthly meetings and weekly updates. Accountability transforms strategic plans into action plans.

Dawn, the CFO in our opening story, learned that although she couldn't predict the future, strategic planning was the process to create it. She expanded her visionary skills by developing a strategic plan to meet her goals. As a new CEO, she is now building on her strategic planning skills by learning to think strategically.

From Strategic Planning to Strategic Thinking

Not long ago, Grace, the CEO of a midsize firm, conveyed how pleased she was with the results of the coaching and training I had done with her executives for the past two years. She then informed me that she needed to hire another, less expensive leadership consultant to coach her lower-level managers.

I congratulated her on focusing on developing her middle managers and then asked her how hiring a new consultant related to her overall strategy. When Grace confessed that she hadn't really thought about it, we discussed the difference between strategic planning and strategic thinking.

Strategic thinking is not the same as thinking about the strategic plan. The strategic plan is an output from a systematic process. Strategic thinking is a way of thinking throughout the day. It is the mindset that helps implement the plan daily. As illustrated in Table 9.2, there are five aspects strategic thinking.[18]

TABLE 9.2

The Five Pieces of Strategic Thinking

1. Focus intention: What do we want to achieve?
2. Use peripheral vision: How are we staying open to other opportunities?
3. See the system: How does an issue relate to the elements of our ecosystem?
4. Connect in time: How should our history influence our destiny today?
5. Test-drive solutions: How could we try this idea?

Focus intention

What do we want to achieve?

"We believe in saying no to thousands of projects so that we can really focus on the few," asserts Apples CEO Tim Cook.[19]

Cook is reminding us that our energy, attention, and time can be focused like a laser…or diffused like a prism. Intent-focused leaders are lasers. They act on what is most important and refuse to allow the scattered spectrum of daily urgencies to distract them. Cook is also telling us that most leaders don't need to do more with less; they need to do less with less by thinking strategically.

Strategic-thinking executives strive to apply Peter Drucker's mandate to be both effective (do the right things) and efficient (do things right) throughout their day, and in that order. They also use the Pareto principle — the 80/20 rule — to focus their organizations on the fundamental few. They don't mistake activity for accomplishment because they know one whale is worth a thousand minnows.

Laser-like leaders who apply strategic thinking capitalize on their most profitable customers, coach their valuable employees, and invest considerable energy in top priorities. Focused executives also limit the number of agenda items at meetings and contemplate their desired outcome prior to most conversations.

As a CEO, Grace is often pulled in many directions by diverse stakeholders with competing agendas. We have worked together to identify and manage her primary strategic paradox (the tension she feels to improve customer service and constrain costs). She's also growing her strategic thinking skills by being more intent-focused in her daily interactions. She is placing her attention on her intention prior to every communication.

One way to increase your focus is to write Morning Pages about the future state of your organization. In fact, University of Virginia's Jeanne Liedtka recommends that you write two cover stories, as if you were preparing a piece for a business magazine, one about where you are and another about how you got there five years from today. One story could be titled "The Dark Ages in My Organization" and describe the difficult issues you currently face. The other, "Renaissance in My Organization," could detail the steps you took to overcome your challenges.[20] These cover stories will help you focus on your fundamental issues and how to address them. (They are not meant for publication.)

Use peripheral vision

How are we staying open to other opportunities?

Athletes who are intent on scoring seldom see their open teammates who may have easier shots. In basketball, it's called forcing the shot. In business, clear direction without flexible execution becomes dogma. An executive who has a strategic direction but lacks peripheral vision is like the narrow-minded leader that Zig Ziglar once told me about — the one who could look through a keyhole with both eyes.

If Grace placed all her attention on her intention, she would lose opportunities that could appear at the margins of her business and interactions. For example, Grace visits her regional offices every quarter to review their progress. When I asked her how she stretched to stay open to regional influences and concerns as she pursued her central business plan, her eyes glazed over.

I explained that healthy peripheral vision encourages executives to keep their eyes wide open *and* pursue their top priorities. Grace decided to decrease the amount of time she spent reviewing her central plan and increase her time with each region's stakeholders (local staff, customers, suppliers) to discuss their issues and opportunities. She also is considering how to implement 3M's famous mandate, adapted successfully by Google, that employees allocate some of their time to work on projects of personal interest. Grace believes that her team members will improve their peripheral vision if they explore their own interests.

To some executives, focusing attention *and* using peripheral vision is an easy balancing act between having a rational plan with clear goals *and* adapting the strategies to meet those goals. To others, it feels like a big stretch.

See the system

How does an issue relate to the elements of our ecosystem?

A systems perspective invites leaders to think about the parts of their organizations, the pattern of the parts, and the relationship among the parts. It is a way of viewing any issue as part of the larger ecosystem.

Unfortunately, many executives think in silos instead of systems. The ecosystem becomes their *ego*system. They walk around with blinders on, like a racehorse focused only on its path. The strategic thinker, on the other hand, sees the relationships among the vertical (corporate, division, business unit) and horizontal (marketing, research and development, manufacturing, supply chain) elements of the organization.

If Grace were thinking from a systems perspective when she considered hiring a less expensive leadership consultant, she would have thought about how her other leadership training and coaching initiatives would be affected by this new hire.

Strategic thinking is not about saying no to silos — it's about saying *know* to silos. It's about knowing when to focus on her silo (in this case, her division) and when to open her silo doors to connect with others.

To help develop this skill, draw circles to represent the various stakeholders that might affect the issue you are thinking about. Then, consider which circles, if brought together to deal with the issue, might provide insights. Where do these circles overlap at the margins? How might you adapt this Venn diagram approach to develop a better understanding about the pattern of these parts or stakeholders?

Connect in time

How should our history influence our destiny today?

"If you're still here after Christmas, I'm going to climb up on that Coke box and hit you." A bank president told me that the lesson he learned from the preacher who uttered those words to him 40 years earlier was not to quit when the going got tough. As a result of the preachers scolding, he dragged himself back to college after Christmas, received his diploma two years later, and went on to become a successful banking executive. This bank president now has the Coke box in his office as a connection to the past.

This is one of the many stories I heard when I taught leaders in Emory University's executive education program. One client of ours, Synovus Bank, requested that its senior executives give a one-hour presentation on their views of leadership as part of the week-long class. Over the years, after listening to dozens of these executives, it became very clear to me that Synovus leaders know how to connect in time. Although they do not live in the past, they do use it. They understand that history shapes destiny. How? By communicating important values and principles through powerful metaphors, symbols, and stories. They know what to remember —and what to forget.

To connect in time, strategic thinkers reflect on the past and use it to influence present decisions. Like a sturdy oak tree, they gain stability from deep roots as they stretch for the sky. If Grace were connected in time, she would have thought about how past leadership training, retreats, and coaching efforts should influence new coaching approaches or different leadership models.

If you want to improve your strategic-thinking skills in this area, consider answering these questions:

- How can I use lessons from our past to remind our team which values are most important?
- What stories from our organization's history can help us cope with all this change?
- Which veteran employees could I hold up as great examples of our rich past?
- How can we celebrate our past so that it builds confidence as we stretch toward the future?

Speaking of stretching, during one ten-year stretch, Synovus was selected as one of the best places to work in the United States.

Test-drive solutions

How could we try this idea?

Unlike those who always try to get it perfect the first time, strategic thinkers often conduct small experiments. They test solutions by trying ideas, gathering data, conducting after-action reviews, and adjusting course. In other words, they are hypothesis-driven.

Those skilled in this approach are able to think both creatively (like an entrepreneur) *and* critically (like a data-driven analyst). They build a culture that promotes learning as a way of working.

HP applied this experimental mindset (called "rapid prototyping" in R&D departments) to explore novel ideas as it researched and developed the ink-jet printer.[21] Leaders at HP used rapid prototyping to encourage their teams to push innovations out the door so that real users could test them as fast as possible. Failure was not only an option for the strategic thinkers at HP, it was welcomed—provided it was fast, small, and learning-oriented.

If Grace thinks experimentally about hiring a coach for her middle managers, she might consider testing her idea by conducting a brief trial coaching session with one of her managers. If Grace is adapts the HP way, she'll understand that there is no failure—only feedback.

The secret of fast progress is inefficiency, fast and furious and numerous failures.

KEVIN KELLY

STRATEGIC THINKING AT WORK

Executives who develop strategic-thinking skills acquire a powerful set of tools to adapt their strategies as they pursue their goals. Leaders who also foster strategic thinking in their teams are well on their way to a sustainable future. I invite you to adapt the following executive tools and questions to accomplish both.

Professor Ellen Goldman identified experiences that led to the development of strategic thinking by studying top strategic thinkers.[22] I've incorporated her findings, and others, into Table 9.3, which consists of several tools to help you expand your strategic leadership skills.

TABLE 9.3

16 Tools to Expand Your Strategic Leadership Skills

1. Apply Pareto's 80/20 rule to focus on the most important issues and priorities.
2. Stimulate strategic thinking in meetings by frequently asking the five questions in Table 9.2.
3. Discuss your team's contribution to achieving your organization's overall goals.
4. Select a mentor to stimulate and challenge your strategic thinking.
5. Make assignments that require your team members to apply strategic skills.
6. Spend more time with colleagues who challenge, stretch, and stimulate your thinking.
7. Define and follow a process to monitor the facts necessary for thinking strategically.
8. Discuss your industry's significant trends and opportunities, and their impact, with your team.
9. Become more engaged in the strategic planning process to become a better strategic thinker.
10. Lead a major project that is complex, capital- and labor-intensive, and requires at least one year to complete.
11. Choose and implement tactics that keep your organization's strategic imperatives at the forefront of your team's minds throughout the day.

12. Schedule regular times to discuss with your team the connection between new initiatives and the overall direction of the organization.
13. Take a helicopter view of what is going on a regular basis.
14. Invite your team to relate the organization's vision to each team member's daily work.
15. Remind yourself to invite people who disagree with you to discuss issues.
16. Play chess.

The world's best chess players are said to be able to envision the game several moves into the future. They also adapt their strategies based on the dynamics of the game.

The AOL and Time Warner executives, by contrast, played checkers. They applied the one strategy they had seen work in the past: consolidation. It also seems they lacked the will or skill to adapt their strategy to meet their goals. In the next chapter, we'll explore how AOL Time Warner also failed to cultivate innovative growth—the second core competency of the visionary leadership style.

We are all in the gutter,
but some of us are looking at the stars.
OSCAR WILDE

CHAPTER 10

Elephants Dancing with the Stars

It would be an unsound fancy and self-contradictory to expect that things which have never yet been done can be done except by means which have never yet been tried.

SIR FRANCIS BACON

The customer looked up from the computer screen. "Dave, this software is fantastic. How did your company come up with it?"

"A few of my sales colleagues and I worked with a recently hired programmer," I said. "This programmer, Ray, is part of our new engineering team at Siemens. They focus on bringing small software products to market fast."

"Well, Dave, I'll buy from you. But only because you're telling me that your company is becoming more innovative and responsive to customers. I still think they are like a lumbering elephant, stumbling in the forest. Still, I'll give you and Siemens a try."

We did obtain that large, medical computer order, but then things went downhill fast. Ray left the following year, and his new team collapsed. The top salespeople, including me, left within two years. West Coast market share for Siemens plunged faster than you could say "innovate or die."

Our elephant had *not* learned to dance—that is, the medical division at Siemens did not know how to cultivate innovative growth.

At that time, Siemens, like many corporate behemoths, didn't fully appreciate what an analysis of 759 companies in 17 countries had found to be the most important factor driving innovative companies: executives who support an innovative culture.[1]

This is the second of four chapters to discuss the four competencies of visionary leadership. As a reminder, those four core competencies are:

1. Adapt strategies to meet goals.
2. CULTIVATE INNOVATIVE GROWTH.
3. Inspire creativity and change.
4. Imagine broadly.

This chapter discusses why cultivating innovative growth is critical to executive effectiveness, and how you can further develop this skill in yourself and for your organization.

Cultivate innovative growth

Innovation is the process of creating value by bringing ideas to the market. Innovation is not, as many believe, the same as creating or inventing products. Creativity and inventions are the parents of innovation. Yet effective executives cultivate a "mind to market mindset" in themselves and throughout their organization because they know innovation is both personal *and* a process. Science says those who fail at this critical visionary leadership competency doom their organization.

When Professors W. Chan Kim and Renee Mauborgne studied product launches within 108 existing companies, they found 86% of those new ventures were line extensions.[2] This means the vast majority of their new products were incremental improvements to existing offerings. While these important line extensions accounted for 62% of the total revenues, they delivered only 39% of the total profits. Meanwhile, the 14% invested in creating new products and industries delivered 38% of the total revenue and a massive 61% of the total profits.

Some executives assert that these results prove the peril of focusing on "incremental innovation." They are wrong. These results, and others, demonstrate the peril of over-focusing on incremental innovation *at the expense* of radical innovation.[3] Effective executives create both incremental and radical innovation by managing the tension between these interdependent imperatives.

Cultivating innovative growth requires that leaders undertake a process of achieving small wins *and* big, hairy, audacious goals (BHAGs) and, in fact, drill it into their DNA — their own and that of the organization.[4] They must encourage both hitting singles *and* swinging for homeruns. How? By launching experiments that bring incremental and new products, services, and processes to fruition.

Visionary leaders who cultivate growth also aggressively seek to grow or improve the business by leveraging their unique ideas with those in other departments or divisions. They carefully cultivate broad support from internal and external stakeholders. They form strategic alliances to accomplish mutually beneficial goals. When I worked for Siemens, the executives were weak in these areas.

Speaking of Siemens, surveys rank Siemens between 34 and 38 (depending on which survey you read) in innovation among the top global companies.[5] The elephant has learned to dance.

You can, too.

A DOZEN INNOVATION-BOOSTING STRATEGIES

Tapping the innovation well is critical for many other reasons besides boosting the bottom line. First, to serve internal or external customers better, organizations need all their team members contributing. The individual strands of string may be weak, but — when twisted into a rope — you have the strength of collective contribution. Second, inviting people to share their ideas to improve policies, process, and procedures motivates them. Increasing engagement increases commitment. Third, a culture of innovation decreases turnover, especially among high-potential employees who see their good ideas brought to life.

To increase innovation so that you can accomplish your growth goals, let's examine how a big elephant like Google dances. Google is consistently ranked among the most innovative company in the world. Adapt the company's ideas to help your team innovate as a way of working.[6]

Budget innovation into the job description

Google managers are required to spend approximately 20% of their time on personal projects that may lead to innovation. Executives hold them accountable for this time in frequent performance reviews. Google staff claim that as many as half of their new products and features flow from this cultural norm.

How should you increase the time invested in brainstorming, creativity, and out-of-the-box thinking—the precursors of innovation?

Eliminate friction at every turn

Google's approach to innovation is akin to improvisational jazz. Any engineer in the company, at any level, can create a new product or a new feature to an existing product. One engineer tells the story of his first month on the job. He complained to a co-worker about the Google e-mail system. His co-worker told him to fix it himself. The next day, the e-mail engineering team reviewed his code. A week later, Google incorporated his changes into the software.

How open are you and your department to implementing new ideas fast?

Let the market choose

Google has no grand design for how new offerings fit together. It lets the market decide. Google's leaders do not worry about identifying the perfect product mix. Their 132 million users are better evaluators of new products.

How could you improve customer involvement in your innovation process?

Cultivate a taste for failure and chaos

Nature teaches us that experimentation is king of the jungle. Google plants a thousand flowers and sees which ones bloom. Google executives ignore the fetters of small failures. In fact, they perceive most failures as feedback. While Nike encourages everyone to Just Do It, Google tells its people to just try it. Google's executive chair, Eric Schmidt, encourages this experimental mindset when he says, "Please fail very quickly—so that you can try again."[7]

How might you encourage this experimental mindset?

Create a collaborative work environment

Google packs offices close together for better communication, conducts all-hands meetings every Friday, and maintains a rigorous interviewing and hiring process.

How could you increase the sense of community and collaboration in your work environment?

Use feedback to stay on track

Google scores employees on 25 performance metrics. The company systematically models the attributes of its highest-performing employees and also continually modifies its hiring approach based on ongoing analysis of performance.

What analytics should you use to keep your team on track?

Let's move from Google, one of Silicon Valley's most successful companies, to Hollywood's most successful studio for a few more lessons that can help your team innovate. Pixar Studios is the creator of extraordinary films such as *Toy Story* and its sequels, *Monsters Inc., Finding Nemo, The Incredibles, Ratatouille, WALL-E,* and *Up,* among others. In fact, every single one of Pixar's films has been a blockbuster.

What's the secret? Unlike most other studios, Pixar never buys scripts or movie ideas from the outside. Pixar doesn't have to import innovation. It has cultivated a community that hires and supports artists throughout the entire movie-making process.[8] Let's look at how Pixar's cultural principles might shine a light on your innovation process.

Promote creativity in everyone every day

A movie contains tens of thousands of ideas: what the characters say, and where and how they say it; the design of the characters, sets, and backgrounds; the colors and lighting; etc. Every member of the 250-person production crew needs to make creative suggestions. Creativity is encouraged and celebrated at every level of the organization *every day*. It is not a single initiative to capture great ideas in a moment of time—it's the way they do things all the time. Take, for example, how Pixar used this idea to influence Disney (which bought Pixar) when Disney added the ride "Luigi's Flying Tires" to its California Adventure theme park. Pixar suggested that riders in the flying tires control the ride. Today, riders tip the tires by shifting their weight, which affects how the jets of air beneath the tires move. It's like an air hockey game with you riding the puck. *That's* involving everyone in the creative process.[9]

How can you promote creative input every day?

Hire creative team players

Most Hollywood studios search for promising ideas, then assemble a group of people to make the movie. Pixar reverses that process. It hires and supports creative people, then nurtures their nature. According to Ed Catmull, co-founder of Pixar, "If you give a good idea to a mediocre team, they will screw it up; if you give a mediocre idea to a great team, they will either fix it or throw it away and come up with something that works."

How do you attract and retain innovative thinking talent?

Gain breakthrough ideas from people, not committees

Pixar executives believe great movies begin with the individuals who come up with a movie idea. They give enormous leeway and support to these individuals and then provide them with an environment in which they get honest and direct feedback from everyone. While the development department in most studios is charged with coming up with new ideas for movies, this is not true at Pixar. Pixar executives believe the development department's job is to assemble a small incubation team to help individuals refine their own ideas to a point at which the team can convince senior executives that their idea has the potential to make a great film. Contrast this approach with most organizations, in which only the R&D team comes up with and develops great product or service ideas.

Obtain honest and true peer review

Pixar has a brain trust that consists of the co-founders of Pixar and eight directors. When directors feel they need assistance, they ask the brain trust (and anyone else they think might help) to view their work in progress. The session is a two-hour, lively, give-and-take discussion focused on making the movie better. It's not ego-driven, and nobody pulls any punches to be polite. It produces results because everyone trusts and respects each other. After the session, the director of the movie decides which ideas to accept or reject. The brain trust has no authority to mandate any changes.

How well developed is your culture of candor?

Communicate with anyone, anytime

Members of any department are free to approach anyone in any other department to solve problems without having to go through "proper" channels. (As an outside consultant, I'm constantly amazed at how internal silos and turf wars block communication.)

Create a unifying vision

A movie needs a coherence that brings together the thousands of ideas that go into a movie. Each of Pixar's movies has a unifying vision that focuses all these ideas into clear directives that the staff can implement. Yet the vision statements of most organizations are boring placards on the wall. The essence of a great unifying vision is one that *stimulates action in a given direction.*

I helped a department within San Diego County create a vision statement (in one hour) during a day-long executive retreat. The associate director told me that they already printed it on their stationery because it gives them direction and stimulates action. (*Through committed and innovative services, we help our customers live high-quality lives in their own homes.*) Another executive presented me with a cup that had the vision her transportation engineers created during our Lunch-N-Learn session a few months ago. (*Building the foundation for moving experiences.*)

Adapting all of the aforementioned lessons—the ideas from Google and the guiding principles of Pixar—will cultivate both incremental *and* radical innovation in your organization. Using the tools in the next section will nourish your innovative mindset.

Innovation is the central issue in economic prosperity.

MICHAEL PORTER

In a six-year quest to uncover the secrets of the innovator's mindset, Professor Jeffrey Dyer and his colleagues studied 3,525 executives and entrepreneurs who had either started innovative companies or invented new products within their own organizations.[10] Their most startling finding was that innovation couldn't be delegated to others or relegated to culture alone.

The most innovative organizations—the top 15%—have top executives who lead innovation by example. These create-value-in-the-market leaders incorporate innovation into who they are, how they lead, and therefore what everyone sees. The innovative culture within these organizations is a by-product of the entrepreneurial executives, who preach only what they practice. The following exercises will help you drive this innovative mindset into your DNA so that it also becomes part of your team.

Find associations

Steve Jobs often remarked, "Creativity is connecting things."[11] Jobs dedicated a portion of his most precious resource, his time on this planet, exploring seemingly non-computer interests. Studying calligraphy and meditation allowed him to make connections few of us could imagine. Jobs understood that innovations blossom in the fertile soil of great associations. What outside interests could you cultivate? How might expanding your interests help grow your ability to categorize and synthesize new knowledge? Can you use Venn diagrams, pictures, and flow charts to illustrate issues or highlight connections?

Ask questions

Meg Whitman, HP CEO (and former CEO of eBay), has worked with many of Silicon Valley's brightest entrepreneurs (e.g., the founders of Skype, PayPal, and eBay). She points out, "They get a kick out of screwing up the status quo.... They spend a tremendous amount of time thinking about how to change the world. And as they brainstorm, they like to ask: 'If we did this, what would happen?'"[12]

In other words, they ask questions that challenge assumptions. These types of questions go beyond those that stimulate incremental improvement (How can we do this better?). Instead, they create radical innovation (How can we try an entirely new approach?).

They also know that a point of view is not the *only* view. And because they aren't attached to one perspective, including their own, they find pleasure in playing the devil's advocate and inviting the "loyal opposition" to discussions. Their open-mindedness stimulates creative ideas and encourages dissent during brainstorming sessions.

Spend a few minutes every day writing down questions that challenge your processes, policies, and procedures. Here are several questions to stimulate an open mind:

- What problem is most pressing in our industry?
- Will solving this problem give us a competitive advantage?
- How can your organization foster more consistent cross-functional collaboration?
- Which community of stakeholders could influence our future growth?
- Which strategic partners or vendors could help us grow the most?
- How could a survey of our best customers give us innovative insights?
- How might we use cross-training to cultivate innovation?
- What can we learn from the most innovative companies?
- How can I network more with our company's best innovators?
- How can we exploit existing products and services even as we explore new ones?

Listen and observe

One of the last meetings I had when I worked for Siemens, prior to accepting a position at UCLA, was with a young product development engineer who asked me to preview an upcoming software release. She spent a few hours watching me flip through the beta version and listening to my feedback. As she shut down the computer and gathered her notes, she startled me by saying, "Thanks for the tons of feedback, Dave. I had no idea you knew this stuff so well."

I smiled and replied, "I think you'll find that our salespeople stay very close to their customers. If you want to know what the market really needs, listen to and watch those close to the customer."

Although it took some time for the medical division at Siemens to learn that "observation facilitates innovation," it eventually did. That's what the most successful entrepreneurs do—they watch behaviors closely. Scott Cook, founder of Intuit, saw his wife was frustrated trying to track the family finances. He combined this observation with the insights he gleaned from seeing Apple's graphic user interface during a pre-launch demonstration of Apple's original Lisa computer. Cook alleviated his wife's pain and captured 50% of the financial software market in his first year by heeding the advice of Hall of Fame baseball manager Yogi Berra: "You can observe a lot by watching."

How can you make observation part of your work?

Experiment

A decade ago, Honeywell, a global, diversified technology and manufacturing leader, was a stumbling giant. Today, it's one of America's most successful companies.[13] Over the past ten years, Honeywell's sales have risen 71% to $37.7 billion, its EPS is up close to 200% to $4.48, and free cash flow has increased by 66% to $3.7 billion.

One of the reasons for its success is that CEO Dave Cote believes in conducting pilot studies and testing ideas—or, as I like to call it, experimenting. We're not talking about Edison or Einstein-type experiments; we're talking about trying things out before rolling them out. For example, when Cote was rolling out the Honeywell Operating System (HOS), modeled after Toyota's manufacturing practices, he tested the program in ten factories, learned what worked and what didn't, tweaked the program, and piloted it in five more factories before even considering deploying it globally.

Honeywell now has more than 260 manufacturing locations globally that are in full-scale HOS deployment. On average, sites deploying HOS that have reached Bronze level maturity have seen productivity improvements of 19 percent; inventory reduction of 25%; quality gains of 70%; an 18% increase for Health, Safety and Environment audits; and a seven-point improvement in on-time-to-request for delivery.

Jeff Bezos has drilled this experimental attitude into Amazon executives by encouraging them "to go down blind alleys and experiment. If we can get processes decentralized so that we can do a lot of experiments without it being very costly, we'll get a lot more innovation."[14]

How can you increase your "test it" mindset?

Network

The insights and innovations that solve many industry challenges often come from thinking outside that industry. That's why top-down innovation doesn't work well as an isolated strategy. Adding an outside-in perspective can help our myopic tendency. Here are a two related approaches to encourage outside-in thinking by expanding your network:

- Expand the membership of those in your circle of influence. Poet and philosopher Ralph Waldo Emerson met with an elite yet diverse crowd known as the Saturday Club. They met once a month for more than 20 years in the Boston area. Members included Longfellow, Hawthorne, Holmes, and Whitman.[15] In his study of 500 industrial giants, Napoleon Hill reminds us that Henry Ford had his most outstanding achievements when he began networking with Edison, Burroughs, and Firestone.[16] What do you get when three media giants (Walt Disney Co., News Corp., and NBC Universal) decide to collaborate? Internet television named Hulu and Hulu Plus!

- Develop relationships with people in different industries. The CEO of a large public agency in Dallas told me (over lunch) that he frequently lunches with business leaders. He believes that understanding their private industry perspective helps him deliver better public services. Similarly, every quarter I attend a meeting of diverse organizational development (OD) experts at a colleague's home. The group consists of leadership professors, best-selling authors, graduate school students, and industry executives. We discuss a variety of professional issues and challenges. I always walk away with new insights that influence my business. How can you expand your network to stimulate more outside-in innovation?

• • •

Cultivating innovative growth is critical to survival because it is the very process of creating value in the market. Effective executives nurture this "mind to market" mindset by growing both the personal (*I need to be more innovative in my thinking*) *and* the process (*We need to build innovation into how we work in this organization*) aspect of innovation.

The first step is an intuition—and it comes with a burst, then difficulties arise. The thing gives out and then…"bugs," as such little faults and difficulties are called, show themselves and months of anxious watching, study, and labor are requisite before commercial success—or failure—is indeed reached. I have the right principle and am on the right track, but time, hard work, and some luck are necessary, too.

Thomas Edison[17]

Edison, one of the greatest inventors (1,093 patents) and innovators (he brought those good things to life), wrote those words in 1878. He exemplifies the lessons we have learned in this chapter from Google, Pixar, Honeywell, and the others. Now, contrast these great innovators to a market position of AOL, as described by Ken Auletta:

> The company still gets 80% of its profits from subscribers, many of whom are older people who have cable or DSL service but don't realize that they need not pay an additional $25 a month to get online and check their e-mail. "The dirty little secret," a former AOL executive says, "is that 75% of the people who subscribe to AOL's dial-up service don't need it."[18]

In our fast-changing world of free wireless Internet access (in fast-food restaurants and coffee shops), AOL has represented the polar opposite of growth through innovation. Unlike Siemens, AOL is an elephant that has not focused on learning to dance. Nor has AOL seemed to inspire creativity and change—the topic of our next chapter.

CHAPTER 11

Think Inside and Outside the Box

Everyone has the spark of creativity in them.
It is the job of the leader to inspire and release that spark.

PAUL SLOANE

A financial services firm in Connecticut hired an outside consulting firm to help increase efficiency. Employees at all levels of the organization submitted more than 1,000 ideas to streamline policies, processes, and procedures. After one of the company's senior IT executives expressed her enthusiasm for the initiative, I congratulated her and then asked her two questions:

1. Where were those 1,000 ideas prior to the initiative?
2. How is your company educating the executives to inspire creativity and change daily so that you don't need another expensive initiative?

She didn't have any answers. What she did have was an organization with a number of well-meaning executives who had inadvertently snuffed out the creative spark in the heart and soul of employees. Her executives lacked the third core competency of visionary leaders—the ability to inspire creativity and change.

1. Adapt strategies to meet goals.
2. Cultivate innovative growth.
3. INSPIRE CREATIVITY AND CHANGE.
4. Imagine broadly.

What's the cost of throwing cold water on employees' creative fire? Increased turnover, poor organizational performance, and eventually growth stagnation and death. How can organizations grow if their employees do not or cannot share creative ideas to help companies adapt to the changes in today's competitive global market?

The answer is, They can't. Just ask Microsoft. Microsoft's stock price has oscillated between $25 and $30 a share for more than a decade. Many call it Microsoft's lost decade. The company has been a late entrant, often last, in almost every new market — search engines, online and portable music and video, mobile phone software, social networking, tablets, and e-books. Apple's iPhone generates more revenue than all of Microsoft's products combined.

What's behind this sluggish performance? According to a behind-the-scenes investigation by Kurt Eichenwald, it's a culture that crushes creativity through a management system called "stack ranking"—an approach that forces each unit leader to categorize certain percentages of employees as top, good, average, and poor performers.[1] That means if you are a good employee on great team, you could be ranked as a poor performer.

Can you imagine a worse way to inspire creativity, change, and collaboration among team members?

Inspire creativity and change

A few Harvard Business School professors invited business executives from highly creative companies (Google, pharmaceutical leader Novartis, design consultancy IDEO, among others) to a two-day symposium to discuss the role of the leader as a catalyst for creativity and change.[2] Their first conclusion: You can't manage creativity, but you can manage *for* creativity.

In other words, leaders must create an environment that supports the creative process in how employees at all levels do their daily work. The company in Connecticut wouldn't need a major creativity initiative if inspiring creativity were part of the corporate culture.

Another key point: Leaders must not confuse innovation with creativity. Although innovation draws on creativity, innovation (as discussed in Chapter 10) focuses on bringing products and services to market.

Inspiring creativity and change, on the other hand, is the ability to transcend traditional ideas, rules, patterns, and relationships to achieve a variety of small and big goals. It's a separate competency because it requires leaders to unleash employees' novel ideas and energy toward daily objectives and long-term targets in all areas of their business.

As my colleague Jodi Walker says, inspiring executives create an environment that motivates employees from the status quo to status go!

Ten tools to inspire creativity

Here are ten tools, adapted from the Harvard conference and my consulting experiences, designed at once to help you create an environment that supports the creative process with your team and avoid pitfalls such as those experienced by the Connecticut firm and Microsoft.

None of us is as smart as all of us

"Capture every fleeting idea," says Sir Richard Branson, CEO of Virgin Atlantic Airways (and hundreds of other Virgin companies). He is reminding us that none of us is as smart as all of us.

To test this principle, Google's founders tracked the progress of ideas that they had backed compared to ideas executed in the ranks without support from above. They discovered a higher success rate among the ideas that emerged from Google's ranks than among ideas that emerged from Google's executives. They concluded that executives need to support a creative process for everyone.

Leaders must have processes to capture new ideas individually and your team's ideas collectively. One of my favorites is to keep a notepad or recording device nearby to capture those fleeting, creative thoughts. Otto Loewi, who won a Nobel Prize for his work in cell biology, offers another way. He had a brilliant idea in his sleep, so he woke up and scribbled his creative insight on a pad. Unfortunately, he could not read his own writing the next morning. (This idea works only if you get out of bed and write your ideas clearly.) Luckily, his idea surfaced in his dreams the following night and he implemented another idea-capturing technique — he got dressed and went to work in his laboratory!

To facilitate team creativity, consider brainstorming during meetings. You can also boost group creativity 100% with what Professor Robert Epstein, visiting scholar at the University of California at San Diego, calls "the shifting game."[3] Here's how to apply it:

- First, give your team members a creative challenge or problem to solve and ask them to work together for five minutes.
- Then shift out of the group and invite team members to work on the problem individually for five minutes.
- Finally, have the group come back together for the final five minutes.

Foster collaborative challenges

The lone inventor is a myth. Linux, Wikipedia, and Mozilla's Firefox web browser are illustrations of collaboration both within the organization and with customers. Network and social structures that are fluid enable this type of cooperation. An organization structure that overemphasizes centralized, top-down hierarchy kills creativity.

Effective executives often give their toughest problems to internal or external social networks. A network's broad experiences, interactions, passion, and varied behaviors create unique insights seldom seen by the solitary inventor. This is one reason that ranking employees relative to peers, as Microsoft and many other organizations do, is so damaging — it creates intra-competition instead of fostering cross-functional collaboration.

Celebrate diversity

Creativity is more likely when people of different disciplines, backgrounds, and areas of expertise share their thinking. The most creative companies engage people from outside their organization who have and respect different perspectives.

If you are on the outside of a house trying to see what's inside, you can only see through your window. If you have different people peer through different windows around the house you'll get a more complete picture of what's inside. A single point of view is no way to see the world.

Don't kill ideas with process

Dr. Mark Fishman, president of the Novartis Institutes for BioMedical Research, reported that when organizations over-focus on process improvement it hurts long-term innovation. He recommends that leaders focus their efficiency initiatives in the middle and at the end of the creative process.

The fuzzy, initial stages of innovation are places to celebrate creative and novel ideas—not to seek efficiency.

Pass the baton carefully

The most passion for an idea resides in its creators. When it comes time to commercialize the idea, the hand-off must be handled with care. The best organizations allow these creative idea generators to stay on the team as it goes through the implementation or commercialization process. This keeps the enthusiasm for the idea high, but only if the tension between the creators and those who commercialize the idea is managed well.

Filter the ideas

For every one idea that generates revenue, nine generate only expenses. Gardens have weeds; so do organizations. Merck's R&D chief, Peter Kim, rewards scientists who bail out on a losing project with stock options.

Filtering ideas lets the people who generated the idea be involved in killing it. Be wary of product evaluation committees, especially if they don't involve the creative people. Their only power is in saying no, so that's what committees do.

Provide intellectual challenge

A study of 11,000 R&D employees found that early-stage researchers—the people with the best and brightest ideas—found their greatest motivation in intellectual challenges, followed by a desire for independence and extrinsic rewards (i.e., salary, benefits, job security).

If you want to inspire your R&D team, give them tough challenges, freedom with a few clearly defined constraints, and a carrot at the end of the stick.

Encourage the pursuit of personal passions

Encourage your people to spend some of their time on projects of their own choosing. While some employees prefer exploiting the present by working on the 42nd iteration of a current product or process, others find motivation in exploring the future by searching for the next big thing. Nurture *their* nature.

Applaud effort — not just results

Professor Kelly Lambert examined the importance of applauding effort, not just results, by studying two groups of rats.[4] One group was placed in a cage filled with little mounds of dirt. Buried beneath these mounds were Froot Loops—the treat of choice for hungry rats. During a five-week period, these "worker" rats learned to dig for their treats. In an identical cage, the second group of rats received their Froot Loops free. These "trust-fund" rats didn't have to dig or work for their food.

After the five weeks, researchers placed a ball made of screen and filled with Froot Loops in each cage. The only food in the cages was in the screen ball. The increasingly hungry rats could see and smell—but couldn't reach—the Froot Loops.

Which group do you think worked hardest to obtain the food in the cage? The worker group spent 60% more time and made 30% more novel attempts to get the Froot Loops compared to the freeloading trust-fund group.

The moral of this story: If you want to increase creative thinking and overall persistence, reward effort—a growth mindset—not just accomplishment.

Praising only goal achievement or talent teaches employees not to try or experiment unless they are sure of success. Can you imagine a gymnast refusing to try a new routine because she feared failure? Stanford Professor Carroll Dweck summarized 30 years of scientific investigation by declaring that we should "teach people to have a growth mindset, which encourages a focus on effort rather than intelligence or talent."[5]

If you want your team to work hard, especially in activities that don't always pay off quickly (such as creativity), reward effort and progress. What you appreciate appreciates.

Interpret failure as feedback

Kim Scott, director of online sales and operations for Google, observed that the Silicon Valley firms that have had the most difficult time managing creativity are those that have been the most successful.

Why? Because they develop an aversion to failure.

Most company cultures reinforce the belief that failure is bad; when it happens, it is best forgotten as quickly as possible. Executives who inspire creativity and change adopt the experiment mentality of researchers: The essence of experimentation is trial, feedback, learning, next trial. Effective executives foster a culture that doesn't focus on failure — only feedback. They believe that failure happens when they don't learn from the feedback.

The problem with the financial services company in Connecticut was that its leaders acted as if creative input was a one-time initiative instead of an everyday way of working. They didn't employ many of these top 10 ideas for cultivating a creative culture.

How will you adapt these steps to inspire creativity on your team?

Inspire change by providing stability

The third competency of a visionary leader is not just about inspiring creativity; it's about inspiring creativity *and* change. As a high-tech firm in the Southeast United States discovered, there's a big difference between advocating change and inspiring change.

Two weeks after announcing a new change initiative, the CEO of this global, high-tech firm conducted an all-hands meeting. He started the meeting by answering a few questions previously submitted by employees. When the CEO addressed one of the "negative" questions that challenged the need for another major initiative, he actually admonished the naysayers for their dysfunctional attitude and declared that he would not tolerate dissent about his new initiative.

The collective wind went out of the sails of everyone at the meeting.

Six months after the all-hands-meeting, a mid-level manager who relayed this incident to me also reported that trust in the CEO had plummeted and that the change initiative was barely limping along.

This disturbing story illustrates one of the many reasons that 70% of all change initiatives fail: low trust caused by pushing change instead of inspiring it.[6] The actual percentage will vary depending on a host of variables (e.g., how one defines success, the scope of the change, whether the change is initiated in times of crisis, the level of buy-in from those affected by the change). Yet, the ugly reality remains that most change efforts fall short of their goals, leaving the slug-like residue of negative consequences (seen in Table 11.1).[7]

TABLE 11.1

Residue of Failed Change

Anger

Lower morale

Increased stress

Diminished risk-taking

Decreased trust in leaders

Less money for other priorities

Subtle sabotage of the change effort

Less commitment to future change initiatives

Although entire books are dedicated to the implementation of change, this section focuses on the essential first step of any successful change effort — minimizing the resistance to change by inspiring employee buy-in. If you gain commitment to change, you have overcome the biggest hurdle to achieving that change.

There are many reasons employees don't accept change, including the one illustrated by the opening story—lack of trust.[9] Table 11.2 lists the top 10 reasons people resist change in the workplace.

TABLE 11.2

Top 10 Reasons Employees Resist Change

1. Lack of trust
2. Economic threats
3. Relatively high cost
4. Fear of personal failure
5. Loss of status and power
6. Threat to values and ideals
7. Resentment of interference
8. Belief that change is unnecessary
9. Belief that the change is not feasible
10. Failure to focus on changing employee behaviors

The first responsibility of a leader is to create mental energy among people so that they enthusiastically embrace the transformation.

N.R. NARAYANA MURTHY[10]

You can avoid the fate of the CEO at that global, high-tech firm by following the four-step process to inspiring change:

1. Begin the journey on common ground.
2. Engage others to increase commitment.
3. Motivate a change in behavior.
4. Lead the change by managing stability.

Begin the journey on common ground

According to the mid-level manager who told me about the all-hands meeting, passive resistance from the silent majority—caused by low trust—is now killing the CEO's change initiative. The CEO chose not to see that the "negative" question was merely feedback telling him that he had not taken the first step of inspiring change.

Many change efforts get off on this wrong foot because executives don't realize that "if you suppress dialogue, you'll miss opportunities to gain [other people's] buy-in."[11] So, if you want to take employees on the journey of change, you must first go to them and begin the journey on common ground.

Contrast the approach of the CEO in the previous story with the one taken by Xerox's Anne Mulcahy when first appointed CEO. She called legendary executive Warren Buffett, who recommended that she spend the first three months of her tenure assessing her environment. He suggested that she meet with key customers and front-line employees before deciding how to implement any change. She followed his advice and earned credit for Xerox's dramatic turnaround.[12]

Lou Gerstner also emphasized the importance of going to others when he took over a struggling IBM in the early 1990s. He urged his top executives to get out of their ivory towers at least once a month to visit customers. Customer feedback led to strategic insight that helped Gerstner right IBM's listing ship.[13]

Anne Mulcahy and Lou Gerstner understood that the first step in inspiring and gaining buy-in to change is understanding the current environment. That environment includes employees' readiness to change, the organization's competitive climate, financial realities, and early feedback about the start of change. Thus, the most effective executives begin the journey by getting in touch with the rank and file.

Here are some simple and powerful tools to help you begin the change buy-in process by staying in touch with your team:

- Increase your management by walking around (MBWA). Listen to hallway, water cooler, and cafeteria conversations during the early stages of the change initiative. Sometimes, "buy-in can be a simple matter of being heard."[15]
- Solicit e-mails directly from employees at all levels. This was essential to Paul Levy as he set the stage for change at Beth Israel Deaconess Medical Center. He personally responded to more than 300 e-mails he received regarding suggestions for improvement as he started a major change at that institution.[16]
- Invite front-line supervisors to survey *their* employees regarding the impact of the change on them.
- Encourage your direct reports to create a worry list and an idea list. Discuss the lists with other executives. Then, let your direct reports know what you can and cannot address on each list.
- Survey customers and the competitive landscape about the need for change.
- Send key team members to visit critical customers who understand the need for change. Let these customers help sell the need for the change.
- Conduct fewer all-hands meetings. When Watson Wyatt Worldwide (now Towers Watson) investigated 531 organizations that had undergone major changes (many of which fell short of their goals), CEOs were asked what they would do differently next time.[17] The most frequent answer: "The way I communicate with my employees."

  Specifically, the researchers found that conducting *fewer* all-hands meetings and more communication with supervisors worked best. Employees view communication from the top with suspicion. They know that messages from senior executives are scrutinized, sanitized, and pasteurized. So, if you want to inspire employees to change, communicate to the people employees really listen to — their supervisors. Conduct frequent face-to-face meetings with small groups of front-line supervisors.

The CEO of the high-tech firm in the Southeast U.S., who admonished employees for submitting a negative question at his all-hands meeting, yelled "charge" as he raced uphill into battle. But when he turned around, he discovered that he was the fool on the hill. He didn't realize that he couldn't lead people through a change if he didn't have them with him as he started the journey. Use these tools to begin your journey on common ground. That way, when you yell charge, your troops will be there when you turn around.

Engage others to increase commitment

An executive in one of our leadership classes stated that the legendary Green Bay Packers coach, Vince Lombardi, engaged others all the time. When I asked how he knew this to be true, he said that he used to be a ball boy for the Packers when he was a young. He explained that Coach Lombardi would frequently ask him—the ball boy—what he would do to improve or change the team.

According to a survey of 22,451 employees in 2,295 organizations, Lombardi was practicing the second principle of inspiring change—increasing engagement increases commitment.[18] Psychologists have been telling us for years that the more input people have about their journey, the more connected they feel to the trip and the destination. If you want your team to commit to the *outcome* of change, involve them in the *process* of change.

The former CEO of Electronic Data Systems (EDS), Dick Brown, understood the wisdom of engagement when he needed to implement an expense-reduction change several years ago. Instead of initiating a board-recommended, top-down, expense-cutting initiative, he "sent an e-mail to 120,000 EDS employees...asked every one of them to save $1,000 [and] saved millions."[19] Very simple can be very effective when employees are engaged in the change process.

Let's review some simple techniques to engage others in the process of change, especially if that change is being thrust upon them.

- Focus on influence: Whenever you detect that employees feel that they are victims of change, conduct the Stephen Covey exercise called "Circle of Influence and Concern."[20]

  Draw a large circle on a whiteboard or flipchart. Inside the circle, near the outer edge, write the word *concern.* Ask team members to brainstorm all their concerns about the change. Write their answers in the circle. Do not discuss or analyze these concerns during this brainstorming process.

  Next, draw a smaller circle in the middle of the big circle. This is your "doughnut hole." Write the word *influence* in this inner circle. Now ask your team members to brainstorm all the factors that they can influence with respect to this change effort. Again, do not discuss or analyze their input at this time.

Finally, ask them in which circle they choose to spend the majority of their time. Explain whichever circle they choose, that circle will expand. Tell the team that although you share their concerns, if they spend too much time complaining about things they can do nothing about, they will spend less time on things they can do something about. Invite them to focus on those things that they can influence.

Carol, an executive in a government agency, engaged her unmotivated managers (who felt like victims of change) using this exercise. After they completed the process, her team decided that because the change was not going to go away, they were going to concentrate their efforts on four tasks they could influence:

1. How to adapt the new budget initiative (i.e., the change) to suit their environment
2. The nature and timing of training needed to implement the new changes
3. Creative and constructive ways to provide feedback to the senior leadership team regarding the impact of the change on their unit
4. Their attitude about the change

- Discuss the immaculate reception: If a tree falls in the woods and nobody hears it, does it make a sound? I believe that the answer to this age-old question is no. Noise is created when a sound wave strikes the eardrum.

  This metaphor teaches us that no matter what change happens in the external environment, we can choose how we receive and process it in our internal environment. If this were not true, everything would affect everyone the same way.

  Here's a simple method to introduce this powerful concept of free will. During a meeting of any size (I once used this technique during a presentation to 100 CEOs), ask people if they get upset when someone cuts them off when they are driving; then ask those people who say yes to stand up. (I find about half of my audience usually stands.) Now, ask everyone these three questions:

  1. Why isn't everyone standing?
  2. How could the exact same incident affect people differently?
  3. Is it possible that those sitting choose to think about getting cut off in traffic differently than those standing?

This simple and profound exercise often leads into a conversation about free will and choice. Without choice, we would be leaves in the river of life, victims of current circumstances. Choosing to respond, and not react, to change reveals the essence of what I believe is the immaculate reception.

It is in the receiving that meaning is made.

If employees feel they are the victims of change, they won't change their behaviors to support the change outcomes. Discuss this concept at one of your meetings. Ask the people on your team if they believe they have free will. Talk about how and when they choose to access and not access their freedom to choose.

As part of the circle of concern/influence exercise, Carol and her team *chose* their attitude about change. They *chose* which circle they wanted to focus on. They *chose* not to be the victims of change that someone else thrust upon them. Expansive executives unleash the energy of their teams toward worthy goals by helping them choose free will.

- Ask expansive questions: When change hits employees, they often ask disempowering questions, such as:
  1. Why me?
  2. Who made this dumb decision?
  3. Why can't our leaders get this change right?
  4. When are we ever going to have time to learn this new system?

I even hear executives ask questions like these when change hits them unexpectedly. The problem is that these disempowering questions lead to dispiriting answers, thereby perpetuating a victim mindset. Instead of helping employees face the challenge of change, these questions let them slip down the deep, dark abyss of woe-is-me thinking.

Disempowering questions leave people in the dark, like an ostrich that sticks its head in the sand, where the view is limited. (Never mind what's sticking up and vulnerable when your head is in the sand!)

Worry often gives a small thing a big shadow.

Swedish proverb

To inspire commitment to change, ask "expansive" questions. These questions motivate employees to move away from victim thinking to meaningful activity because they encourage employees to access their free will. Here are those four disempowering questions asked earlier turned into expansive questions:

1. How can I make the best of this situation?
2. What evidence do decision makers need to see that might get this decision changed?
3. How could my customers show our leaders how to get this change right?
4. How can we make learning this new system fun?

See how expansive questions lift us out of "sinking thinking" into possibility thinking. The view is better and the options more abundant when employees choose to take their heads out of the sand.

Here are eight generic expansive questions that increase buy-in to any change that hits you or your team during the day:

1. How does this change fit into the big picture?
2. What does my irritation about this change teach me about me?
3. How can I choose to see this change differently?
4. What's my lesson in this messin'?
5. Who can help me deal with this change?
6. How can I let go of my attachment to the old way?
7. How can I shine my leadership talents during these dark times?
8. What expansive questions could I ask myself to feel better right now?

Effective executives are like stars, shining their light at night. Expansive questions amplify that light.

The future always begins today.

- **Create a culture using norms:** One of my last projects as an executive at UCLA was to lead a technology transfer program. The program was designed to exchange our faculty know-how for deeply discounted equipment needed to do our research.

  After both the equipment vendor and our UCLA team had agreed to the terms, we each delivered our agreements to our respective legal departments. A few weeks later, the vendor delivered the agreement with the few minor changes requested by its lawyers. I forwarded their document to our legal department and waited...and waited...and then waited some more.

  It took a year of phone calls, e-mails, and personal visits for me to extract our agreement from UCLA's legal department. Their norms of risk avoidance and poor customer service grounded our institute's entrepreneurial spirit.

Norms are the mini-culture of a group. They are "the way we do things around here" and consist of the rules of engagement, often unwritten and unconscious, that regulate how employees behave within their teams. Our faculty's entrepreneurial norms supported the many changes and projects we undertook to achieve our vision. Yet when our projects encountered the snail-paced norms of UCLA's legal department, our norms caused more friction than progress.

The moral of the story is that norms, like gravity, are always at work; the only question is, Are they working for you or against you? Do they support or hinder your change efforts? If change affects the entire organization, leaders must ensure that the culture—the company-wide norms—will support the change.[21] On the other hand, if you are striving to get buy-in among your own team members in a smaller unit, create behavioral norms that support the change locally.[22]

- Don't just broadcast—communicate: Don, a mid-level manager in the travel industry, lamented that his team felt that company executives were sugarcoating their message about a new change initiative. He feared that lack of candid communication from the top was decreasing trust below.

  An OnPoint Consulting survey of 655 employees concluded that open and honest communication from top executives makes change easier, even when the executives don't have complete information or good news.[23] In my subsequent conversation with Don, he indicated that his executives were confusing broadcasting with communicating. Broadcasting scatters a message in all directions. Communication, on the other hand, is a process by which information is exchanged. The most effective communication strategies about change include four critical elements:

  1. Open dialogue in small meetings and brief one-on-one encounters
  2. Frequent discussion about the facts
  3. Transparency regarding how decisions are made and applied
  4. Behaviors by executives that communicate their words in action

  Broadcasting and communicating both have their place. Yet leaders must not confuse one for the other, as the executives in Don's organization did.

The way to do is to be.

Lao Tzu

Motivate a change in behavior

Joan, a front-line supervisor from a large insurance company, complained to me that many of her high-performing colleagues were distraught after a corporate policy change was announced. She moaned that the senior executives had no idea how the new policy was damaging employees' commitments to a major change initiative that was being implemented.

When I quizzed senior executives about the policy change, they asserted that the policy change was needed to support the major change initiative. I told the executives that instead of motivating employees to change behaviors to align with the major initiative, my impression was that their misguided new policy was motivating employees to quit. (Two of those who complained the loudest have quit.)

In a survey of 5,100 global business leaders, the American Management Association (AMA) found that one of the major reason employees don't buy into change is that the executives do not focus on changing those specific behaviors that align with the change.[24] Joan's leaders were so focused on changing a policy that it blinded them to the importance of motivating employees to change behaviors required by their major change initiative.

There is no organizational change without individual transformation. That's because organizations don't change — people do. Unless employee behaviors support the change initiative, long-term change is as stable as a house of cards on a windy day.[25] Joan's senior executives failed to execute the third step of inspiring change — motivating team members to change their behaviors. Here are several tactics to help you construct a solid foundation of changed behaviors:

- Communicate a sense of urgency logically and emotionally: Urgency comes from the Latin *urgentia,* meaning pressure. Good leaders increase the pressure to change behaviors by sharing with employees the data that proves the need for change. Effective executives illustrate logically and emotionally.

  Dan Cohen tells the story of the procurement manager whose project team discovered that the company purchased 424 types of gloves when the company actually needed only three types. To communicate logically and emotionally, the manager collected all 424 gloves, put a price on each, and stacked them in the boardroom so that senior leadership could tangibly see and feel the cost of this inefficiency.[26]

Increase the pressure to change behaviors by discussing issues with team members affected by change. Use these questions to guide the discussion:

- What if we don't change?
- Why do we need to change now?
- What will the change look like?
- How will this change affect how employees do their jobs?
- Who are the opinion leaders we need to convince first?
- How can we help employees feel the negative consequences of not changing?
- What is our process for celebrating changed behaviors?

- Experiment with small change during major initiatives: Don't fall victim to the fallacy of the big bang fix—the mistaken notion that all change must be big change. Nature teaches us that experimentation is king of the jungle. Whenever possible, conduct small experiments before rolling out any major initiative or during the change itself. Learn from each trial. The knowledge gained from trial and error is the feedback that keeps you on track toward your goal.

- Make changed behaviors and progress visible: During the early phase of a major change initiative, my colleagues interviewed 64 employees about the upcoming change. When asked what would encourage behavioral change, the number-one recommendation from the employees was, "Seeing how the new system would actually work."

  This suggestion takes the experimental approach a step further by inviting leaders to make the progress visible. Pat employees on the back when they try new approaches, develop novel ideas, remove obstacles, and take small steps toward changing behaviors. Employees are inspired when they see progress rewarded. Celebrate these small wins to send the signal that management is paying attention to small steps.

- Be the change you wish to see: This statement reminds us that employees comply with what they hear, but they commit to what they see. This is especially true during crises because heightened emotions anchor the learning people are observing.

  For example, when I worked for Siemens, senior executives announced a major change initiative designed to increase collaboration among divisions. Yet when I implored my boss to solicit cooperation from one of the divisions to help me book a large order, he told me that the other division's executives wouldn't collaborate with us because they were under too much pressure to reach their own quarterly sales numbers.

So much for my commitment to the senior executives' "knocking down silos" initiative. The company's response under pressure left an impression for all to see.

> *Every move you make, everything you say, is visible to all. Therefore, the best approach is to lead by example.*
>
> JOSEPH TUCCI[27]

- SET REALISTIC GOALS AND OBJECTIVES: I was a member of the dean's goals committee when I was at UCLA. The dean wanted us to create a plan to accomplish his vision — for the UCLA School of Medicine to become *the* preeminent medical school in the country by the end of the decade. At the time, UCLA was ranked eight or nine, depending on which survey you reviewed.

  The dean's goal was so lofty that most of the committee members did not believe it was achievable. They therefore did not put forth any serious effort to develop a plan. They went through the motions by giving the dean's initiative *lip* service but very little *hip* service. Nothing ever came of our halfhearted plan to be number one. Last time I checked, the school was ranked 13 out of 138 U.S. medical schools.

- ESTIMATE RESOURCES ACCURATELY: Employees have a specific capacity to handle change. Too much change overwhelms them. Yet many organizations push one change after another without assessing the ability of people to digest the change.

  A middle manager in one of our leadership classes said that her high-tech firm currently had three major organizational change initiatives affecting most of its employees. The resources required to implement these changes were severely underestimated and the capacity for people to absorb them was overestimated. She told senior executives that her employees were at the breaking point. They didn't listen.

  The middle manager also told me that her company just lost its largest client because it didn't pay enough attention to this client's needs. By miscalculating the resources needed for all their change initiatives, senior executive failed to consider the impact all the change would have on the company's clients.

- Be a meaning-making machine: "We're grateful to the ironworkers for helping make our patients' and families' lives just a little bit better, and their stays at the hospital a little bit more fun," says Todd Johnson, vice president of facilities at Seattle Children's Hospital. "What started out as a simple gesture to one patient family became something that touched many people's lives."[28] For weeks, ironworkers for Local 86 spray-painted children's names on the steel girders being used for the "Building Hope" expansion at Seattle Children's Hospital.

  As the construction project neared the end of this phase, the children thanked the ironworkers by designing T-shirts for them. Ironworkers returned the favor by distributing 400 of their end-of-project T-shirts emblazoned with "I'm on the Beam" to the youngsters.

  The ironworkers made meaning out of their work. They understood that the *why* is the steam behind the *what* of change.

  John Hammergren, the CEO at U.S.-based healthcare company McKesson, made meaning out of one of his company's change initiatives by emphasizing that every employee was, or would someday be, a patient in the healthcare system—in other words, McKesson's end user.[29]

- Focus on what you want: Don't think of a red apple. Don't think of a red apple.

  What just popped into your mind? You probably thought of a red apple, right? Why? Because the brain cannot work on the reverse of an idea.[30] We move in the direction of the dominant images that we place (or let others place) in our minds.

  Therefore, it is important when communicating change that you focus on what you want more than what you *don't* want. This does not mean you totally ignore problems, obstacles, or mistakes. It does mean emphasizing the specific behaviors, skills, and outcomes that support the change—at least according to 127 female bowlers in Wisconsin.

  Professor Daniel Kirschenbaum and his colleagues at the University of Wisconsin studied the importance of focusing on what you want by assessing the impact of positive versus negative self-monitoring in novice bowlers.[31] In their study, 127 women bowlers learned the seven key components of effective bowling (called "Brain Power Bowling" in this study). Researchers then divided the women into two groups for five weeks, gave them rating sheets, and provided the following instructions:

- Group 1 — Positive Self-monitoring. After bowling each frame, review the seven components of Brain Power Bowling. For those components that you do well, put a number from 1 to 3 in the box corresponding to that component (1 = good; 2 = very good; 3 = excellent). If you did not do a good job on a particular component, leave the box blank. Before making your next approach, remind yourself of the correct way to complete the components.
- Group 2—Negative Self-monitoring. After bowling each frame, review the possible errors you made by not following the seven component principles of Brain Power Bowling. If you made any of these possible errors, put a number from 1 to 3 in the box corresponding to that error, denoting how poorly you did (1 = terrible; 2 = very poor; 3 = poor). If you did not make an error on a particular component, leave the box blank. Before making your next approach, remind yourself of the errors you might make on the components.

Thus, Group 1 (positive self-monitors) focused on getting what they wanted, and Group 2 (negative self-monitors) focused on avoiding errors. Five weeks later, Group 1 improved its scores 100% more than Group 2 (an average of 11 pins).

How much more would the members of your team be motivated to align their behaviors with those needed to support the change initiative if you consistently focused on what you wanted?

- Rewrite the job description: In a rapidly changing environment, job descriptions and employment policies should include flexible language that encourages team members to develop talents and behaviors needed to support change. During IBM's transformation, CEO Lou Gerstner changed IBM's policy of lifetime employment to one of lifelong employability — if employees developed the behaviors and skills mandated by their new landscape.

Lead the change by managing stability

The soapy, wet rags danced across my front windshield as I drove into the car wash. Instantly, my 90-pound German shepherd leaped from the back to the front seat. His big brown eyes screamed at me, "Dad, what's that?"

"It's OK, Comet." I stroked his head as the car darkened.

Within seconds, the gigantic brushes attacked the car from all sides.

Comet scrambled from the passenger seat onto my lap, shaking. His eyes, glued to mine, cried, "I'm not OK!"

I held him tightly, stroked his head, and sang his favorite song: "That's our good boy Comet; Comet is a good boy. . . ." He stopped shaking and panting.

Minutes later, we exited the car wash. That's when it occurred to me that Comet stopping shaking and panting because I was able to give him security; he handled change because I gave stability.

Old dogs can learn new tricks if given comfort. Stability provides the security needed to feel comfortable about change. Therein lies the paradox. The fourth step to inspire change is to lead that change by managing stability. All those "change agents" and books telling executives to drive change are only half right. Too much change without stability drives people over the edge.

If executives don't give employees something to hold onto, employees cling to their old habits of thinking and working. When the change is too much, the water cooler talk and social media channels are ablaze with naysayers. These comments are from employees who seek a firm foundation because they feel they are on shaky ground:

- It will never work.
- This too shall pass.
- Why do they have to hit us with so many changes?
- Can't we get one right before we start the next one?
- I won't be able to get my job done without the old system.
- I'll never learn this new way.

The paradox of growth

Professor Thomas Lawrence and his colleagues summarized 15 years of change research: "Initiating and maintaining continuous change in an organization requires a foundation of stability. Understanding that paradox is crucial."[32] Thus, the final step in inspiring employees to change invites executives to construct a platform of stability. One way to manage stability is by discussing growth curves with your team.

Professor Charles Handy, from the London Business School, suggests using an S-shaped growth curve (or sigmoid curve) to help explain this stability-change paradox.[33] I've adapted his approach as I've taught the following step-by-step approach to thousands of executives during the last two decades. I invite you to try it to increase buy-in.

1. Draw a sigmoid (or S) curve on a flipchart or whiteboard, such as the one shown in Figure 11.1.

FIGURE 11.1
Sigmoid Curve

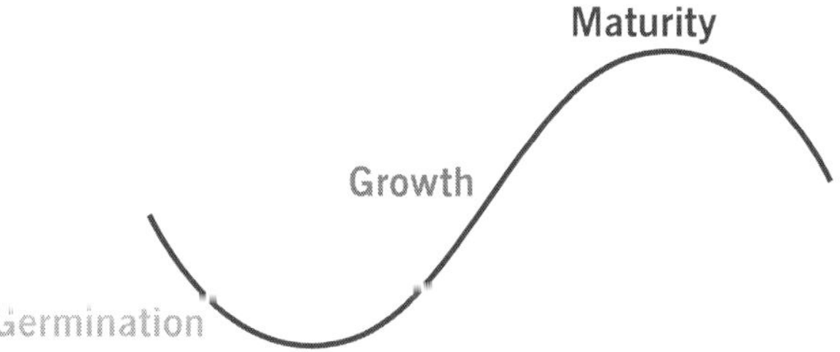

2. LABEL THE CURVES and explain each section of the curve:

- GERMINATION is where new ideas are born and innovation is encouraged. R&D occurs here, although it's usually more research than development. There are heavy investments of time, money, and effort with little initial return. This is the work the garden needs before the plants can grow. Tilling the soil, planting the seeds, fertilizing, and watering are all necessary to move into the next stage.
- GROWTH occurs when the product takes off. The market accepts the new product and sales are great. When sales blast off, it is often hard to meet demand because the process, policies, and people are not in place yet. Production is often strained at this time because operations and plans are not fully implemented. Toward the end of the growth phase, sales start to slow down. The crop is ready to harvest.
- MATURITY is that time in the product's life when demand levels off. The competition has joined the field and affected market share. The crop is harvested and people wonder how they'll make it through the winter.

3. ASK THE TEAM WHAT TO DO WHEN MATURITY IS REACHED. Of course, people will say that a new curve is needed. Ask them where this new curve should start. They'll probably indicate that this second curve needs to begin during the growth phase of the first curve, as illustrated in Figure 11.2. Next, ask the team a series of questions, such as:

- How well accepted is this new, second curve?
- Is there any tension between the first and the second curve? (When they answer yes, draw a line between the curves as seen in Figure 11.2. Label that line Tension, and define it as "the state of being stretched.")
- How have you experienced these growth curves at work and at home?

FIGURE 11.2

The Stability-Change Curves

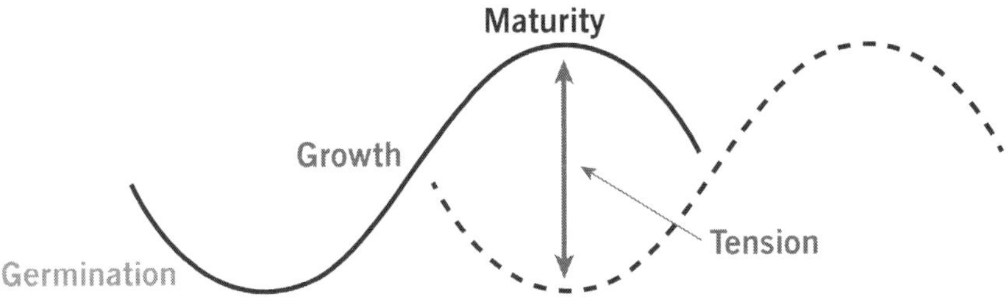

4. Discuss the two curves and the tension between them, especially as it pertains to people's own life experiences. Help them understand certain key ideas using, again, a questioning strategy. Don't lecture—if you say it, they doubt it; if they experience it, they'll believe it.

- Referring to Figure 11.2, curve one is the stability curve, while curve two (dotted line) is the change curve.
- The stability curve funds/finances the change curve.
- You need both curves to survive.
- There is a recurring tension between the two curves. We all need to stretch when we feel pulled by the stability and change paradox.
- Different groups in the organization value and defend different portions of the curve.
- Different leadership styles need to be emphasized at different phases of the curve. While visionary and commanding skills (the preferred styles of adventurous pioneers) are needed during the germination phase, more rational and empowering skills (the preferred styles of organized administrators) are needed during the growth and maturity phases. Of course, executives need all four styles, but effective executives accent specific styles to meet the unique demands at different phases of growth. Context matters.
- In rapidly changing business environments, the length of the cycle gets shorter. One reason is that global competition demands both continuous improvement programs (frequent small changes) and major change initiatives (episodic transformation). This means that employees are spending more time managing the tension between the old (stability) and the new (change).

- Rigid organizational structures do not function well in dynamic environments. They lack the agility to adapt rapidly to a whitewater environment. Professors Christopher Worley and Edward Lawler from USC remind us that only organizations built to change will last.[34]
- Employees stretch toward the new (the future) when they are grounded in history (the past).
- Life is a series of growth curves. Going to college, getting married, having children, loved ones dying, children growing up…all these life transitions are illustrations of growth curves. The essence of *The Hero's Journey*[35] is the story of growth curves.

5. Ensure employees understand the need for both stability and change by the end of this discussion. The final step is to encourage employees to decide what norms and behaviors would give them a feeling of security during the change – how to build their platform of stability. The ten behaviors identified most in our leadership classes are:

- Align rewards with desired behaviors.
- Nurture new norms that support change.
- Encourage employees to remove obstacles.
- Celebrate short-term and tangible successes.
- Develop a vision that gives direction and stimulates action.
- Compose an influential team of leaders to provide visible support.
- Brainstorm with employees about how they benefit from the change.
- Establish clear roles and responsibilities for those affected by the change.
- Engage in ongoing communications that emphasize why the change is urgent.
- Affirm those values that are grounded in who we are as an organization and make sure these values are practiced by all leaders.

The value of explaining growth curves to gain buy-in to change was best summarized by Analog Device founder and former CEO Ray Stata (a recipient of the Annual Creativity in Electronics Lifetime Achievement Award), when he explained:

> [T]he S-curve is always there. The whole idea of the birth, maturity, and death – whether it's technology or whether it's products, or markets, or organizations – ultimately is about companies and people. Right? Everything's got a life cycle.…So I'd say that's another key thing about being innovators and staying alive because today the record shows that the

average life expectancy of Fortune 500 companies in the United States is 40 to 50 years. And it has a lot to do with the fact of the S-curve, and the fact that business strategies and technologies...are running out of gas, and people just haven't anticipated those points of inflections adequately to have answers to continue on into the future when death strikes things that had been so successful in the past. So, nothing fails like success, so being able to go beyond your current success and create new success has always been a challenge for our industry, and will continue to be.[36]

Executives who fail to inspire creativity and change as the norm lead their organizations on a Titanic voyage. Their sinking may be slow (Kodak) or fast (People Express Airlines). But disaster is assured for those who don't know how to adapt their policies, procedures, and products in stormy seas.

A voyage of discovery awaits executives who tap into the creative talents of their teams. Smooth sailing is almost assured if they then inspire employees to change by beginning the journey on common ground, engaging them throughout the change, motivating changes in behavior, and leading the change by managing stability. Listed below are 13 more tools to help you on your journey.

TABLE 11.3

13 Tools to Inspire Creativity and Change

1. Encourage entrepreneurial and creative thinking on your team.
2. Separate idea generation from idea evaluation.
3. Develop norms to stimulate creativity during your meetings.
4. Increase the fun factor with your team.
5. Stimulate brainstorming on your own and with others.
6. Reward people who challenge the status quo.
7. Ask them to give you at *least* three ideas, instead of asking for three ideas.
8. Encourage a more "what if" mindset with your team.
9. Give people something to hold onto to get them to change.
10. Explore unfamiliar areas outside of your comfort zone.
11. Imagine what the world could look like if it were completely different.
12. Practice the art of noticing the extraordinary in the ordinary.
13. Write three pages of non-stop, brain-dump Morning Pages.

AOL Time Warner executives tried to make the merged company function well enough to create value for its shareholders and deliver a compelling value proposition to its customers. Yet, they inspired neither creativity nor change. The tools listed in Table 11.3 are a virtual checklist of everything the company's leaders didn't do. The result? The company lost nearly 90% of its market value over the course of a decade.

Although AOL Time Warner executives had a big picture in mind, they didn't know how to imagine broadly—the subject of the next and last chapter in this section on the visionary leadership style.

CHAPTER 12

Go Big or Go Home

They are ill discoverers that think there is no land, when they can see nothing but sea.

FRANCIS BACON

My eyes bulged, I took a deep breath, and—as calmly as I could under the circumstance—I stated the facts: "Dr. Froelicher, we have multiple PVCs."

He took hold of the patient's arm on the treadmill and barked, "Stop the treadmill—get the crash cart."

As I bolted out of the room to get the crash cart, out of the corner of my eye, I saw the patient collapse. Three steps down the hall my brain screamed: *The crash cart is in the treadmill room with the patient!*

I rushed back into the room just in time to see Dr. Froelicher, defibrillator paddles in hand, deliver the shock to the patient. The jolt worked, and the patient responded immediately.

After the hospital code team had wheeled the revived patient out of the treadmill room, Dr. Froelicher took me aside and asked why I ran out of the room. "I panicked," was my pathetic and honest answer.

Instead of firing me (I was, after all, just recently hired), he shocked me by replying matter-of-factly, "It happens to a lot of people during their first code. What do you think about taking a course in advanced life support?"

I muttered how much I would appreciate a second chance.

What happens to you and your team after difficult experiences? How much time do you take to reflect on what happened, why it happened, and how to decrease the chance it happens again? We don't learn from experience unless we reflect on the experience.

Every emerg*ency is an opportunity for leadership to* emerge.

After years of working closely with Dr. Victor Froelicher at UCSD, it became clear to me that one of the reasons he was so effective as a leader (and cardiologist) was that he possessed a broad imagination. By this I mean that he had a helicopter view, valued diverse perspectives, and reflected on experiences. He also had interests in a broad range of topics, ranging from the arts and politics to exercise and philosophy.

Dr. Froelicher was strong in the fourth competency of visionary leadership, and this is the fourth and final chapter describing those competencies. As a reminder, those four competencies are:

1. Adapt strategies to meet goals.
2. Cultivate innovative growth.
3. Inspire creativity and change
4. IMAGINE BROADLY.

IMAGINE BROADLY

The importance of seeing the big picture, which includes taking time to reflect, was also demonstrated by Dr. Timothy Hoff of the University of Albany, who studied the ability to learn from medical errors in three different hospital units (surgical suites, emergency rooms, and intensive care units).[1]

He found that ICUs had the better environment for correcting errors because the physicians and nurses used what little downtime they had to step back, listen to a variety of opinions, and then decide how to improve. Leaders in the surgical suites and emergency rooms did not make the time to make improvements. Their unwillingness to take or make time to think about the lessons learned or the long-term consequences trapped them in a more error-prone workplace.

Sound familiar?

Executives who fail to take the helicopter view do not see the forest because they often over-focus on the trees. They also have limited time horizons (deal only with today) and constrained interests (focus only on this issue). Ironically, this narrow-minded thinking is evident in the expansion of the specialists. Lawyers, physicians, professors, and many other professions celebrate the sub-specialist — the expert who focuses on the bark on the trees.

I experienced the problem of over-focusing on the part at the expense of the whole when my mom was diagnosed with lung cancer. My siblings and I had a terrible time getting the all the sub-specialists to agree on which follow-up tests and treatment were best. When I complained to one physician about not seeing the big picture, he lamented that he was just doing his part. My brain screamed, *That's the point. If everybody's only playing their part, who's taking care of the whole?*

Leaders like Dr. Froelicher, those in the ICU, and you — that's who. Organizations need executives who can zoom in and zoom out, stretching when they feel pulled too much by one or the other. A broad imagination opens the mind to reflect on old experiences and be receptive to new information.

GE discovered the importance of executive imagination when it undertook an in-depth study of how companies grow organically.[2] The company reported that imagination was one of the key characteristics of executives in the most successful companies. GE now evaluates its leaders on imagination (and creativity) during performance reviews.

The capacity to absorb

A broad imagination is critical because executives need to draw upon practical and powerful ideas from a reservoir of knowledge that must be refreshed with a stream of diverse experiences and perspectives. Dr. Froelicher was a voracious reader (from science fiction to scientific journals), lover of music, avid exerciser, and movie buff. Steve Jobs was a Zen Buddhist who studied calligraphy and believed in making time for retreats. Jobs' broad imagination reinvented not one, but four entire industries: smart phones, music, digital movies, and PCs.[3]

A breadth of information feeds the depth of the imagination, which leads to a high absorptive capacity — the ability to value, assimilate, and apply external information to an organization's internal goals.[4] Companies with high absorptive capacity are more innovative.[5] Their leaders have learned to take in and use new information to conquer their challenges and achieve their goals.

The following sub-sections describe how you can broaden your imagination and enhance your organization's absorptive capacity.

Broaden your imagination

Here are seven practical tactics to broaden your imagination:

1. Volunteer for a project that will expand your horizons: For example, your organization probably supports various charities. If so, why not volunteer to be on the committee — and if not, why not volunteer to start such a program?
2. Travel to unfamiliar vacation spots: Last year my wife and I embarked on our first cruise. This was a big stretch for me because I didn't think being on a boat surrounded by a sea of food for a week

would help me maintain my weight. (Surrounded by food, I have the discipline of a polar bear in a fish farm!) Of course, we had a great time. We experienced the majesty of the great state of Alaska, hiking glaciers and taking a plane to the interior. (And I only gained two pounds.)

3. Read international publications with global perspectives: *Financial Times* and *The Economist* are easy to find and digest, and the range of other international options is as diverse as the United Nations. Watch the BBC World News on a regular basis.
4. Expose yourself to new experiences: In *The Artist's Way,* Julia Cameron recommends that once a week you go on an artist date. Go to a museum or new store, or hike new terrain—anything that gives you a new perspective on what you deal with every day.
5. Study a new topic: What have you always been interested in, but not made the time for? How could your interest in the arts, a new sport, a particular reading genre, or a new hobby expand your horizons?
6. Study the giants: Read about great inventors, thinkers, and leaders such as Darwin, Einstein, Edison, Churchill, Gandhi, Curie, or any of the scores of influential people who have made an impact by using their imaginations.
7. Study those you would emulate: The list of books and articles about the world's most innovative companies—including Google, Pixar, Apple, 3M, Procter & Gamble—is practically endless.[6]

Reflection is a precursor to transformation.

Successful visionary executives

As you think about the qualities of visionary thinkers, what names come to mind? Who are the business, religious, and historical leaders that were and are visionary? Executives in our classes often identify Bill Gates, Sir Richard Branson, Steve Jobs, Nelson Mandela, Martin Luther King, Albert Einstein, Madame Curie, and other names you'd recognize.

Now, reflect on the responsibilities that you must engage in throughout the day. Which duties are associated with a visionary thinking style? In the space here or on another page, please brainstorm the answer to the following incomplete sentence for one minute. When I say brainstorm, I mean just that: Just write, and don't process, over-think, or let your pen stop. Keep your hand moving for one minute.

I need to use visionary thinking at work when ________________________

____

____

____

How did you do? Did you get a feel for whether you use, or need to grow, this visionary style? How and when to apply this style depends on your specific responsibilities. Use the questions in Table 12.1 to further stretch in those situations where you feel pulled by your rational competencies.

TABLE 12.1

14 Questions That Expand Big-Picture Thinking

1. How well and how often do you use your intuition?
2. What can you do to access your internal wisdom more productively?
3. When can you spend more time in reflection?
4. How can you stimulate your curiosity?
5. What can you do to avoid the quick-fix solution when problems surface?
6. How can you better anticipate what others will think and do?
7. How can you increase the variety of your interests and experiences?
8. Which community agency or outside organization might give you a broader perspective?
9. How often do you pause and reflect on the big picture and the long-term before expressing an opinion or communicating with others?
10. How can you explore different cultures through travel, reading, or personal contact?
11. How might you increase your exposure to a variety of different departments?
12. What projects might give you wide international experience?
13. Do you have a meeting-free day?
14. When will you set aside time to think every day?

Executives who have strong rational leadership styles sometimes find this focus on the visionary competencies somewhat uncomfortable. Some of the information in this chapter may have seemed fuzzy, especially when you are overwhelmed by deadlines, customer expectations, or shareholder demands. That's understandable.

But remember this: It is managing the tension between the visionary and rational styles under pressure that helps lopsided leaders stretch when they feel pulled. It's not the abandonment of the rational style in favor of the visionary style (or vice versa) that enables stretching instead of snapping; instead, it's the judicious application of one when the other threatens to take over. This expansion happens when you understand, choose, and practice the appropriate competency associated with that style.

The next two sections explore how to manage the tension between the other two opposing and interdependent leadership styles in the XLM — empowering and commanding.

Section IV

How Empowering Executives Take Care

March 11, 2011, Japan experienced an earthquake that was the country's worst disaster since the U.S. military dropped atomic bombs on Hiroshima and Nagasaki. The 3/11/11 earthquake, with a magnitude of 8.9, generated a tsunami that, along with the quake, killed at least 16,000 people while destroying more than 129,000 buildings and damaging another 950,000.

The Fukushima Daiichi nuclear energy generating station, as well as Japan's other nuclear generators, survived the quake. It nearly survived the tsunami. But Fukushima Daiichi couldn't survive its executives who failed to access the four competencies of the empowering leadership style:

1. Engage others.
2. Motivate teamwork.
3. Communicate trust and empathy.
4. Serve ethically.

On every count, executives responsible for ensuring the safety of Japan's nuclear energy program and its citizens failed. They did not engage the right people, motivate teams, or communicate with each other. Nor did the executives communicate with the citizens of Japan, the nuclear energy authorities of other countries, the public safety responders, or citizens of countries that would be affected by the meltdown of three of Fukushima Daiichi's six reactors.

In those failures, they breached their obligation to serve ethically. Just ask the plant's employees, more than 300 of whom received hazardous doses of radiation.

According to physicist Amory Lovins:

> [Japan's] rigid bureaucratic structures, reluctance to send bad news upwards, need to save face, weak development of policy alternatives, eagerness to preserve nuclear power's public acceptance, and politically fragile government, along with TEPCO's very hierarchical management culture, also contributed to the way the accident unfolded.

Two weeks after the 3/11 earthquake, elevated radiation levels from Fukushima Daiichi were detectable throughout the northern hemisphere. Within a month, monitoring stations throughout the southern hemisphere reported elevated radiation. Water used to cool the melting reactors flowed back into the ocean; more than 18 months after the disaster, radiation continued to leak into the Pacific and tuna caught off the coasts of Washington and Oregon showed traces of cesium from Fukushima Daiichi. The area around the Fukushima Daiichi station will remain uninhabitable for decades, and scientists expect hundreds of people will die earlier than they otherwise would because of their radiation exposures.

Empowering leadership could not have prevented the earthquake or the tsunami. However, it could have ameliorated the risks that either event would damage Fukushima Daiichi. Since an earthquake and tsunami were entirely predictable, applying the competencies of the empowering style could have limited the damage, and the resulting meltdown and subsequent releases of radiation after the disaster. It's rare that we can point directly at leadership as literally making a difference in life-or-death situations. The next four chapters will explore how executives can develop four competencies to avoid major, as well as everyday minor, disasters.

CHAPTER 13

Love 'em or Lose 'em*

Leadership is the art of getting someone else to do something you want done because he wants to do it.

DWIGHT D. EISENHOWER

ENGAGE OTHERS

To be successful in a global and competitive environment, executives need to tap into the energy, ideas, and expertise of all their employees by empowering them. Jay Conger's analysis of 51 studies concluded that empowerment leads to improved innovation, work satisfaction, buy-in to change, teamwork, and overall performance.[1]

The first of the four core competencies of empowerment stresses the importance of engaging others, and the risks of failing to engage, as illustrated below by Terry's story.

Terry delivered results. He rose quickly in the sales organization, from district manager to regional sales manager to senior vice president. As the senior VP, Terry was not afraid to shake things up in the complacent, bureaucratic company known for quality but sorely lacking in innovation. He had the power to git-r-dun, and he used it.

Every year, Terry changed the sales compensation plan based on his perception of the market and the salespeople's performance. About four years ago, a group of disgruntled salespeople met among themselves to discuss how *they* felt about the compensation plan and how they would like to tweak it to make it fairer.

When Terry discovered they had met, he scolded them in front of the entire sales and marketing division. He hammered away that he was in charge—not them—and that he would not tolerate "insubordination."

---

*Although the chapter title is the same as the excellent book by Beverly Kaye and Sharon Jordan-Evans, none of the ideas in this chapter are from the book because their focus is on retention, while this chapter emphasizes engagement.

During the next few years, most of these top salespeople and sales managers chose to leave the company. Market share dropped rapidly. Last year, the CEO fired Terry.

The employees who relayed this story to me are convinced that Terry's major problem was that he did not complement his command-and-control leadership style with a strong empowering style. Specifically, Terry failed to engage others and suffered the cost of employee disengagement.

You do not lead by hitting people over the head—
that's assault, not leadership.

Dwight D. Eisenhower

The cost of disengagement

Terry's employees told me that they seldom felt engaged when they worked for him. He dictated instead of delegated, blamed when he could—and should—have coached, and rarely involved them in decision-making. While he occasionally asked their opinion, he seldom followed through. His direct reports were not fooled by his "illusion of inclusion." As meaning disappeared from their work, they quit.

Employee engagement is defined as the connection employees have to their jobs, careers, and organizations that leads to value-added effort. When engagement is high, employees go the extra mile to get the job done. When this connection is missing, employees comply but seldom commit. Executives like Terry, who push for results without engaging others daily, are driving with one foot on the gas and one on the brake.

Despite the importance of engaging others, a Towers Watson Global Workforce Study[2] of 32,000 employees found that only 35% are fully engaged in their work—that is, they go the extra mile most of the time. In addition, the study also reported:

- 22% are unsupported: They are often engaged, but obstacles and resources cause problems.
- 17% are detached: Seldom engaged, they rarely go the extra mile.
- 26% are disengaged: They've already quit, but forgot to tell you.

This means that on any given day, 65% of employees worldwide fall somewhere in the engagement gap—the often-considerable gulf between what employees are capable of contributing and what they actually contribute. Terry's low engagement behaviors pushed his managers and his top salespeople into this muddled middle of engagement. It cost his organization, and eventually him, dearly.

How much does it cost you?

According to Gallup, the cost of lost productivity due to disengagement is $300 billion in the United States, $286 billion in Germany, and $6 billion in Singapore.[3] Research estimates that the U.S. economy runs only at about 30% efficiency because of a lack of engagement.[4] Can you imagine walking into an organization and telling 65% of the employees to go home early every day?

That's what executives do when they don't engage their managers and employees daily.

Organizational strategies to engage others

A core set of workplace elements crosses borders and cultures.[5] It makes a difference in driving better employee engagement, regardless of where a company operates.

Development opportunities

One such element is a dedicated emphasis on learning, skill enhancement, and career development. If executives could take just one step to increase engagement everywhere they operate, this would be it. In every country, virtually without exception, the availability of training opportunities and the ability to access such training to improve skills are core elements in driving engagement. The equation is straightforward:

> Build skills • Advance in one's career • Increase pay and reward opportunities • Maximize earnings potential

Employees understand the relationship across these elements. They rely on their employer to make that relationship available to them. When it is established, available, and clear to them, they increasingly accept their responsibility to develop themselves — and, therefore, their organization's value — on their own.

Leadership visibility

Another element is visible senior executive involvement. Employees need to see and hear from their top executives regularly. They need to understand their organization's mission, vision, and growth strategy, and how their efforts and activities contribute to it. And they need to believe that their leaders are being forthright in their dealings with them.

Effective front-line management

Part of senior leadership's visible commitment is effective front-line management and supervision. Employees turn first to their immediate supervisors for advice, support, direction, and help with problem-solving.

If their supervisors cannot deliver, employers are at far greater risk for both higher (undesirable) turnover and increased disengagement. Companies that recognize the manager's role in delivering results invest significant time and effort in tools to help them take on that role effectively.

Equitable compensation and benefits

Another essential element of senior leadership, though less visible, is a well-considered compensation strategy. Unlike Terry, effective executives customize "comp and ben" appropriately for different segments of the workforce, and then ensure the effective implementation and communication of the strategy.

Employees are far from a homogeneous group when it comes to the specific nature of the rewards that matter to them. The values they place on different aspects of their deal—both monetary and non-monetary—vary considerably, depending on their stage in life and career, their personal and professional ambitions, and their culture and geographic location, among other factors.

Executives need to understand what different groups of people value, at what points in time and why, so they can effectively optimize their investments and ensure they are getting the appropriate return in terms of retention and discretionary effort. In the absence of senior leadership, reward strategies can become as meaningless as most mission statements—well-intentioned philosophies without teeth in terms of follow-through.

Reputation management

Finally, there is the company's reputation as an employer. Think of it as the sum of the preceding elements. Companies that invest in leadership, management, career development, and relevant rewards will position themselves over time as employers of choice. Reputation proved a core driver of engagement and retention in almost every country surveyed in the Towers Watson global workforce research.

As an executive, you may be able to influence the organizational factors described in the previous sections. Let us now consider the four individual strategies that you and your managers can definitely control in order to engage your employees:

1. Increase meaningful work.
2. Delegate—don't dictate—work.
3. Involve others in decision-making.
4. Care about what other people care about.

Increase meaningful work

Don was a successful senior executive with an insurance firm. When I say successful, what I really mean is that he had all the appearances of success. He had money, prestige, friends, family, and three homes. But he wasn't very happy at work. At age 60, he retired to take care of an aging, ailing relative. He told me that he never experienced such fulfillment as when caring for his aunt. Ron had found much more meaning in his new "career" as a caregiver.

People spend about one-third of their lives at work. As demographics and the nature of work have shifted, many people are reevaluating the role work has in their lives. Compared to past generations, employees today search for jobs that have significance—that provide a sense of satisfaction and meaning.[6] This is why the correlation between life satisfaction and work satisfaction is strong.[7]

Of course, you don't want your employees to retire or quit their day job to find meaningful work (like Ron or those who worked in Terry's organization). The question is, How can you help them find more meaning in their current work?

Meaningful work is "the ability to earn a living doing that which satisfies an individual's psychological, spiritual, and social sense of purpose and contribution." Table 13.1 shows the four key elements of meaningful work, and the respective tactics to achieve each.[8]

TABLE 13.1

Key Elements of Meaningful Work

The sense of self:

- Bringing one's whole self (mind, body, emotion, spirit) to work
- Recognizing and developing one's potential
- Knowing one's purpose in life and how work fits into that purpose
- Having a positive belief system about achieving one's purpose

The work itself:

- The act of performing—mastering one's performance
- Challenge, creativity, learning, continuous growth
- The opportunity to carry out one's purpose through the work
- Autonomy, empowerment, and a sense of control over one's environment

The sense of balance:

- The balance of work self and personal self
- The balance of spiritual self and work self
- The balance of giving to oneself and giving to others
- The balance of family self and friendship self
- The balance of individual self and supportive others

The sense of contribution:

- Using one's skills, strengths, and talents to serve others
- Making a difference
- Making the world a better place
- Feeling part of something larger than ourselves
- Experiencing mutual benefit—"By helping others, I help myself"

Although it is not entirely your responsibility to make work meaningful for employees, it is in your best interest to *help them put more meaning in their work*. I recommend that you distribute Table 13.1 to your employees and invite them, individually and collectively, to brainstorm ways to increase the meaning in their work.

In a study of 7,700 workers, researchers also found the following techniques to boost engagement:[9]

- Develop a plan with employees to help them master all aspects of the job.
- Present them with challenging and creative tasks.
- Provide a sense of autonomy and control.
- Measure the impact of their work on the organization and various stakeholders.

- Discuss how their duties affect customers and make the world a better place.
- Offer diverse and continuous training.
- Encourage mentoring and sabbaticals when possible.
- Allow employees to seek fresh assignments and career changes.

These researchers cited above also point out that Marriott International offers leaders opportunities to take on a second, lateral role while decreasing a few of their current responsibilities. The challenging assignments increase cross-functional collaboration and engagement. Other organizations, such as Lincoln Electronic, employ cross-training programs that allow employees to change jobs based on factory production requirements. Intel's employee database tracks skills learned and needed, which helps match mentors to employees who want to grow. Both mentor and mentee take a class to clarify expectations, roles, and goals, and then formalize the relationship with a signed agreement.

As you facilitate the process of integrating more meaning in work using these tools, how surprised will you be when you can report increased performance and retention based on your employees' improved engagement?

Delegate — don't dictate — work

Employees who are not engaged don't mind the boss telling them what to do and how to do it. High-performing, engaged employees hate it.

One the fastest ways to lose engaged employees is to dictate their work instead of delegating it. Dictation subtracts from the power people feel they need in order to influence events and circumstances swirling around them. Engaged employees equate dictating with micromanaging. It sucks the wind out of their sails. Executives often don't even realize that their managers perceive them as occasional dictators.

How do your direct reports perceive you?

To assess the perception of your people, conduct a brief one-on-one meeting with each of your direct reports. Ask them to identify their essential job functions (EJFs)—those key responsibilities that are the essence of their jobs. Invite them to tell you where you need to let go in each of their EJFs. In addition, ask them where they see you working on tasks that you could delegate.

Combine their suggestions with these six fundamentals of effective delegation when you're discussing an assignment:

- Explain *what* needs to be done.
- Discuss *why* it needs doing, by relating it to the big picture.

- Agree on a deadline (*when*) after discussing employees' current workloads and priorities.
- Ask if they know *how* to do it, and with whom to work (if others should be involved).
- Invite them to tell you how they want you to check on their progress.
- When their assignment is complete, conduct a brief after-action review to discuss objectives desired, results achieved, and lessons learned.

Involve others in decision-making

I was teaching a group of middle managers leadership skills when someone asked me a question about compensation plans. I replied that it was not my area of expertise and asked others in the group if they had any suggestions. Their wonderful insights stunned me. In that moment, I realized I needed to ask more questions in class to tap into the wisdom of the crowd.

How often do you tap into the wisdom of your crowd?

Executives who increase engagement seldom need to show that they are the smartest people in the room (even if they are). They ask lots of questions because they know they are not wiser than the collective wisdom of their team. They involve others in decisions, and delegate those decisions and the accountability for them to the lowest possible level in the organization.

As one of the world's largest power companies, AES owns and operates a diverse, growing portfolio of worldwide generation and distribution businesses with the capacity to serve 100 million people. In an interview with *Harvard Business Review,* former Chairman Roger Sant remarked that AES fully engages its employees so "they have total responsibility for decisions."[10]

I encourage you to solicit input from others in your decision-making whenever possible, especially when it affects them. This approach will boost engagement *and* yield better decisions. And remember—just because you ask for the opinion of others doesn't mean you always have to follow it.

Care about what other people care about

Cavett Robert, the founder of the National Speaker Association, is credited with saying, "People don't care how much you know, until they know how much you care." To which I add, it's about caring "about what they care about."

I learned that second part from coordinating research for Dr. Vic Froelicher at UCSD. As our research grants began winding down (our projects were scheduled to conclude within the year), I asked Vic if I could take classes at a local university to prepare me for my next job. Unfortunately, I discovered the university offered the classes I needed only during the day—conflicting with my working hours. When I told Vic of my dilemma, he said not to worry about my work for him and to focus on my classes. He said he knew I would find some way to get my work done.

Vic demonstrated that he cared about what I cared about. It was no coincidence that I worked extra hours at odd times to fulfill my work obligations.

How could you increase employee engagement by showing your employees that you care about what they care about?

Dead men working

While cycling down a bike path near Venice Beach, California, I saw a group of workers from the Los Angeles County Probation Department in orange jumpsuits whacking and pulling weeds from the sides of the path. As I slowed down and watched, I couldn't help but notice that they all seemed to be going about their tasks in a stupor. It was as if I was cycling through a movie playing in slow motion—*Zombies at Work*.

As I peddled home, I wondered how many employees felt chained to their jobs, complying with their boss instead of committing to their work. I wonder how you will use the tools discussed in this chapter to engage your employees and avoid the "dead men working" syndrome.

The engagement payoff

Let's close with the good news about engagement. The Corporate Leadership Council surveyed 50,000 employees at 59 global organizations and found that increasing an employee's level of engagement improves performance 20% and reduces the probability of departure by 87%.[11] I encourage you to adapt the ideas in this chapter, summarized in Table 13.2, to improve engagement in your organization.

TABLE 13.2

Guidelines to Engage Others Organizationally and Individually

- Demonstrate an interest in employee well-being.
- Help employees improve their skills and capabilities.
- Emphasize that the organization has a reputation as a good employer.
- Encourage the appropriate amount of decision-making authority.
- Do whatever you can to ensure that salary criteria are fair and consistent.
- Facilitate collaboration across business units.
- Maintain a focus on satisfying customers.
- Demonstrate that the organization's long-term success is a high priority.

Sadly, the leadership of the Fukushima Daiichi nuclear plant failed almost across the board on these engagement strategies. Most nuclear energy workers in Japan are contractors working for relatively low wages and at relatively unskilled positions compared to their counterparts in other countries. Although many plant workers made heroic sacrifices to stop the disaster from getting worse, the executives could have done much more to engage these employees well in advance. These employees also seldom felt motivated to work as a team, which is the subject we explore in the next chapter.

CHAPTER 14

Can't We All Just Get Along?

Teamwork is the ability to work together toward a common vision. The ability to direct individual accomplishments toward organizational objectives. It is the fuel that allows common people to attain uncommon results.

ANDREW CARNEGIE

MOTIVATE TEAMWORK

There's an old story about President Abraham Lincoln once summoning a newspaper reporter to the White House. As the reporter entered the Oval Office, President Lincoln was petting Fido, the family dog.

After introductions, the president said, "Son, I've been reading some of your reports about the Civil War. I don't think you have your facts right."

"Well, Mr. President, that's what my sources tell me," the reporter said.

Just then, Fido sauntered across the room. Lincoln pointed at the dog and said, "If I told you that the tail on my dog was a leg, how many legs would my dog have?"

The startled reporter blurted, "Mr. President, if you told me that tail was a leg, your dog would have five legs."

"No," replied the president, "Just because I told you the tail was a leg doesn't make that tail a leg. My dog would still have four legs. Just because a source tells you something is true doesn't make it true."

Just because someone tells you that you have a team doesn't make it a team. A team is a group of people working together toward a common goal. If you are not working together toward a common goal, you don't have a team. You may have a single-leader work group, but that is not a team.

Effective executives know how to create and motivate teams to achieve the goal. This is the second of the four empowering leadership competencies, and the focus of this chapter:

1. Engage others.
2. MOTIVATE TEAMWORK.
3. Communicate trust and empathy.
4. Serve ethically.

TEAMS AND THEIR FLAVORS

The first, and most fundamental, question to ask before putting a team together is whether you actually need a group of people to come together to achieve a common goal.[1]

If you *do* need to create and then motivate a team, you then must decide what kind of team you and your organization need to assemble. The five most common types of teams are functional, cross-functional, self-managed, virtual, and top management. Each of the five types of teams has a unique place in an organization.

Functional teams

These teams are typically work units (e.g., the sales team, maintenance crew, SEAL Team Six). They usually work together for an extended time and have a leader who has direct authority over the performance of the team.

Cross-functional teams

These project-oriented teams come together to accomplish a specific goal by a given date. They include team members with specialized skills from various functions throughout the organizations (e.g., operations, engineering, finance, IT) who must juggle their responsibilities to the team with their duties in their functional area. The appointed leader of a cross-functional team seldom has direct authority over the team members' other priorities.

Self-managed teams

These teams are assigned a specific responsibility, such as producing a product, administering a policy, or providing a service. Much like a functional team, self-managed team members usually have similar backgrounds. However, their leaders do not have direct authority over the team members.

Virtual teams

These teams are similar to cross-functional teams, but their members work in different physical locations (buildings or countries) or at different times (in shifts or in different time zones). Virtual teamwork is on the rise because of globalization and organizational partnerships. Virtual teams are enabled by technologies (e.g., videoconferencing, low-cost conference calling) that facilitate communication anywhere, anytime.

Top management team

The TMT includes the members of an executive team who report directly to the leader of an organization. They often assist the leader in making strategic decisions, managing complex change, and implementing succession plans.

Why teams fail

The increasing complexity and interdependence of work, as well as the need for flatter and more nimble organizations, fueled a dramatic rise in teamwork over the past two decades. The vast majority of organizations — about 80% — organize employees into teams. Yet 82% of all teams "fall short of their intended goal."[2]

Consider the U.S. government's sluggish responses to the oil spill in the Gulf of Mexico and Hurricane Katrina, the failure of teamwork to prevent the 9/11 tragedy, or the explosion of Space Shuttle *Columbia.* As another example, a survey of 261 nurses at four Midwest hospitals revealed that poor teamwork in emergency departments and intensive care units was responsible for poor patient safety.[3]

Why do so many teams fail so often?

Teams of all types fail when they do not address the eight major challenges[4] that confront teams, as presented in Table 14.1.

TABLE 14.1

8 Major Challenges That Confront Teams

1. Align clear team goals and roles with organizational strategies.
2. Ensure that the team possesses and uses the skills to accomplish the goal.
3. Overcome internal and external communication barriers.
4. Obtain continued support from the organization.
5. Connect effectively with external stakeholders.
6. Cultivate trust and accountability among team members.
7. Define effective norms.
8. Demonstrate leadership.

To overcome these challenges, the next section discusses what science reveals are the best practices of effective teams.

How to create effective teamwork

Empowering executives understand how to orchestrate diverse individuals into high-performing, energized teams that work well internally and with other groups. These leaders employ a number of specific tactics that help them reach their common goal. Of course, it all begins with setting a clear goal.

Set a clear goal

The goal must lead to specific objectives and create a sense of urgency. The more urgent, relevant, and meaningful the goal, the more dedicated the team. Linking the goal to the organization's priorities creates the laser-like focus that lights a fire within team members.

The mayor of a mid-size city hired me to increase teamwork on the city council. When I interviewed the seven city council members individually, I discovered that each of them had their own goal for the coming year. However, they had not set a clear team goal. There was no teamwork because they all had their own agendas. During a retreat, we set a goal that the entire team agreed on:

We will increase economic development 20% by this date.

Once your team has a clear goal, frequently remind them and your internal and external stakeholders of the connection between the team's goal and the organization's priority. This maintains their focus and the support of the organization. Consider starting your team meetings by stating the goal, inserting the goal as a footer in all of your team communications, and reporting on the team's progress at executive meetings.

Select the right team members

We form a team because no single person possesses the knowledge to accomplish our goal. But what kind of knowledge do we need on a team? Frank LaFasto and Carl Larson did an analysis of 6,000 team members and leaders and found that the selection criteria for team members should include both working knowledge and teamwork attributes.[5]

Working knowledge refers to the specific skills and experience needed to solve problems and carry out project-related tasks.

Teamwork attributes include openness, supportiveness, action orientation, and a positive personal style. Openness includes the willingness to be on the team only as long as the team needs the team members' skills.

Team leaders should also assess the skills of the members throughout the cycle of the team and identify opportunities for learning, coaching, or changing team members. At Siemens, our sales team constantly upgraded our skills to keep pace with the waves of changes in healthcare technology. The few who refused to ride the waves drowned.

MIT Professor Deborah Ancona and her colleagues remind us that it is also important to choose team members who are skilled at managing relationships *outside* the team, according to an analysis of 169 teams.[6] This external focus is critical in obtaining resources, acquiring information, connecting to new initiatives, and linking to other relevant groups (e.g., senior management, user stakeholders, other departments, customers). Effective team leaders pay very close attention to managing these boundary-spanning, interdependent activities. Do you?

Create metrics with the team and each member

You can't manage what you don't measure. The right metrics confine the inevitable conflict that arises on most teams to what is relevant and strategic. Conflicts, when they arise, should remain cognitive and task-focused, instead of oriented on emotions or relationships.

Metrics also provide a dashboard for team members and senior management to monitor collective and individual performance. They facilitate role clarity, prioritization, and accountability.

Sharing real-time information related to these metrics during meetings is the feedback that keeps teams on track.

Encourage contact

Familiarity breeds compatibility in teams. When researcher Lee Fleming analyzed 17,000 patents, he discovered that frequent and informal social interactions among team members improved the value of a team's output.[7] At UCLA, the director of our institute encouraged us to celebrate every conceivable holiday as a team and attended our numerous team picnics. How can you encourage informal social interactions among your team?

Define norms

A norm is a standard, model, or pattern regarded as typical. In organizations, norms are the rules (often unwritten) that dictate how team members behave—"it's the way we do things around here."

Successful team leaders discuss and define which norms need clarity (e.g., meetings, communication, managing conflict, contribution quality, decision-making or problem-solving processes) and then create specific rules, behaviors, and measures with the team for each of these areas.

There are some simple actions you can take to create norms within a team. If done throughout an organization, this process can transform an entire culture:

- Engage everyone on the team to brainstorm the answer to this question: For us to achieve our goal, what behaviors do we need to demonstrate?
- Select the four to seven behaviors that surface most frequently, such as communicate priorities, manage conflict, recognize and reward behaviors, and coordinate with others.
- For each of the behaviors identified, invite your team to brainstorm answers to this question:

  Imagine you're on a team that has excellent ______________ (*insert the behavior you want to define*). What rules are in place and specific actions are people taking?

  As they offer answers, write these norms on a flipchart. Don't process the information at this point, just brainstorm answers to the question. Process and refine their ideas after brainstorming. These norms become the rules that the team agrees to follow.

  Example: The city council members decided they needed to create norms that encouraged respect. Thus, as an outcome of this process, their norms emerged as follows:

In order for us to increase teamwork by demonstrating mutual respect for each other, we hereby agree to:

1. Pay close attention to, and stay focused on, the goal or issue being presented.
2. Include every member of the council in the process.
3. Share our ideas openly and invite opposing ideas from others.
4. Make sure we respond to important inquiries in a timely manner.
5. Maintain civility in all verbal and nonverbal communications with one another, in public, private, and electronic discussions. Be aware that our expressions and behavior often communicate more than our words.

- ASK YOUR TEAM MEMBERS HOW TO MEASURE AND CELEBRATE PROGRESS as they implement the norms. What we focus on expands. Sometimes just going through the process of defining the norms and bringing them to the surface is its own reward. Like a thermometer poster that tracks the progress of a fundraising campaign, make your goal and the progress toward it easy for everyone to see. Discuss, applaud, and reward the baby steps that individuals and the team take on the journey.
- DECIDE WITH YOUR TEAM HOW TO RECOVER when someone makes a mistake by failing to follow a norm. You don't learn to ride a bike by reading about it, and everyone falls when trying something new. How will your team members help each other get up when they fall?

Emphasize a learning culture

Teams that train together achieve more. This is one of the keys to team success according to Ancona's analysis.[8]

In addition to learning from each other, challenge the group with information from external experts to remind them to search outside their own borders for new ideas, information, and experience. Make learning an agenda item at many of your team meetings. Invite the team members to come up with different ways to educate one another.

Delegate decision-making

Responsibility without authority is lame. Interference with the team's work is perceived as micromanaging and lowers team morale.

Expansive executives leave the authority to decide how to reach the goal with the team. Team leaders also need to ensure that team members have the authority to complete their tasks.

Develop an environment that supports execution under pressure

In Chapter 13, we were introduced to Terry, the senior VP who was a strong-commanding/low-empowering leader. Under pressure, he became even more commanding, exhibiting what's often referred to as a dominant response pattern. He relied on the behavior patterns that were most deeply ingrained in his response repertoire. Unfortunately, Terry is like many executives. His lopsided leadership when stressed creates a negative impact on teams and their projects.

Think about a time when you've observed people in a stressful meeting with a high-commanding leader. Every time I've been in that situation, the group defers to the leader. Terry's story and the research suggest that's a universal occurrence.

It's like a player who tries to take over the entire game by himself in overtime. He does so at the expense of executing plays with his team. Although the media likes to highlight end-of-the-game heroics by individual stars, teams that defer to their star players for long stretches seldom win championships. Team sports and organizations require both teamwork and individual contributions to win.

This isn't to say executives should never access their commanding skills to push the team. Just like a star player who occasionally takes over the game, there are times that the leader must step up and make difficult or unpopular decisions. That is what American explorers Meriwether Lewis and William Clark did in June 1805, when they came to a fork in the Missouri River.

Forced by the impending mountain winter to press on, Lewis and Clark determined to "set out early the next morning with a small party each, and ascend these rivers until we could perfectly satisfy ourselves...."[9] When they returned to camp, they met with all their men and asked for opinions, as was their custom. The overwhelming team consensus was to follow one river. After much discussion, Lewis and Clark overruled their men and made a different—and what turned out to be the correct—choice.

This is just one anecdote among many to demonstrate there are times to lead by taking over. If it becomes your dominant response pattern under pressure, however, you will experience a silent mutiny from the neglected majority.

Decreasing involvement
increases detachment.

Ancona's research shows that the most successful teams develop processes that encourage involvement. And they do so not just within the team, but also in the connections to important stakeholders outside the team. She recommends integrative meetings that access the diverse expertise of the members.[10] These effective meetings provide an environment in which team members share information, make transparent decisions, manage conflict productively, and use scheduling tools to communicate deadlines visually.

Involve the team in implementation

A high-tech firm in Silicon Valley jokingly referred to "throwing the project over the wall." Marketing would do its part and throw the project over the wall to the engineers, who would then complete their portion and throw the project over the wall to manufacturing.

Multiple hand-offs were killing their projects. There was no team ownership of the overall project. Because the nature of their projects required the projects to be handed over to different departments, I suggested that they involve a few core team members during most phases of the project. The goal would be to increase continuity and the probability that the hand-offs, thus implementation, would succeed.

It worked. Their projects have become much more successful because the firm no longer drops the baton during the hand-off.

Pay attention to team achievement

That which is appreciated appreciates.

If you want teamwork, reward team accomplishments, not just individual achievement. Brainstorm with your team how to applaud, praise, and reinforce team progress as well as individual contribution.

One of the companies at the forefront of teamwork is Cisco. It has gone through a radical reorganization to empower leaders and decentralize many decisions.[11] Cisco also created a network of cross-functional and international councils and boards empowered to fund projects and launch new businesses, thereby greatly expediting innovation. The company invests heavily in social networking applications. It promotes an open-source culture by encouraging employees to blog, upload videos, and tag their strengths in their Facebook-style internal directory.

"Collaboration this way helps the world community solve big problems," says Cisco VP Jim Grubb. "If we can accelerate the productivity of scientists who are working on the next solar technology because we're helping them together, we're doing a great thing for the world."[12]

In today's world, collaborating across internal and external borders requires virtual teamwork.

Increase virtual team success

A virtual team is one that has members in different physical locations or working at different times. One of the major trends in business is to get more work done via virtual teams. If you have not been a leader of a virtual team yet, rest assured—your time is coming.

Despite growing prevalence of virtual teams, studies show that senior managers judged only 18% of these teams highly successful.[13]

How successful is your virtual team?

Although many of the team issues discussed previously affect virtual teams, research reveals ten specific tactics (detailed in the following subsections) that target virtual team's performance. Applying any or all of these ten strategies and tools places virtual teams in the top 18% of teams. How can you adapt them to put your team in this highly successful group?

Balance the numbers

In a study of 62 six-person teams, Josh Hyatt found that the number of team members at different locations affected overall virtual team performance.[14] Having an equal number of team members at each location had the most positive effect. Having two different-sized sub-groups triggered negative dynamics. The investigators explained that imbalance breeds instability, except when only one member was physically isolated from the rest of the team. In these isolated cases, it appears that having an individual isolated in one location produces a positive "novelty effect."

If you need to staff a virtual team, make sure you have equal numbers (unless placing one person in a remote location makes sense).

Clearly define the scope

When teams are able to meet face-to-face on a regular basis, it's easier to work out any ambiguities in the project. Meeting in person less often, as in the case of virtual teams, mandates that the scope of the project, the expected deliverables, and the time frame be exceptionally clear.

Create a core team

The optimal size of a virtual team is the one that has the requisite knowledge and skills to fulfill the team charter. However, that can lead to a large, cumbersome team. Furthermore, the technology that facilitates virtual team interaction (i.e., groupware) can make it *too* easy to add team members.

One option is to create a core group of ten or fewer team members. Then, if this core team needs additional knowledge or skills, they can choose to bring others in on an ad hoc basis. If the core team needs to be a large, consider breaking it into a sub-teams and assign specific aspects of the project to each sub-team based on skills, not personality.

Choose an effective team leader

Effective virtual team leaders must be able to manage the organizational, cultural, and physical distances that separate team members and create communication barriers.

Team leaders should also have credibility based on proven skills in leadership, conflict resolution, and project management.

Develop norms

As previously defined, norms are the rules that dictate how team members behave. Ask your team members to brainstorm areas in which they need to create norms to complete the project successfully.

Virtual teams should create norms regarding the use of groupware (i.e., collaborative software), etiquette on the Internet ("netiquette"), and which tasks require true collaboration versus individual attention.

Adopt data-driven decisions

Without data, we are nothing but wandering opinions. Worse, contrary opinions without facts often degenerate into personal attacks. Data-driven discussions allow team members to debate facts, not opinions or personalities.

Rotate meeting locations

Rotating locations of face-to-face meetings and the times of conference calls sends the message that every team member is equally valued.

Conference-call on your own phone

Have you ever been on a conference call with the home or central office where several people are gathered around the speakerphone, but you were at a remote location dialing in? How does that feel?

Virtual team members who call in remotely can neither hear the side banter nor see the body language of the other people. They often feel left out.

Whenever possible, conduct conference calls in which each and every person on the call is on his or her own phone.

Make it visible

Set milestones for the project. When teams reach these milestones, celebrate and make their accomplishment visible to others. Put it in your organization's newsletter, on the website and bulletin board, and anywhere else your people look.

A great example: A CEO of a multi-billion-dollar construction company showed me his company's *quarterly* milestones brochure, which illustrated graphically the 35 projects his teams were currently working on.

Increasing visibility increases ownership and a sense of teamwork, especially for virtual teams.

Learn about each other

Virtual team members need to know a lot about each other to tap into each other's talents. Executives must facilitate this learning through meetings and collaborative software.

For example, advertising agency Ogilvy & Mather created an internal online community using its own IT-developed software. It contains an updated database of each employee's responsibilities and passions, as well as the many projects the company is (and has been) involved in.

The Keys to Effective Top Management Teams

In an increasingly turbulent and complex work environment, the success of any organization is more dependent on the *team* at the top than any one person at the top. The heroic executive leading the charge from on high has been supplanted, or at least significantly augmented, by the top management team (TMT) in the most effective organizations.[15]

The TMT differs from other teams in that it must manage the conflicting agendas of diverse stakeholders, deal with an enormous amount of ambiguous information, and decide on specific courses of action (unlike other teams, which are usually given very specific projects or tasks).

The TMT's role is to provide the executive talent required to address complex issues, stimulate creative ideas, discuss numerous options, decide on the strategic direction, and engage managers at all levels of the organization in the successful implementation of the strategic imperatives.

Despite the importance of TMTs, considerable research shows that they, like other teams, often fall short of executing their duties. Their failures are usually caused by an inability to resolve conflicts, avoid groupthink, surface assumptions, share information, manage the tension between self-interests and organizational interests, or gain commitment to execution.[16]

For years, researchers looked to understand these problems by studying the diversity of the TMT. If the TMT had a better mix of characteristics (e.g., age, tenure, education, ethnic background, size, functional experience), perhaps the team would perform better. The research tells us that increasing diversity alone seldom increases team effectiveness — but improving the process does.

The team process is how the team members interact with one another and make decisions. The process is very similar to norms discussed earlier. Here are a few tips to help improve your TMT's process.

Know when to let the team lead

When members of the team have the same amount of information available to them (referred to as *symmetric information*), the leader should minimize his or her input by letting the team lead the discussion.

Executives who reveal their positions during the early stages of discussions inhibit the free flow of ideas because team members may defer to the leader's position. If, however, certain members of the team have unique information that they do not freely share (one of the executives I coach calls it hoarding information), the leader needs to take more control of the process by encouraging people to share their information, asking those without information to discuss their concerns, and testing for understanding.

Know when to lead the team

If the team members understand how to manage the tension between self-interests and the interests of the organization (referred to as *symmetric interests*), the leader should encourage participation in decision-making, problem-solving, and consensus-building.

However, when the leader is dealing with executive team members more focused on their own interests than the organization's (i.e., *asymmetry*), the leader must limit self-serving discussions by making the final decision in this situation.

Build transparency and fairness into a decision-making structure

In situations when team members are not sharing information and too focused on their self-interests, the leader needs to create a fair, transparent, and structured decision-making process.

Effective leaders often assign a devil's advocate to ensure that team members express perspectives without feeling pressure to conform to groupthink. Leaders can also create cross-functional teams that dismantle natural coalitions. After the Bay of Pigs fiasco in the early 1960s, U.S. President John F. Kennedy's administration implemented these tactics. They helped him deal effectively with the subsequent Cuban missile crisis.

Develop harmonious working relationships

Not long ago I was coaching a member of a TMT. He complained that one of his colleagues had unfairly criticized his team's work during an executive team meeting.

When I asked him how he handled it during the meeting, he said he chose not to say anything for the sake of harmonious team relationships. When I asked him how he was going to handle it after the meeting, he said it was "water under the bridge" and that "it was time to move on."

I reminded him that water under a bridge rises fast during a storm and can knock that bridge down. I suggested that he discuss his concerns with his colleague one-on-one. He chose not to.

By choosing not to effectively deal with conflict, this leader is damaging the process of behavioral integration—the harmonious relationship among team members and overall group cohesion. In a study of 116 TMTs, Professors Abraham Carmeli and John Schaubroeck reported that TMTs with higher behavioral integration made better strategic decisions, which led to improved organizational performance.[17]

I hope to persuade the senior executive I am coaching to work on his process of managing conflict for the sake of the TMT and organization.

The four fundamental drivers of team motivation

My first job after graduate school was coordinating research at the University of California at San Diego. I had the privilege of working with an extraordinary team led by a luminary leader, Dr. Victor Froelicher. In four years, our small, productive, and highly motivated team published 33 major research papers. Several members of our team went on to become leaders in their respective fields.

What accounted for such productivity, effectiveness, and motivation?

The latest research in neuroscience, biology, and psychology confirm that Dr. Froelicher created an environment that fulfilled the four fundamental drivers of human motivation. If you want extraordinary leadership results, you need to satisfy these desires, too.

Professor Nitin Nohria and his colleagues from Harvard surveyed employees at 300 Fortune 500 companies.[18] They found that you can MOTORvate your team if you know the ABCDs of what drives them:

- Acquire
- Bond
- Comprehend
- Defend

Acquire

This driver relates to our desire to acquire physical goods, positive experiences, and social status. It is relative—that is, we compare what we have to others. It's as if we are driving down the highway and checking to see how fast everyone else is going. We judge our progress toward our goal by looking at those around us.

Many leaders think they are meeting this motivational driver if everyone receives the same rewards or perks, regardless of their contribution.

They are wrong.

Treating everyone equally is not fair unless everyone is performing equally. Dr. Froelicher succeeded because he clearly connected rewards to performance. For example, we could not go to scientific meetings unless the conference accepted our research papers for presentation. The rule was clear and fair: If you didn't conduct excellent research, you didn't attend scientific meetings.

How could you satisfy the desire to acquire in your high performers?

Bond

Human beings have an internal impulse to connect to others in small groups, such as our families, as well as larger collectives, including organizations, associations, and nations.

At work, employees who feel proud of an organization are very motivated. At UC San Diego, Dr. Froelicher fostered bonding among co-workers by having Friday afternoon parties and occasional picnics at the beach, and encouraging us to exercise together. In addition, we frequently collaborated with other divisions. We attended their meetings, invited them to ours, and shared best practices.

How might you motivate your team by building more camaraderie, collaboration, and cross-functional communication?

Comprehend

We all want to make sense of the world. We become frustrated when things don't make sense.

At work, people try to satisfy this desire by making meaningful contributions in areas of interest to them. Google allows its people to spend time on pet projects. We satisfied this drive at UCSD because Dr. Froelicher gave us wide latitude in the type of research each of us could conduct. We were encouraged to investigate areas that we found interesting and meaningful. We also contributed to each other's comprehension by educating each other at our numerous staff and research meetings.

How could you increase job flexibility and lifelong learning on your team?

Defend

We all want to defend our property, positions, and accomplishments. This drive is rooted in the fight-or-flight mechanism that has evolved during millions of years. In a competitive market, knowing what threatens your turf is essential and motivating.

Henry Ford II ran Ford Motor Company for decades after World War II. Unfortunately, he almost ran it into the ground by refusing to defend his company against Japanese competition well into the 1980s. Xerox committed the same error around the same time. You can't defend yourself if you don't acknowledge the competition.

Exceptional leaders don't deride young upstarts and emerging markets. Top leaders, like those at P&G and Unilever, defend their turf by exploiting the present and exploring the future. At UCSD, understanding that we were competing for very limited research funds kept us very motivated. We were acutely aware of what others were doing in our area of research.

How can you use market conditions, threats, and opportunities to motivate your team?

One piece of advice: Don't worry if you are unable to fulfill all four of these fundamental drivers of human motivation to the degree you would like. Employees understand that there are limits to the boss's ability to influence all four of these areas.

What else motivates employees?

Researchers have studied motivation at work for more than a century. They have surveyed hundreds of thousands of workers regarding what factors they consider most important in their work. Before I show you these results, let's first assess your knowledge in this area.

Rank the following factors in the order of importance you think your team members would put them, with 1 being the most important, 2 being second most important, and so on.

____ Working with people who treat me with respect
____ Interesting work
____ Recognition for good work
____ Chance to develop skills
____ Working for people who listen if you have ideas about how to do things better
____ Chance to think for myself, rather than just carry out instructions
____ Seeing the results of my work
____ Working for efficient managers
____ Challenging job that is not easy
____ Feeling well-informed about what is going on
____ Job security
____ High pay
____ Good benefits

Did you complete the test? Are you ready to see how your answers compare to hundreds of thousands of workers? OK, here are the results.

Read the list from top to bottom.

That's it. The list is *already* in the order of importance, according to Professor William Cohen.[19]

Most leaders in my classes rank the last three factors near the top of their list. However, when they realize that they can't always guarantee job security, pay, or benefits, it's actually better that these factors are at the bottom of the list. The very things executives can influence the most are near the top.

How might you use this list to motivate your team?

One executive told me that he asked his team members to rank the items in order of *their* individual preferences. Then, he met with each person and discussed how he, the executive, could better meet that team member's individual needs.

• • •

The executives at the Fukushima Daiichi nuclear power plant demonstrated that their top priorities were cozy relationships with their regulators, relative freedom from public oversight, and maintaining face instead of being honest. Motivating teamwork to prevent or manage the disaster was not even on their list. Nor was communicating trust and empathy, the leadership competency we'll explore in the next chapter.

CHAPTER 15

Trust Me

The problem with communication is the illusion that it has occurred.

GEORGE BERNARD SHAW

"I'll get back to you on that."

I uttered these famous last words to a graduate student at UCLA when I was selling for Siemens. I never did get back to him. I don't remember why. I probably just forgot.

Not a big deal, right? It wasn't as if he was the person buying the equipment from us—he wasn't even influential in the buying process.

Two years later, when I became chief administrative officer of an institute at UCLA, my failure to follow through came back to bite me. This graduate student became a young professor in our institute and told my boss, the director of the institute, that he preferred not to work with me on any projects because he didn't trust me. *Ouch!*

An executive without trust is like a captain with a crew of cynics—they question every decision you make.

How well do you communicate trust and empathy to your team? If you're not sure, this chapter is for you. It presents the third of four competencies of the empowering leader.

1. Engage others.
2. Motivate teamwork.
3. COMMUNICATE TRUST AND EMPATHY.
4. Serve ethically.

COMMUNICATE TRUST AND EMPATHY

One reason trust is difficult for executives to maintain is that there is more than one kind of trust. In fact, there are four categories of trust within any organization:[1]

1. Strategic: Is there confidence that senior management is setting the right direction?
2. Organizational: Can employees rely on the organization itself?

3. Personal: Do employees have confidence in their manager?
4. Team: Is there trust among members of a team?

If any one of these takes a hit, it often bleeds into the others.

Trust is defined as the decision to be vulnerable to the actions of others, based on an expectation that they will perform a particular action. A careful reading of this definition provides another clue as to why trust is slow to build, difficult to maintain, and easy to destroy:

1. Trust is a *choice* to rely on others.
2. Trust puts us at *risk*. Without vulnerability, trust is not needed.
3. Trust involves a *prediction* about the intentions or behaviors of another person.

Professor Robert Hurley from Fordham University surveyed 450 executives from 30 global companies and found that half of them didn't trust their leaders.[2] Another survey of 12,750 U.S. workers at all job levels and in a variety of industries[3] came to these conclusions:

- 39% of employees at U.S. companies trust their senior leaders.
- 45% of employees say they have confidence in the job being done by senior management.
- 43% of employees say they trust the way their company manages change (e.g., restructuring, downsizing, merging, expansion and growth).

The cost of mistrust

This epidemic of low trust infects employee morale, retention, recruitment, productivity, sales, customer service, product quality, and the long-term financial performance of the organization.[4] Low trust creates deception, opposition, and unhealthy competition within organizations. That's why the Bible lectures us that "a house divided against itself cannot stand."

Low levels of trust have profound implications for leaders at all levels of an organization. When Professors Tony Simons and Randall Peterson studied 100 CEOs and executive teams, they found the teams whose members distrusted one another were less effective in collaborating and endorsed strategic decisions less strongly.[5] Low trust at the executive level degenerates into poor teamwork and decreased buy-in, and damages strategic implementation.

When trust is low, employees don't work through the everyday disagreements and difficulties they encounter. They don't collaborate because they don't think it's worth the effort.

Professor Kimberly Merriman and her colleagues studied 49 business-school teams that collaborated on four-month projects.[6] They found that team members who reported lower levels of trust in their colleagues preferred individual-based rewards. People don't want their pay based on their colleagues' efforts if trust is low. (Yet 85% of Fortune 1,000 companies use some form of team based pay.) If trust is low, individual pay is the way to go.

Speaking of pay, does fostering trust pay off? According to researchers Dennis and Michelle Reina, organizations in which front-line employees trust senior executives show a 42% higher return on shareholder investment compared to low-trust organizations. In addition, when trust is increased, job satisfaction improves and employees equate that with a 36% pay increase.[7]

In an analysis of studies involving 27,103 individuals, Professors Kurt Dirks and Donald Ferrin showed that trust correlated strongly with employees' satisfaction with leaders, job satisfaction, organizational commitment, turnover intentions, belief in information provided by the leader, and commitment to decisions.[8]

Common causes of low trust

Let's examine the six most common causes of broken trust and how to repair each.

The undiscussable

Mr. Gerrosi was my eighth-grade science teacher. Before we left school for the summer, he had a big nose, like a moose. When we came back, he didn't.

During the first week of class, he commented, oddly, that he did not believe in *any* medical operations. I stared at his downsized nose, still scarred from the surgeon's summer knife, and blurted, "Wasn't your nose job an operation?"

I spent the next week staying after school, in detention, contemplating the concept of the "undiscussable."

Organizations, like classrooms, have undiscussables. The more there are, the lower the trust. One way to measure this enemy of trust is to ascertain if employees discuss sensitive issues in meetings the same way they discuss them after work in the bar.

You can increase trust by discussing what was previously undiscussable. One high-performing management team I worked with actually had a stuffed moose as a mascot. Any team member could pick up the moose and plop it on the table during meetings to bring up a sensitive issue without any fear of retribution. Unlike Mr. Gerrosi's classroom, the team had a process for letting the moose loose.

Do you?

Inconsistent verbal and nonverbal communication

It happens at all levels of the organization, thereby affecting all four categories of trust—strategic, organizational, personal, and team. When what executives say is not congruent with how they act, employees don't feel safe asking questions, speaking their minds, challenging assumptions, raising issues, or seeking help.

Researchers at Harvard University surveyed nearly 1,300 employees, customers, investors, and suppliers to understand the nature of trust with various stakeholders.[9] They found that stakeholders' trust goes up when they see espoused values communicated in both words and deeds.

Inconsistent standards

After dinner at a national sales meeting, I observed the senior vice president of sales leaving the hotel with a first-year salesperson. One of the other first-year salespeople, Don, told me that although he had sold more than that departing peer, he was confident that the senior vice president was going to select his dinner buddy as rookie of the year.

During the awards ceremony, Don cynically smiled at me when his prediction came true. Later, Don told me that the company never published the criteria for selecting who received the sales awards. Therefore, he and his sales colleagues believed politics and the good-old-boy network was the process used for awards.

When people do not believe in the process, they'll never believe in the outcome of that process.

Light is the best disinfectant. The best way to avoid Don's (and his colleagues') perceptions of inconsistent standards would have been to publish standards by which the company made its sales awards.

This is why *Forbes* turns to Audit Integrity, an independent financial analytics company, when compiling its annual lists of "Most Trustworthy Companies" and "Least Trustworthy Companies." One of the key measures Audit Integrity uses to assess organizations is based on the transparency of publicly filed documents. Audit Integrity's rating system identified problems at Lehman Brothers, Washington Mutual, and American International Group (AIG) years before the financial meltdown of those organizations.[10]

Misplaced benevolence

It's easy to fire a jerk who underperforms. But have you ever seen well-liked employees perform poorly yet keep their jobs?

I can guarantee you that the underperformer's colleagues and direct reports all wonder why there's a double-standard. Not applying the same standard of performance to all employees by tolerating incompetent employees, no matter how nice they are, is a trust-buster.

At one of my consulting engagements, it was a sad joke in the company that managers passed around poor performers from one unit to another. This company so over-focused on its "culture of caring" at the expense of accountability that the new president asked us to focus our leadership curriculum on creating a culture of candor to complement (not replace) its caring mores.

Unfortunately, neither the president nor our new leadership program survived. Some cultures just can't handle the truth. The company's share price has plunged from $12 to $3 in the last few years, and many of their executives still don't understand that trust wilts if poor performers are not weeded out.

By the way, most poor performers receive false feedback, which is why they are often shocked to learn that anyone thinks they have any performance issues. If they ever get fired, their most common objection is, "Look at my great performance reviews!" Lack of candor is a precursor to low trust. It explains why so many managers find themselves sitting in HR offices with lawyers discussing wrongful termination lawsuits instead of getting their work done.

Don't let that happen to your managers. Employees will not trust you or your organization unless you honor the company's performance review systems by telling the truth.

Failure to delegate

Allowing employees to work independently is difficult for some executives, especially if the boss has a tendency to be a perfectionist, workaholic, or micromanager. High-performing employees often interpret this as a lack of trust in their skills.

A senior executive I coach, Casey, had this exact problem. One of his high-performing direct reports, Douglas, actually told me that he did not trust Casey because he felt micromanaged. Casey later told me that he received an e-mail from Douglas praising Casey's improved delegation skills. Trust is being rebuilt as Casey learns to delegate instead of dictate.

It's not your mediocre performers who leave when they feel micromanaged—it's your best performers.

Consistent corporate underperformance

If a company does not meet the financial expectations set by its executive team, investors lose confidence, stock prices plunge, and employee trust falls. Set realistic expectations and communicate the why behind those expectations.

He who does not trust, will not be trusted.

LAO TZU

Beyond these six most common causes of mistrust, researchers have identified a number of other factors (listed in Table 15.1) that damage trust.[11] Ask your team members if any of these issues affect your organization.

TABLE 15.1

10 Other Trust-Busters

1. Changing values to get things done
2. Randomly changing goals without explaining why
3. Eliminating office desks for those who travel
4. Making claims that are not likely to happen
5. Taking actions that are judged unfair
6. Treating goals as more important than values
7. Over-focusing on superstar performers or charismatic leaders
8. Not demonstrating commitment to organizational values
9. Not holding all personnel accountable for mistakes
10. Failing to provide honest feedback about job performance

How to build and maintain personal trust

Actions speak louder than words. This section details ten actions you can take to become more trustworthy.

Don't gossip

In surveys of more than 100 organizations, researchers found that gossip was the number-one killer of communication trust.[12]

Here is a rule of thumb: If you are talking about someone and you're not discussing specific performance issues or complimenting him, you are probably gossiping. If someone comes to you and starts gossiping about another employee, I encourage you to tell that person to work it out with that other employee.

The president of a healthcare group once told me that his job demands that he talk about others because he needs to discuss the medical performance of colleagues. He also said that he hates gossip. So he tried an experiment of not sharing the names of the doctors whose performance he was discussing—that is, he kept the conversations anonymous.

It worked. He felt that if he didn't use their names, it wasn't gossip. Perhaps there are times when you, too, need to talk about an employee and can avoid using that person's name.

Improve the right competencies

Employees trust executives who have managerial competence, while customers and suppliers award increased trust when they perceive technical proficiency. Which competencies are you working on to boost trust?

Keep personal information confidential

Ask people if they want information to be confidential at the beginning of private conversations. Honor their wishes.

Demonstrate loyalty

Give credit to others frequently, and take the responsibility when it's yours to take—especially when the finger is pointing at someone innocent.

Admit mistakes

Do it early and take ownership of the consequences of your mistakes.

Don't oversell

Enthusiasm to please or persuade often causes executives to over-commit and under-deliver. Pause to consider the consequences before committing to another task, project, or initiative.

Share information ASAP

Tell your team everything you can, as soon as you can. When you can't tell them, tell them that you will tell them as soon as you can.

Increase the right kind of transparency

Transparency usually increases trust. However, transparency can actually diminish trust if inappropriate information is disclosed. For example, disclosing executive bonuses to front-line supervisors may hurt trust, especially if there is no perceived link between pay and performance.

Create trust norms

Ask your team to brainstorm responses to this challenge: Describe what a team with high levels of trust would look like to you.

Talk about me *and* we

Count the number of times you say I/me instead of us/we. By focusing on us/we, you'll be demonstrating empathy, another essential leadership skill (discussed later in this chapter).

And a bonus practical tip to increase trust: Next time you utter those famous words, "I'll get back to you," make sure you do.

How to repair strategic and organizational trust

If, despite all your efforts to maintain trust, you discover trust has been damaged in your organization, follow these principles.

Prescription without diagnosis is malpractice

First, find out what happened:

- When did it happen?
- Who knew what, when?
- What caused the drop in trust?

We see only the tip of the iceberg

The mass of the iceberg and the currents that control it are beneath the surface. What we *don't* see controls what we *do* see. Therefore, find out the depth and breadth of the loss of trust. Is it isolated to a particular person, unit, or event?

Personal responsibility increases "respond-ability"

Most Americans never forgave former U.S. President Richard Nixon because he never took personal responsibility for the loss of trust he caused (in him, the presidency, and the government) during the Watergate scandal.

Once you know what has caused the drop in trust, quickly tell your employees that you accept responsibility for allowing this trust-busting incident to occur. You don't need to have a complete plan in place at this point; however, it is critical to tell people what you know, that you accept responsibility for it, and when you expect to know more.

Create your trust-building plan

Determine the changes that need to take place to restore trust. Start by answering six questions:

- Who needs to be involved in these changes?
- What difficult conversations need to occur, and who needs to talk to whom?
- How will you make decisions differently?
- How might you make information or processes more transparent?
- Do reporting relationships need to change?
- Which of the norms need tweaking?

Implement your trust-building plan

Use the answers to the questions in the previous section, and the numerous ideas discussed throughout this chapter, to put your plan into action.

Communicate empathy: Do you feel like they do?

We had already biked 120 miles through Sequoia National Park in two days. I was shocked that my legs felt strong as we made the final dusty push through 20 miles of hot, windy roads to our hotel in Exeter, California. I took the lead to be the "windbreaker" for my friend Mike. (In cycling, the lead rider works a lot harder.)

I heard his labored breathing as I bolted by, my resilient legs urging me to stay up front for a long time. Two minutes later, Mike passed me. I thought, *What's he doing? I know he's really tired. I feel great. Why doesn't he let me do more of the work at the front?*

As I started to move to the front again, Mike barked at me to stay back and let him do the work. I backed off, shocked at his over-reaction. *Why is he pissed at me?*

A few miles later, I found out.

We stopped to refill our water bottles. Although he was dead tired, Mike said he needed to spend time in the lead. I told him my legs felt strong and I didn't mind letting him draft as I stayed in the lead. Mike replied that he didn't feel good about himself unless he was contributing by doing his fair share of the work.

He apologized for yelling. And I apologized for being clueless about his need to share the load by being at the front. I had not exhibited empathy.

How empathetic are you, especially when you and your team are working hard? Do you feel what they feel?

The dictionary defines empathy as "the ability to identify with and understand somebody else's feelings or difficulties." The quintessential example of empathy was Counselor Deanna Troi, a character on the award-winning TV series *Star Trek: The Next Generation.* She was an empath—a person highly skilled in identifying and understanding feelings. Her role was to help the officers and crew understand what was going on within themselves and others so that they could make better decisions.

Leading researchers in the field of emotional intelligence (EI) have found that social intelligence, especially empathy, is critical to effective leadership.[13] Unfortunately, high-level executives—typically hired for their strong self-discipline and drive—often get fired because they lack empathy under pressure.

Have you ever watched a leader drone on in a meeting as the attendees become increasingly detached? Have you seen executives texting away in meetings, oblivious to what is being discussed or the impact their behavior has on others? Have you ever tried to have a conversation with someone, only to shuffle away knowing that his cup was so full with his own issues that he didn't hear you? Did you hear about the top performer who shocked her organization by announcing her resignation?

Each of these common scenarios illustrates lack of empathy. Leaders who drone on or text during meetings are not in touch with what others are feeling. Leaders who do not pay attention to subtle emotional clues during conversations also fail the empathy test. And people seldom quit their job—they usually quit their boss. Research on more than 4,000 leaders teaches us that when peak performers leave unexpectedly, their boss is usually an empathetic lightweight.[14]

Empathetic executives recognize and meet the emotional needs of diverse stakeholders. They work hard to understand how their customers, colleagues, and employees feel. Here are specific ways you can enhance your empathy skills.

Develop a personal vision for change

Write a clear picture of the empathetic person you want to become. Describe in rich sensory detail what it means to be a more empathetic person. The more sights, sounds, smells, and feelings you use to paint your picture of empathy, the better.

Answer these additional questions to paint your empathetic self-image: What will you observe at work as you become more empathetic? How will people respond to you? How will that make you feel?

Become a better listener

When stressed, people seldom hear us unless they feel heard. Most executives who want to improve empathy need to develop better listening skills. Leaders often receive low scores from peers and subordinates on behaviors such as "encourages others to express their views, even contrary ones" and "patiently listens to other opinions, perspectives, and beliefs without prejudgment." To be heard, listen well.

Watch your words

How often do you end your meetings (with individuals or groups) with this question: "Is there anything else you want to discuss?" If you want to be more empathetic, change the word "anything" to "something."

In a clinical environment, medical researchers found this simple change eliminated more than 75% of all unmet patient concerns, and the amount of time the patient spent with the doctor was not affected by asking the better question.[15]

Keep a log of your daily successes and failures

Use it to help you notice when and how you practice new empathy behaviors.

Work with a mentor

Identify someone at work perceived as very empathetic. Ask if you could work with that person during the next several months to grow your skills. Executives I coach often have an internal mentor at work also — a coach and a mentor is a great one-two punch.

Use daily reminders

Identify current habits that you can link to the new behaviors you want to augment. For example, if you take notes during meetings, you might write the word *empathy* at the top of your notepad to help remind you to be empathetic during meetings. Every time you look down to scratch a note, you'll see your reminder.

Celebrate small successes

Reward yourself whenever you experience small progress using or growing your new skill. One medical director that I coach rewards her progress by walking to the cafeteria for a frozen yogurt. Another leader at a Hollywood studio takes a mid-afternoon nap after she makes progress toward her goal. That which gets rewarded gets repeated.

Empowering executives communicate trust and empathy in thought, word, and deed. They listen patiently to other's opinions, maintain confidentiality, and promote candid dialogue. Trusted and empathetic leaders withhold their comments until the end of discussions because they "seek first to understand, then to be understood," as Stephen Covey recommends.

• • •

We've seen that blatant failure to communicate trust and empathy can have dire consequences. Few things are as terrifying to humans as the idea of radiation exposure. From the post-war monster movies to comic-book superheroes, we are constantly exposed to the message that radioactivity is a silent and horrible killer.

The executives at Fukushima Daiichi demonstrated no greater failure of leadership than their failure to communicate trust and empathy to the people most affected by the meltdown of the reactors.

Many of the executives I have coached have also had "trust issues." However, they successfully used the tools in this chapter to boost trust and empathy. Things got better because they got better. The same will be true for you.

Unfortunately, the executives at Fukushima Daiichi also missed several chances to do the right thing before and after their disaster. They failed to serve ethically, which is the last competency of the empowering leader and the subject of last chapter in this section.

CHAPTER 16

Do the Right Thing

The leader is the servant of his followers in that he removes the obstacles that prevent them from doing their jobs. In short, the true leader enables his or her followers to realize their full potential.

MAX DE PREE

SERVE ETHICALLY

The colossal failures of Enron, WorldCom, Tyco, Fannie Mae, Freddie Mac, and the many financial institutions responsible for the economic tsunami that swamped the world were all failures of ethics. Although it's popular to blame the leader at the top, it was not one person who made one error, at one point in time, creating these disasters. Many corporate and public leaders at numerous levels made countless unethical decisions, over extended periods, to produce a flood of financial calamities.

These leaders created cultures that permitted and often supported unethical approaches to work. Executives who do not dedicate themselves to constructing ethical environments are building castles in the sand at low tide.

The dictionary defines ethics as "the study of the general nature of morals and of the specific moral choices to be made by the individual in his relationship with others."

My definition is a lot simpler: *Ethics is what we should do.*

When we discuss what executives should do, ethics is elevated from merely following the law to doing the right thing. Just because something is lawful does not mean it is ethical. Before the Civil Rights Act of 1964, discrimination based on race was lawful in the United States. It was lawful —not ethical. Presently, it is also lawful to gossip, give a lousy performance review, and lie at work.

The law is the floor of ethics: It's necessary for a firm foundation.

Effective executives aspire higher. They stretch to serve ethically, the fourth core competency of empowering leadership:

1. Engage others.
2. Motivate teamwork.
3. Communicate trust and empathy.
4. SERVE ETHICALLY.

THE HIGH COST OF LOW ETHICS

I attended a one-day class on ethics at a local university to hear how others teach this topic. The professor made the point that leaders fail ethically because they put their own interests above the organizations—they're greedy. He asserted that self-interest was the cause of our current "corruption eruption" (as Moises Naim, editor in chief of *Foreign Policy* magazine, called it).

I asked how self-interest could be the cause of ethical lapses when it leads to self-destruction. I pointed out that the professor's argument was contradictory.

Executives who act unethically do so because they act only on their *short-term* self-interests. Their failure is of time, not of focus. Leaders who act unethically seldom consider the long-term negative consequences of their behavior. If they did, they would see that it is in their self-interest to do the right thing—to serve ethically.

One reason it is in an executive's self-interest to serve ethically is that good employees leave if executives exhibit low ethics. A global study of more than 9,700 employees in 32 countries confirmed this high cost of low ethics.[1] Researchers were able to separate employees into four major categories:

- Loyal (34%): Loyal employees demonstrate behaviors that make your organization successful. They work hard, stay late, do whatever it takes to serve customers, and recommend your organization to their friends and family as a great place to work.
- Accessible (8%): Accessible employees tend to demonstrate the same behaviors as loyal employees. However, for reasons unrelated to loyalty, they often leave within two years (e.g., because of a spouse's job transfer, childcare needs, or other personal issues).
- Trapped (31%): Trapped employees want to leave their jobs, but for a variety of reasons (e.g., no other job opportunities, children in school, lack of confidence) feel they can't leave.

- High-risk (27%): High-risk employees are actively seeking other jobs during work hours. It's probably no surprise that 60% of this high-risk group would not recommend their organizations as good places to work.

Of the all employees who described their organizations as ethical, 55% were loyal, while only 9% of those who questioned their companies' ethics were in the loyal group. High ethics lead to loyalty, which decreases turnover. Put another way, one of the high costs of low ethics is employee churn.

What does it cost to replace an employee? Depending on the position, the cost of recruiting, interviewing, hiring, and training an employee is usually between $5,000 (to replace a front-line employee at a retail store) and $100,000 (to replace that must-have IT manager).

But turnover is only one of the many costs associated with low ethics. There are also huge legal, productivity, reputation, morale, sales, and opportunity costs. How much time, money, and effort did U.S. President Bill Clinton have to spend defending his unethical, although perhaps not illegal, affair with Monica Lewinsky? He could have invested the same resources in achieving his ideological and political goals, rather than helping his competitors achieve theirs.

Put Ethics to Work for You

Uncle Burt reached into his back pocket and pulled out his wallet. He fumbled for another five-dollar bill and then slapped it on the bar. He directed his soft, raspy voice toward the bartender and said, "When you get a chance, get my nephew another beer."

As he settled back onto his stool at the bar, I blurted out, "Burt, I got my draft card yesterday." It was 1973, and though the Vietnam War was winding down, the draft was alive and well.

"Well, what are you going to do?" The war-decorated Marine's blue eyes stared at me.

He was a second father to me. I didn't want to disappoint him. Yet, I had to tell him the truth. "Uncle Burt, I don't want to go to Vietnam and die. Don't we have relatives in Sweden or Denmark?"

"You're not going to go to Sweden or Denmark, Dave."

"I'm not? Why?"

"Because" — he put his muscular left arm around me, squeezed hard and smiled — "I know what kind of kid you are. The kind that will always do the right thing."

I wish I could tell you that Uncle Burt was right, that I've always done the right thing. I haven't. I've *tried* to do the right thing, but—as most of us do—I've made a few mistakes along the way. (It turns out I never had to make a decision about the Vietnam War because the war ended before my draft number was called.)

I'm convinced that one of the reasons I've been able to do the right thing most of the time is because of my lifelong love of practical philosophy. There are three practical and ethical philosophies—utility, duty, and virtue—that can help you serve ethically.

Utility

One approach to making ethical decisions is to emphasize actions that provide the most good and least harm for the greatest number.

This utilitarian approach asks you to weigh the impact of your decisions on the many stakeholders who often have conflicting interests, such as your customers, employees, shareholders, the community, and the environment.

Utilitarian executives consider the consequences of decisions by asking, "How can this decision produce the greatest good and least harm for the most people?"

Duty

Philosopher Immanuel Kant emphasized ethics based on our duty to our fellow humans.

The Kantian approach asks us to do the right thing using principles as the criteria for action. It invites you to answer this question: "If everybody was compelled to practice the principles I'm using to make this decision, what kind of environment would we have?"

Virtue

This approach to ethics teaches us that a leader's decision should be consistent with specific virtues or values that provide for the development of humanity. These values enable us to act according to the highest potential of our character.

A virtuous leader asks, "What kind of person will I become if I do this?" or "Is this action consistent with my highest values?"

All three of these philosophies can help increase ethical behavior. Yet, I have found the virtue approach is what helps executives the most. The next section summarizes the research showing how four specific and practical values can help you serve more ethically.

Executives who educate themselves and their employees about the importance of ethics benefit by focusing on virtue. Professor Kim Cameron from the University of Michigan Business School and his colleagues surveyed 804 individuals from 18 U.S. organizations, representing 16 different industries. All but two of these organizations had downsized within the previous three years. The researchers found that organizations that scored higher in virtuousness achieved significantly better organizational performance, despite downsizing.[2] Specifically, they reported that organizations that were driven by core values experienced greater innovation, improved customer retention, higher product quality, and lower employee turnover —all leading to greater profitability.

In addition, research by the World Bank found that contrary to the "efficient grease" theory (i.e., pay bribes to increase efficiency), leaders who pay bribes actually spend more time negotiating regulations with bureaucrats and eventually pay higher costs.[3]

There are many values you could, and probably should, embrace based on the objective evidence that values are a precursor to executive success.[4] My review of the research reveals that you will get the biggest return for your effort by focusing on these four:

1. Honesty
2. Integrity
3. Equity
4. Humility

Is honesty still the best policy?

Honesty is defined as "freedom from deceit" and "adherence to facts." Professor Robert Cialdini and his colleagues at Arizona State University found that the cost of dishonesty is very high.[5] They reported that 80% of consumers surveyed said that their perception of the company's honesty had a direct impact on their decision to purchase goods or services from the firm, while 76% indicated it would affect their decision about accepting a job there.

The researchers also found increased illness, absenteeism, and turnover in cultures when employees perceived a mismatch between the values claimed and values demonstrated. Instead of practicing what we preach, the data tells us to preach only what we practice.

You can avoid these high costs and create a culture of honesty in your team by learning from Ginger Graham.[6] Shortly after she was named president and CEO of a $300 million medical device manufacturer, the entire U.S. sales force was waiting for her presentation at the national sales meeting... and they were angry. Revenue and market share were declining, while manufacturing and customer costs were on the rise. Spirits were down and trust in management was nonexistent in this once-stellar company.

As she approached the podium, Graham decided to take a different approach to her presentation. She opted to talk honestly about what everyone else was discussing at the water cooler: "I've always heard about what a wonderful company this is, but frankly, that's not what I see. What I see is deteriorating morale, disillusioned customers, and finger-pointing. I see a place where R&D and manufacturing are practically at war. You folks in sales blame manufacturing, while R&D blames marketing. We're all so busy blaming each other that nothing gets done. No wonder our customers are furious with us."

The initial response to the new CEO's frank comments was shock. Then emotions changed. People began nodding in agreement. By the time Graham finished, they were shouting their approval and giving her a standing ovation. It was the beginning of her odyssey of honesty.

Ginger Graham used seven powerful practices to inspire more honesty:

1. Assign employee coaches to executives.
2. Report the whole truth.
3. Ask the rank and file for help.
4. Tell stories.
5. Solicit honest feedback.
6. Illustrate the cost.
7. Show you care.

Our own odyssey of honesty begins by seeing how each practice works.

1. Assign employee coaches to executives: Graham assigned each of her executives a coach from the non-managerial ranks. She asked these rank-and-file coaches to uncover employee perceptions about the executive's honesty, approachability, responsiveness, and other qualities. The coaches met with the executives quarterly to deliver their reports. The executives then met with each other to hold each other accountable to act on this honest feedback.

Who should coach you?

2. Report the whole truth: Despite what Jack Nicholson's character testified in *A Few Good Men*, most employees can handle the truth. Not

only can they handle it, they hunger for it. Graham's team began talking with—not at—employees about everything that previously was discussed only in senior management meetings. Topics included sales goals, financial performance, product milestones, key competitive information, market trends, problems, opportunities, successes, and failures. The company disseminated information and discussed it at all-hands meetings, as well as staff meetings throughout the organization.

How can you communicate more directly and honestly with your team?

3. Ask the rank and file for help: When employees have the right information, they can come up with very effective and efficient solutions to difficult problems. Graham gives the example of a product launch that went so well that the executive team was on the verge of asking people to work seven days a week, three shifts a day, including Thanksgiving and Christmas, to meet the explosive demand.

Instead of making this unreasonable demand, the leaders called a meeting of all their employees. They discussed their success by relaying powerful stories about how their new product delighted patients and physicians. Then they asked the employees how to meet the extraordinary production demand. When the possibility of working long hours throughout the holidays came up, one woman asked: "Could you wrap our Christmas presents?"

"We'll do more than that," the executives volunteered. "Give us your lists and we'll hire people to shop for you."

Graham reported that within half an hour, the employees came up with a variety of ways to manage the tension between meeting production goals and meeting their family needs during the holidays.

What difficult problems could—and should—your team solve with you?

4. Tell stories: The "hire people to shop for you" story became a powerful tale about asking others for honest input, subsequently repeated in other company meetings and private conversations. Retelling emotional stories weaves the lessons into the very fabric of an organization. That is a story's higher purpose—to create cultural norms.

Winston Churchill was famous for promising "blood, toil, tears, and sweat." If you want more honesty, tell stories about people who deliver honest messages in tough times. In addition, encourage people to discuss their own standards of honesty (by, for example, recalling the Ten Commandments or signing an honor code) to decrease dishonest behavior.[7]

What stories should you tell?

5. Solicit honest feedback: If you want to ensure that honesty is alive and well in your team, use feedback to stay on track. Graham implemented the "hot seat" feedback session. Each member of the executive management team sits on a tall stool in front of peers. One by one, these peers bring up the shortcomings they had observed in the other executive and offer suggestions for improvement.

Graham points out that, initially, these were very unpopular sessions. Over time, people came to understand that feedback is neutral. Feedback literally means "information returned to the source." It is up to the leader to choose how to think about it. Graham concluded that the hot seat was the most powerful tool for building mutual accountability and honest communication that she had ever seen.

How might you adapt this tool to increase honesty on your team?

6. Illustrate the cost: Why do people steal supplies, time, and other non-money assets? Researchers tell us that "non-monetary exchanges allow people greater psychological latitude to cheat" because they don't see these assets as having real value.[8] Stealing supplies, backdating stock options, falsifying financial reports — these unethical practices seem like Monopoly money to many people. They don't seem to be wrong because the people seldom see the true cost of their behavior.

How could you illustrate the true cost of a dishonest action so that others care about it?

7. Show you care: Caring about what is important to your team has a side benefit: When caring goes up, dishonesty goes down.[9]

Researchers studied 768 employees of a U.S. telemarketing company, each of whom called potential donors to request contributions for a non-profit organization. To make sure employees did not inflate donation pledges (on which their bonuses were based), managers monitored the employees by contacting a fraction of the donors to confirm their pledges. Although employees received bonuses for exceeding their pledge targets, they also had "bad calls" (unconfirmed pledges) deducted from their pay. During the study, researchers manipulated the amount of monitoring reported to the employees because they wanted to know if dishonesty increased when monitoring decreased.

The short answer is yes.

The long answer is also yes, but a substantial number of telemarketers did not cheat even when they were monitored less frequently. When investigators then measured employee attitudes toward their employer, they found that those employees who had poor attitudes about the company logged 79% more bad calls than those who had positive attitudes about the company. The employees who had positive attitudes scored higher on statements such as "The company cares about me." Employees who feel cared for were more honest.

If honesty is not *the* best policy, at least it is a very profitable one — as is integrity.

Psst! Your integrity is showing

An insurance company executive once told me that he believed his team members demonstrated high integrity because they talked about issues during meetings the same way they talked about those issues at the bar at night.

I applauded this state of affairs and reminded him that transparency is only the first step of integrity. If leaders don't follow lip service with hip service, they are transparent hypocrites. Honesty asks for the truth; integrity demands transparency and consistency.

Although people have talked about the importance of integrity for centuries, Professor Tony Simons from Cornell University actually measured the impact of integrity on the bottom line.[10] He and his colleagues surveyed more than 6,500 employees at 76 hotels to assess the consistency, or lack thereof, between what a leader said and did. They evaluated integrity by asking questions such as, "Does my manager deliver on promises?" and "Does my manager practice what he/she preaches?" They correlated the employee responses with the hotels' satisfaction surveys, personnel records, and financial records.

They discovered that an improvement of a mere 0.125 points on the hotel's 5-point integrity score (that's one-eighth of a point on this 5-point scale) increased the hotel's profitability by 2.5% of revenues. This translated to a profit increase of more than $250,000 per year per hotel. No other aspect of manager behavior had as large an impact on profits. It pays to walk the talk.

The researchers pointed out that although integrity is a simple concept, improving and maintaining integrity is a challenge for a multitude of reasons.

- Sticky labels: It takes a long time to earn the reputation as a straight shooter, but only one misstatement to get labeled a hypocrite.
- Conflicting stakeholders: Constantly managing the competing, and often contradictory, demands of numerous stakeholders can create the perception of inconsistency. For example, you might be working with your front-line supervisors to improve quality while at the same

time discussing staff reductions with your boss to meet financial objectives. When word gets out to the rank and file, all they see is low integrity.

- CHANGE: When people are bobbing around in a sea of uncertainty, they look for stability. They cling to the security of the old, the tried and true, and the way we were. New policies, initiatives, management teams, and other changes often feel like inconsistencies (i.e., low integrity) to employees.
- MANAGEMENT FADS: One CEO told me that he refuses "to lead by bestseller." He said too many of his CEO colleagues jump on the hottest management trend — and he's right. The average U.S. company committed to using between 11.4 and 14.4 of the popular management tools and techniques during the 1990s.[11] Yet 82% of the 276 executives surveyed agreed that "most tools promise more than they deliver." These fads fade fast: 90% of Fortune 500 companies adopted quality circles when they were popular, and 80% abandoned quality circles within five years. Employees question integrity when leaders endorse unproven "flavor of the month" management fads. Healthy skepticism succumbs to employee cynicism.
- SHIFTING PRIORITIES: Adjusting to a complex, dynamic economic environment is critical to a leader's success. Unfortunately, when executives do not communicate the changing priorities well, employees do not perceive the changes well.
- BLIND SPOTS: A vice president of safety told me that his CEO always tells him that safety is a top priority. Yet, he lamented, safety is never discussed at the CEO's senior management meetings. We seldom see our own inconsistencies. That's because we have a natural tendency to view our behaviors as consistent with espoused values. If there is an inconsistency, we rationalize to diminish it. This is the essence of the theory of cognitive dissonance, which states that people are motivated to reduce any disconnect between what they do and their attitudes, beliefs, and values.

Employee actions are echoes of executive communication.

Now that we know why maintaining integrity is a challenge, here are six tactics you can apply to build and sustain your own, and your team's, integrity:

1. CREATE A STRAIGHT-SHOOTING TEAM: Invite your team members to help define what integrity means and looks like from their point of view. Involve them in the establishment of integrity norms and procedures

that promote consistent high standards and accountability. Strive for transparency in what you do and the processes used to make decisions.

2. COMMUNICATE: Use all forms of communication to inform your team that they must not compromise the organization's integrity or their own to meet goals. Discuss difficult issues that could cause lapses in integrity in your meetings on a regular basis.
3. DISCIPLINE CONSISTENTLY: Employees must see that leadership holds senior executives, middle managers, and front-line employees to the same high standards. Reprimand anyone who violates established standards.
4. REWARD FREQUENTLY: Applaud those who successfully meet difficult challenges or crises with integrity. Discuss integrity issues during performance reviews. Use bonuses and pay raises to reinforce the importance of integrity.
5. ESTABLISH SUPPORT SYSTEMS: Make it easy for employees to anonymously report financial, legal, and ethical concerns. In addition, conduct an annual employee survey that asks questions such as:
   - Is integrity compromised by business pressures?
   - Are company leaders' verbal commitments to integrity reflected in their actions?
   - Do leaders discuss ethical issues at regular division/department meetings?
6. MINIMIZE CHANGE: Employees suffer from change fatigue when leaders flood them with new policies, initiatives, or management fads. Although waves of change are necessary in a competitive and global marketplace, ensure that your changes are strategic. Remember, strategy is as much about saying no as it is about saying yes. If everything is important, nothing is strategic.

Finally, it is important to understand that integrity requires authenticity. It's no use faking transparency—leaders who try to "fake it till they make it" seldom make it over the long haul. Scientists at the University of North Carolina, Harvard, and Duke conducted a fascinating series of studies demonstrating that people who try to fool themselves often lie to others.[12]

These researchers recruited 85 women to participate in four experiments involving counterfeit consumer products. In one experiment, all subjects were given expensive Chloé sunglasses. However, half of the women thought they were wearing fakes. When the women then performed tasks that provided opportunities for lying and cheating, the women who thought they were wearing fakes (even though they were authentic) cheated 70% of the time. By comparison, the group that knew it was wearing authentic sunglasses cheated "only" 30% of the time.

In the other experiments, researchers discovered that the effects of deceiving oneself extend beyond the self. It turns out that the more we try to fool others, the more we also believe others are trying to fool us, even when they are not. Those who commit a fraud assume everyone else is engaged in the same kinds of deceptions.

Maintain your integrity by being authentic in all you think, say, and do (and even in what you wear).

The equity in your process

Consider two companies experiencing layoffs. Tyrell Corp. provides a safety net for laid-off workers that includes a generous severance package, extensive outplacement counseling, and continuing health insurance for a year. Yet senior management never fully explains the rationale behind the layoffs or the process used to eliminate jobs. Nine months later, Tyrell is mired in numerous wrongful termination lawsuits and another round of layoffs due to low productivity.

Cyberdyne Systems Corp. does not spend nearly as much money providing a safety net for its laid-off workers. However, senior management explains the strategic reasons for the layoffs on many occasions prior to implementation. Managers at all levels make themselves available to answer questions and share their concern for all those affected by the layoffs. Management also works closely with HR throughout the process. Nine months later, none of the laid-off employees at Cyberdyne has filed a wrongful termination suit and performance is better than it was before the layoffs.

What made the difference between these two companies? Although Cyberdyne did not spend as much money on the severance package as Tyrell, Cyberdyne invested heavily in process equity.

Equity, the third value required to serve ethically, is "the quality of being fair or impartial." Cyberdyne employees felt the company had treated them fairly—that there was equity in the layoff process. Professor Joel Brockner points out that when leaders practice *process equity,* often called "process fairness," employees support new strategies, promote innovation, and boost the bottom line.[13] When companies fail to practice process fairness, they pay the high cost of low ethics.

Professor Brockner cites a study of nearly 1,000 people that found only 1% of laid-off employees who felt that they were treated with a high degree of process fairness filed a wrongful termination lawsuit. In contrast, 17% of those who believed they were treated with a low degree of process fairness sued. The researchers calculated the cost savings of practicing process fairness is about $13,000 per employee.

In addition to keeping companies out of legal hot water, paying attention to process equity in decision-making cuts down on employee theft and medical malpractice suits.

People don't retaliate because they don't get what they want. They lash out because they don't receive adequate explanations about the process that led to those undesired outcomes. To increase equity in your team, it is important to address the three components of fairness:

1. Input fairness: How much input do employees feel they have in decision-making? Do their opinions count?
2. Decision fairness: Are decisions based on accurate and unbiased information? Is adequate notice given? Is the process transparent? Are decisions consistent with espoused values and previous decisions?
3. Implementation fairness: Does management explain why it made a decision? Does it treat employees respectfully by listening empathetically as leaders execute the decision?

There are actions you can take to address all three components of process fairness whenever you implement a major decision:

- Engage employees early in the process: Select a group of well-respected managers and ask them to interview a large number of employees from different parts of the company to learn about the pluses, minuses, and consequences of implementing the major decision. Increasing engagement increases commitment.
- Show the data: Show the employees the data used to make a decision. The more transparent the process, the more buy-in to the outcome of that process.
- Explain the why behind the what: Let employees know why the organization made the decision and what other alternatives leaders considered. Employees may comply when they know the *what,* but they'll commit when they know the *why.*
- Practice two-way communication: I once consulted with a $20 billion company whose CEO stated, "Anything worth communicating is worth over-communicating." Unfortunately, he confused communicating with broadcasting. He had no mechanism to detect responses to the signals he sent. His major change initiative failed miserably and he

was fired. Feedback keeps you on track because it allows for early and frequent course correction. Effective executives find multiple channels to listen to the employees' perception of fairness during any change.

- WARN AND EDUCATE LEADERS: Executives who deliver difficult news must be warned about the negative emotions employees will feel and educated as to how to manage these emotions productively. Educating leaders at all levels about process equity is critical—both for the leaders and their employees.

Process equity is how employees view the fairness of an organization's decisions. In addition to looking at the overall organization, employees also peer over their cubicles to judge the ethics of equity related to others—what I call *person equity*.

Equity theory as it relates to individuals was originally presented as a theory of motivation by behavioral psychologist John Stacy Adams in the early 1960s.[14] His theory explains how employees compare what they get (outcomes) to what they give (inputs) in relation to their colleagues. It's illustrated by the following equation:

$$\frac{\text{my outcomes}}{\text{my inputs}} = \frac{\text{your outcomes}}{\text{your inputs}}$$

The theory states that I am motivated, often subconsciously, to resolve any discrepancy when I rate my ratio of outcomes (salary, perks, recognition, job security, promotions, responsibilities, etc.) to input (effort, time, loyalty, personal sacrifice, etc.) and compare it to your ratio.

For example, assume my outcome is 100 (an arbitrary number that represents what I get out of my job) and my input is 120 (an arbitrary number representing what I put into my job). Furthermore, I perceive your outcome and input to be 100 and 80, respectively. Thus, my perception of the ratios would be as follows:

$$\frac{100}{120} = \frac{100}{80}$$

The first observation I make is that I perceive that we both receive equivalent outcomes—we both get approximately the same salary, perks, and recognition. However, my 120 input compared to your 80—a discrepancy of about 40% in the ratio—tells me that I believe I am putting more effort, time, and personal sacrifice into the job than you are.

Equity theory and common sense tell us that I am motivated to resolve this discrepancy (i.e., make the ratios equal) by executing one or more of the following tactics:

- Ask for a raise, flexible hours, better responsibilities, or recognition to increase my outcomes.
- Ask you to work harder and to put in more time (to "do your fair share") to increase your input from 80 to 120.
- Decide to work less myself to decrease my input from 120 to 80.
- Decide to leave.

Here are a few practical tips to put this theory to work for you and your team:

- Employees tend to think in terms of total input and outcomes: This means you need to find out what is most important in each of these categories for each of your team members. For example, I'm coaching a mid-level manager who just agreed to receive lower pay in exchange for more flexible work hours.
- The value employees place on different inputs and outcomes is quite varied: This is another reason for obtaining frequent feedback from your employees regarding their perceptions on inputs and outcomes. Cultures in different countries also value equity differently. For example, researchers have found that, in general, Eastern European countries value "ascribed status" more than achieved status. Thus, employees in Eastern European countries accept nepotism and paternalism more than in the West.[15]
- Executive compensation deserves a close look: CEO pay in the United States was 42 times that of the average employee in 1980. It has since risen to approximately 364 times the pay of the average worker. Workers at all levels think of the equity ratio, usually subconsciously, when they see these numbers and shake their heads in disbelief.
- Individuals who feel they receive more outcomes than they deserve seldom seek to decrease their pay or perks: More often, they inflate their perception of their inputs. This is why you may see highly paid executives defend their pay by comparing what they do to top athletes or popular musicians.
- The comparisons employees make are not just between themselves and their co-workers: They also compare themselves to external influences, such as employees in other companies and industries. Knowing what your competitors and complementary industries pay is important for this reason.

Remember that equity comes in two flavors:

- Process equity is the manner in which employees evaluate how fairly the organization implements major decisions and initiatives.
- Personal equity is how individuals compare their ratio of outcomes/inputs to someone else's ratio.

Ethical leaders keep both in mind to guide their fair treatment of their team members.

Humility — wimp, whiner, or winner?

George Harding, a renowned patent attorney, had been hired by the John Manny Company of Rockford, Illinois, to defend its reaping machine against a charge of patent infringement. Harding thought it best to hire a local lawyer who understood the Chicago judge who would try the case. He picked a young, ambitious lawyer named Abraham Lincoln.

It was a poor choice.

Lincoln was delighted to accept the work in the summer of 1855, six months after losing the race for U.S. Senator from Illinois. He was paid a retainer and promised a substantial fee when he finished the work. He was also excited to have the opportunity to practice law with well-trained, highly educated East Coast lawyers.

Within weeks of hiring Lincoln, Harding received word that the case had been transferred from Chicago to Cincinnati. This allowed Harding to team up with the lawyer he had wanted all along — Edwin Stanton. Unfortunately, Harding did not tell Lincoln about hiring Stanton. So, Lincoln devoted himself to developing his case throughout the summer.

Lincoln arrived in Cincinnati in late September, with his lengthy brief in his lanky hands. When he met Harding and Stanton as they left the court, Stanton pulled Harding aside and whispered, "Why did you bring that long-armed ape here? He does not know anything and can do no good." Stanton and Harding turned away and walked on down the court hall.

During the next several days, Stanton made it perfectly clear that Lincoln was to remove himself from the case, which Lincoln did. Nevertheless, he remained in Cincinnati for a week to hear the case. Although Lincoln stayed and ate at the same hotel as Stanton and Harding, they never asked him to join them for a single meal or to accompany them to or from court.

As he prepared to leave Cincinnati, despite suffering what anyone would consider a supreme insult at the hands of Harding and Stanton,

Lincoln told one of John Manny's partners that he was so impressed by the two lawyers' sophisticated arguments and thorough preparation that he was going back to Illinois to "study law."

Besides re-dedicating himself to studying law, Lincoln had another response to Stanton's insults. Six years after the trial, and the first time Lincoln had seen Stanton since the trial, President Lincoln offered Edwin Stanton a cabinet position as his Secretary of War.

How would you have responded to such mistreatment?

Lincoln's humility helped him achieve extraordinary results. Author Doris Kearns Goodwin asserts that every member of Lincoln's administration was better known, better educated, and more experienced than he was. In addition, Lincoln placed all three of his rivals for the 1860 presidential Republican nomination in his cabinet.[16]

Are you humble enough to surround yourself with superior people?

Humility is a "modest opinion or estimate of one's own importance or rank." It helps leaders direct their ego away from over-focusing on the "me" and toward the greater cause of the "we." Humble leaders, like Abraham Lincoln, are able to subjugate their ego for the good of the team.

In his groundbreaking book *Good to Great,* author Jim Collins revealed that only 11 CEOs of the 1,435 companies studied possessed what he called "Level 5 leadership." A Level 5 leader is one who "builds enduring greatness through a paradoxical blend of personal humility and professional will."[17]

Level 5 leaders demonstrate personal humility through:

- Compelling modesty: They shun public adulation and seldom boast.
- Quiet, calm determination: They rely on inspired standards, not charisma, to motivate.
- Channeling ambition: They prioritize the company's success, not their own.
- Spending more time looking out the window than in the mirror: They properly apportion credit for the success of the company to the leaders, managers, and front-line employees who are responsible for it. They do not allow deflated self-esteem or an inflated ego to shut down their openness to feedback.

How can you apply Collins's research to consistently demonstrate humility?

The opposite of humility is arrogance. During the Great Recession, while millions of Americans suffered on Main Street, many leaders on Wall Street didn't seem to understand the importance of humility. The former CEO of Merrill Lynch, John Thain, resigned after media reports that he spent $1 million to decorate his office and paid billions of dollars in executive bonuses just days before Bank of America bought his shattered firm on the orders of the Federal Reserve.[18]

Contrary to Thain's example, many leaders act with great humility. John Edwardson, former CEO of CDW, a $10 billion company that sells to IBM, HP, and other computer manufacturers, demonstrated his humility by not taking himself seriously. He made regular bets about the company reaching certain goals and, if he was wrong, he shaved his head and grew mutton-chop sideburns.[19] Edwardson's humility also translated into visibility and availability. His office had a large picture window through which employees could watch him work.

Former UPS CEO Mike Eskew captured the spirit of humility when he often reminded everyone that he was only one of 360,000 people who worked at UPS. Similarly, the chief executive of W.L. Gore & Associates, Terri Kelly, lives her multibillion-dollar company's "no titles" policy by describing herself as an associate when asked what she does.

Humility is the ability to keep your accomplishments in perspective. It is, as Pastor Rick Warren says, "not thinking less of yourself; it is thinking of yourself less."

As you travel your path of extraordinary leadership and develop the four fundamental values of serving ethically, you will be humbled by the number of ethical dilemmas you'll face. I encourage you to use the XLM as a practical tool that integrates the diverse philosophical approaches of the four leadership styles into an ethical decision-making process, as seen in Figure 16.1. Think of it as a moral compass to guide your journey. Asking these questions when you face an ethical dilemma will not tell you what to do. The answers, though, can help you frame the conversation, illuminate your options, and consider the consequences.

FIGURE 16.1

An Ethical Decision-Making Process

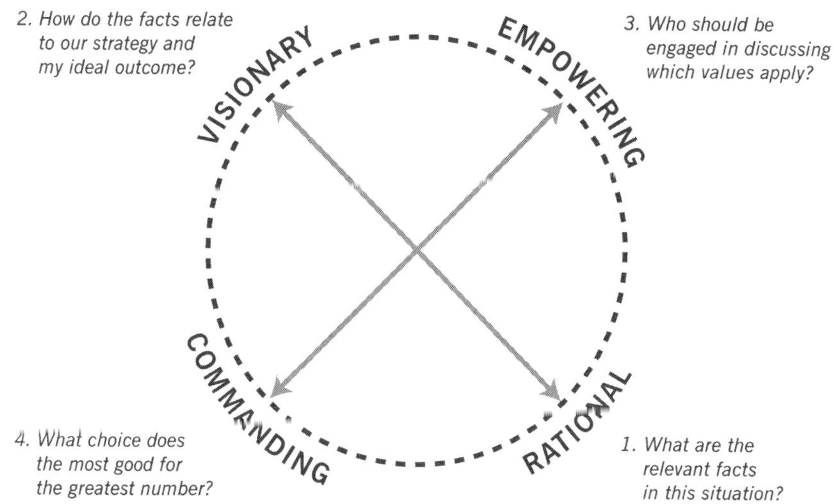

We have learned that the empowering executive is one who engages others, motivates the team, communicates trust and empathy, and serves ethically. As you reflect on this description, what will you do to increase your skills in these areas? Table 16.1 lists 17 actions that executives have taken to expand their empowering leadership.

Which of these recommendations could help you?

TABLE 16.1

17 Actions That Expand Your Empowering Skills

1. Encourage employee career development with specific goals and plans.
2. Ensure that team members have the tools to do their best every day.
3. Demonstrate that you care about what others care about.
4. Ask employees how you can help them make progress on their tasks, projects, and priorities.
5. Avoid blocking your employees' progress by changing goals, being indecisive, or withholding resources.
6. Involve employees in decision-making whenever possible and avoid micromanaging.
7. Foster two-way communication with employees about organizational issues.
8. Recognize the contribution each team member makes at least once per week.
9. Hold all employees accountable for the quality of their work.
10. Delegate tasks and conduct after-action reviews to help others grow.
11. Make time to coach your high-potential employees.
12. Celebrate success after completing major projects.
13. Encourage team learning as part of the culture.
14. Be compassionate and learning-oriented when mistakes occur.
15. Walk the talk by preaching only those things you already practice.
16. Ask more questions and listen patiently to diverse perspectives.
17. Become more of who you really are.

• • •

The nuclear tragedy following Japan's earthquake and tsunami demonstrated in the most powerful terms possible that dedication to learning and employing the competencies of an empowering leader are essential.

However, this servant-style of leadership is not the only kind of leadership required to address the multiple paradoxes of being a 21st-century executive. The next section of this book describes how to apply the four commanding competencies in a manner that complements your empowering style.

Section V
How Commanding Executives Take Charge

Case studies about the mortgage-driven collapse of the global banking industry in 2008 will be researched and written for decades to come. The bankruptcy of iconic global brands, the widespread consumer pain, the massive government intervention, and the failure of public institutions to punish the irrational financial exuberance are too big a collection of targets to pass up.

One example has already been studied in detail by government regulators, politicians, and news reporters: Washington Mutual, better known as WaMu. It grew from a modest, stable regional institution to the country's largest savings and loan on the basis of mortgages of such questionable value that when the bank failed, it was the largest bank failure in American history. WaMu's investors lost every penny they'd sunk into it when it was sold to JPMorgan Chase, shortly after WaMu was forcibly taken over by the federal government.

The person widely considered responsible for WaMu's explosive rise and collapse is Kerry Killinger. His performance as WaMu CEO offers a cautionary tale about the problems associated with taking one leadership competency to its most extreme without accessing opposing and complementary competencies. This section describes the four core commanding competencies:

1. Execute with passion and courage.
2. Embrace ambiguity and paradox.
3. Regulate the emotions.
4. Choose responsibly.

Killinger was certainly passionate and courageous. He believed so passionately in the power of unconventional loans to earn a return for the bank's shareholders that his mortgage brokers aggressively marketed such loans—so aggressively, in fact, that a 2003 audit found fewer than 25% of WaMu's loans were secured adequately.[1]

Unfortunately, Killinger did not excel in the other three commanding competencies. His inability to manage the risk and profit paradox was instrumental in the WaMu collapse. His ability to regulate his emotions was so limited that his bank's "long-running marketing campaign—'The Power of Yes'—came to define the bank's culture and establish it in the minds of consumers as the lender that never said no."[2]

And as for not choosing responsibly, it is perhaps best demonstrated by the fact that Killinger boosted his own compensation to more than $100 million, even while, according to the Washington Post's Steven Pearlstein:

> [T]ime and again, subordinates warned Killinger about ridiculously risky lending practices, poor mid-level management, inadequate information systems and risk-management controls—even widespread fraud. And time and again, Killinger failed to take interest in these problems or insist that they be fixed. His way of dealing with them was to refuse to acknowledge them for as long as possible and then declare that they had been dealt with, eventually cutting himself off from anyone who insisted on bringing them up.

Of course, our goal in this section is to help you avoid Killinger's fate by developing and applying the four competencies of the commanding style, while keeping an eye on the opposing and complementary empowering style.

CHAPTER 17

Git-R-Dun

Come to the edge, He said. They said: We are afraid.
Come to the edge, He said. They came. He pushed them,
And they flew…

GUILLAUME APOLLINAIRE

Greg was organized, likable, and communicated well. He earned a promotion to director of finance after three good years as a mid-level manager. When I interviewed his direct reports, they indicated that they always knew what to do because Greg excelled at clarifying objectives and expectations. Team meetings ran like a Swiss watch. He included his managers in decision-making and delegated well. He also fostered an environment of creativity and openness to change.

As the economy worsened, strategic priorities changed and the CEO required more productivity from the finance department. Greg's weaknesses began to show. Three of his middle managers failed to improve productivity. They also missed project deadlines, became less responsive to their colleagues' needs, and failed to engage their own team members in dealing with the difficult times. Complaints about poor leadership from Greg's front-line supervisors escalated. Employee turnover skyrocketed as morale plummeted.

Greg eventually counseled his three managers individually, but they didn't improve because he didn't hold them accountable for implementing any improvement plans. Greg's colleagues became increasingly agitated about his inability to generate the new analysis and reports required to deal with the tough times. He was also slow to address his peers' concerns and the contagious, emotional conflict within his own team.

Six months later, Greg was fired (*deselected* is the fashionable term these days).

What do you think his major problem was?

If you guessed that he lacked a few of the four critical competencies of a commanding executive, you get a gold star.

Unlike Greg, executives highly skilled in this leadership style work extremely hard to fulfill commitments, especially under pressure. They drive for results by pushing themselves and others to accomplish tasks on time and take calculated risks. Their straightforward and candid approach feels like a spring morning after a cleansing rain the night before. These are the keys to executing with passion and courage — the first competency of the commanding leadership style.

> *Getting things done through others is a fundamental leadership skill. Indeed, if you can't do it, you're not leading.*
>
> LARRY BOSSIDY AND RAM CHARAN[1]

EXECUTE WITH PASSION AND COURAGE

Greg's major problem was that he failed to execute. The word *execute* means "to perform; to carry out; to put into practice." This leadership competency is concerned with being conscientious about getting the job done, accomplishing goals every day — and every week, month, and year — through others. Greg was unable to focus his team's work on the CEO's new strategic priorities.

How well do you execute your boss's priorities?

To execute strategic priorities means different things to executives at different levels of the organization. If you are a senior executive, it means implementing your strategic plan. (We will discuss that topic later in this chapter.) On the other hand, if you are a mid-level executive, execution means focusing your team's efforts on those activities your boss says are most important to the organization (which, of course, should relate directly to the organization's strategic priorities). If your boss fails to specify his priorities, it's your job to discover them by asking questions such as:

- What is most important to you regarding my team's performance?
- What metrics will you use to evaluate me/us during my performance review?
- How does your boss measure your success?
- What must my team accomplish to help you achieve your goals?

Only after answering these questions do you have the necessary information to become a laser beam whose energy and time are focused on strategic priorities.

The essence of daily execution is self-management—how we choose to use our time. Notice that I didn't say time management. We cannot manage time—we can manage only ourselves. If we want to execute well, we must manage ourselves well.

The following sub-section details six simple yet powerful steps to daily execution. This six-step process is a summary of the best self-management tips gleaned from decades of absorbing time-management books, seminars, and programs, as well as listening to practical tips from thousands of leaders who have shared their ideas during my classes.

I'm confident the process will work for you and your team, because when I analyzed a decade of feedback from participants who told me which ideas from our classes helped them the most in the workplace, these six self-management tools were at the top:

1. Look at your GPS once a week.
2. Write one SMART goal for the week.
3. Prioritize your to-do list every morning.
4. Block out time to work on your B priorities every day.
5. Manage your energy—not just your time—every day.
6. Adapt—don't adopt—these steps to your system.

Look at your GPS once a week (every Monday morning—two minutes)

A GPS gives direction by providing an overall picture of the journey. Every Monday morning—and only on Monday morning—invest two minutes reviewing a document that provides the overall direction of your department, division, or unit. This document could be the executive summary of your department's strategic plan, business plan, or operations plan.

If you are not able to obtain this type of document, then review your boss's priorities. It's critical to remind yourself what is strategic at the start of the week because it's too easy to get caught up in the urgency of the day and lose focus on what is most important. For example, if your leader has told you that retention is her priority this year, reminding yourself of this fact every Monday morning will help you focus some of your energy in that direction throughout the week. In practical terms, this may mean investing the time to coach one of your top performers or preparing fully for a performance review.

It's easier to say no when you have a compelling yes.

Write one SMART goal for the week (every Monday morning—two minutes)

Every Monday morning—and only on Monday morning after reviewing your GPS—write one SMART goal that you will accomplish this week. A SMART goal is one that is:

- Specific
- Measurable
- Attainable
- Responsible
- Timed

Of course, you will accomplish a lot more than just this one goal during the week. However, writing a SMART goal after you've just reviewed your GPS will encourage you to make progress on an important goal during the week. This simple technique minimizes the tendency to get caught up in the crisis of the day without making progress on what is important.

If we continue with our example of focusing on retention as an important goal, examples of your SMART goal for the week might be:

- I will ask a star performer to facilitate this week's staff meeting and conduct an after-action review with her.
- I will complete the performance review of Lee Jones by this Friday.

Prioritize your to-do list every morning (Monday through Friday—three minutes)

When you walk into your office Tuesday through Friday, the first task (but third on Mondays) is to prioritize the day's to-do list. I recommend using the ABCD designation:

A = Important and urgent (a critical report your boss needs today)

B = Important but not urgent (a critical report your boss needs by the end of next week)

C = Urgent but not important (a colleague's urgent voicemail begging you to attend a last-minute meeting...of the annual picnic committee)

D = Not urgent and not important (a colleague's voicemail inviting you to attend next month's meeting...of the picnic committee, if you have time)

To decide whether a task is important, answer this question: Does it lead you down the path displayed by your GPS? In other words, is the task related to your boss's or your unit's strategic priorities?

To decide whether a task is urgent, consider this question: Is it highly time-sensitive? A task is urgent if it is pressing from a time perspective.

Labeling a to-do list this way forces you to recognize *every day* that there are critical distinctions among your tasks. Consider the difference between As and Cs. Do you ever confuse the important with the urgent?

For example, a mid-level IT manager at the Federal Reserve Bank announced in class that all of his internal customers were important. I asked him if he had any Chicken Little internal customers, who are always running around saying that the sky is falling if his IT support people didn't call back immediately. He answered yes.

I then asked him if these Chicken Little requests should be treated the same as the needs of internal customers working on his boss's critical project. He shook his head no. In fact, the entire class agreed that some of their internal customers were more important than others. If every demand is important, none is strategic.

The failure to distinguish between As and Cs also rears its ugly head when we arrive at work early, find ourselves staring at a long to-do list or full e-mail in-box, and then decide to tackle a number of urgent items just to get them off the list or clear out our in-box. A half-hour later, we've crossed six items off our list, but haven't done anything important. We have confused activity with accomplishment.

Effective executives who execute with passion and courage are not seduced by checking things off a long to-do list. In fact, they seldom look at a long list.

Effective executives stay focused on important tasks by creating a daily to-do list from their long to-do list. They then label each task on their daily to-do list A, B, C, or D. They seldom look at that long list. Mack, a mid-level executive who learned this approach in class, told me later that labeling his daily to-do list has significantly increased his effectiveness and dramatically decreased his stress.

Time is not money; results are money.

Block out time to work on your B priorities every day (Monday through Friday—one minute)

I met with a CEO a few weeks ago who reported that an action we agreed he should take was on his "to do" list. I told him I'd be happier when I saw it on is calendar.

Once you know your ABCs, you must find at least one hour/day of uninterrupted time to focus on a B priority. Block out this time on your calendar. It is critical to work on your Bs before they become As—otherwise, they become emergencies (another name for As).

It is much more expensive in terms of time, money, and stress — not to mention quality — to work in emergency mode. That's one of the main reasons you need to block out time every day to make progress on your B priorities.

It is often difficult to find time to work on Bs, as opposed to As and Cs, because the urgent nature of As and Cs cause them to act upon us. Conversely, we need to "be proactive," as Stephen Covey says, if we want to make progress on Bs. Covey places B tasks — those tasks that are important but not urgent — in Quadrant II, which he calls the Leadership Quadrant.

If you need to convince yourself of the importance of uninterrupted time, think about this: Have you ever lost track of time as you were working on an important project? You've done that, right? Of course — we all have. You had the mental momentum of a snowball rolling downhill.

Now contrast that with a time you were trying to make progress on an important task but were constantly interrupted by instant messages, e-mails, phone calls, or co-workers stopping by to chat. Every time an interruption ended, you asked the exact same question as you restarted the task:

Where was I?

You then had to backtrack, review what you had previously accomplished, and try to get back in the flow again. Intuitively, you already understand that it takes more effort to get going than keep going.

How much does each interruption actually costs? Researchers at Microsoft were surprised to discover that it took 15 minutes for employees interrupted by an e-mail to return to the suspended task because of the tendency to wander off and browse the Internet or reply to other messages. Professional workers spend 28% of their time handling these interruptions, at a staggering cost of $650 billion per year in the American economy alone.[2]

Effective executives do first things first
and they do one thing at a time.

PETER DRUCKER[3]

Speaking of interruptions, remember the HP researchers (in Chapter 8) who found that the IQ scores of multitaskers dropped 10 points?

In fact, neuroscientists tell us that there really is no such thing as multitasking. When you attempt to multitask, what you are doing, actually, is moving from one task to another rapidly, says Rene Marois, a neuroscientist and director of the Human Information Processing Laboratory at

Vanderbilt University.[4] You are not doing multiple things at the same time; you are doing multiple things in rapid succession.

And you are usually doing them poorly.

Of course, not all tasks have the same degree of complexity. You can talk on the phone with friends while cleaning dishes or folding laundry without either task suffering. However, if you try to watch television and listen to your spouse at the same time, you probably have discovered that you do neither well.

This illusion of multitasking applies not only to daily activities, but also to the number of projects or major priorities employees can handle. In a study of executive recruiters, researchers at MIT, New York University, and Boston University concluded that the optimum workload was four to six projects that lasted between two and five months each.

Manage your energy—not just your time—every day

The problem with most time-management advice is that it only helps you maintain your schedule. It seldom helps you maximize your energy. It's like planning a trip using your GPS without paying attention to how much gas you need to get where you're going.

Imagine an athlete who routinely shows up for games tired, hungry, or thirsty, and then proceeds to play the entire game without any time-outs. What kind of performance would you expect? How well would that athlete perform under pressure? What might be the impact of this dysfunctional behavior on the athlete's career and team?

If you and your team fail to maintain your energy throughout the day, you are running the race without the energy reserves needed to hurdle those daily obstacles. Over time, you will experience a drop in productivity, morale, and employee retention.[5]

If you want to execute with passion and courage, you need to manage your schedule and yourself by maintaining your energy. This requires that you replenish your mind and body throughout the day. Listed below are several practical tips to help you "mind your mind" and "nourish your body" so that you have the energy to meet the challenges of your day.

Finally, brothers, whatever things are true, whatever things are honest,
whatever things are just, whatever things are pure,
whatever things are lovely, whatever things are of good report;
if there be any virtue, and if there be any praise, think on these things.

PHILIPPIANS 4:8

Step 1. Mind your mind: Have you ever seen a star athlete conduct himself poorly off the playing field and then apologize to his teammates for being a distraction? Why? Because athletes understand their negative behavior may cause their teammates to take their eye off the ball — to lose focus. Athletes know how important concentration and mindfulness is to execution. They realize that there is a strong mind-body connection. (Reflect on a recent dream or nightmare you had to convince yourself of the impact your mind has on your physiology.)

The editors of *Investor's Business Daily* (*IBD*) have spent years analyzing leaders in all walks of life. They report that the number-one trait responsible for turning dreams into reality is how leaders think. Be positive, think success, and avoid negative environments is how *IBD* describes minding the mind.[6]

In his study of 500 industrial leaders such as Henry Ford, Thomas Edison, and Harvey Firestone, Napoleon Hill discovered that a positive mental attitude was critical to success.[7] Executives who execute with passion and courage seldom focus on what they do not want. Like athletes, they maintain their energy by placing their *attention* on their *intention.* They engage in a number of daily, mindful behaviors that keep them focused on what they do want.

Do not conform any longer to the pattern of this world,
but be transformed by the renewing of your mind.

Romans 12:2

Here are some tactics that will help you keep your mind focused and renewed. Pick a few that will work for you.

- Review your values and big-picture goals daily: Your values and goals set your rudder for the day. Keep the big picture in mind to take the sting out of those little pinpricks we all experience every day.
- Make positive connections: The people who surround you influence how you think. Spend time with those who tell you the truth and lift you up. They are the ones who leave you thinking, *I like me when I'm around them.* Select your friends and social media connections carefully. Limit the time you spend with people who are optimistically challenged (what some call "negaholics").
- Keep learning: Successful leaders are lifelong learners. They take courses, read books, subscribe to their customers' magazines, join

professional associations, and ask lots of questions. Your customers, products, and environment are constantly changing. Spend an hour a day soaking up new information to stay current and positive. Father Anthony deMello, a Jesuit priest, writes, "The one thing you need most of all is the readiness to learn something new."[8] Stay motivated by being open to most things, attached to few.

- Tell stories: At one executive retreat, the CEO kicked off the meeting by reading a two-minute motivational story. I encourage you to occasionally start your meetings (and perhaps dinner at home) by reading a humorous or uplifting story.
- Be thankful: Several years ago, I woke up in my hotel room in Anchorage, Alaska, feeling exhausted and emotionally drained from traveling and teaching all week. I decided to go for a short, early morning jog before my last Friday class in an effort to recharge my batteries. Within minutes of leaving the hotel, I found myself jogging alongside a cemetery. As I passed row upon row of tombstones, I realized that everyone buried in that cemetery was dead. I was not. It was, in fact, another fine day on the planet. I had much to be thankful for. So do you. Make a list of things you are thankful for. Whenever you are feeling negative, count your blessings... or tombstones in a cemetery.
- Listen to uplifting audio programs in your car: The average commute in the United States is approximately 20 minutes each way, which translates to 10,000 minutes (167 hours) of commute time every year. Are you spending or investing your commute time? Investments go up in value over time. Don't let those grains of time slip through your hourglass. Review the high-quality audio programs available at sites such as www.thegreatcourses.com. Invest in yourself during a portion of your commute time.
- Write positive affirmations: Write an affirmation or quote on a 3"x 5" index card. Keep it with you and read it throughout the day.
- Turn off the TV earlier: Read an uplifting book for at least a few minutes before you go to sleep. You want to have something other than the nightly news dancing around your brain all night.

- MEDITATE DAILY: At a recent coaching session, I told an executive named Mitch that his team and colleagues were unhappy with his inconsistent emotional intelligence. He needed to even out his highs and lows. Those around him, I said, were always trying to find the best time to approach him. "Is he in a good mood or bad mood?" was the silent question that echoed in halls surrounding his office. My feedback was not well received — but not for the reason you might think. On that day, I had back-to-back-to-back meetings and didn't take time to meditate or catch my breath before meeting Mitch. Because I was not grounded when I delivered the difficult news to him, I presented the message in a way he couldn't hear it. This is a major sin for an executive coach. I am convinced I could have avoided this poor feedback incident had I engaged in my normal practice of meditating at least 20 minutes a day, which I've done for the last 35 years.

Before you object and say you don't have time to meditate daily, meditate on this: Bill George, former CEO of Medtronic, and Bob Shapiro, former CEO of Monsanto, meditated regularly throughout their very successful careers. They knew that taking a short break every day allowed them to recharge their batteries and increase their effectiveness and efficiency. They managed their energy, not just their time. Table 17.1 is a summary of the numerous benefits of meditation, according to researchers at the University of Redlands.[9]

TABLE 17.1
Why Meditate?

Meditation enhances brain functioning:

- Increases activity in left pre-frontal cortex (seat of positive emotions, happiness)
- Decreases activity in right pre-frontal cortex (seat of negative emotions, anxiety)
- Produces high amplitude gamma wave synchrony (expanded awareness, alertness, insight)
- Improves learning and intellectual capacities

Meditation enhances psychological functioning:

- Increases production of endorphins
- Decreases stress hormones (cortisol, adrenalin)
- Eases post-trauma symptoms among military veterans
- Reduces aggression, hostility, and recidivism among prisoners
- Alleviates depression
- Helps in treatment of eating disorders
- Helps in obsessive-compulsive disorders
- Contributes to overall sense of happiness (e.g., gratitude meditations and journaling)

Meditation enhances physical health:

- Helps in dealing with chronic pain
- Helps in weight loss and fitness
- Helps in alleviating heart problems

Meditation enhances work performance:

- Less absenteeism
- Greater cooperation and collaboration
- More focused attention on tasks with increased effectiveness
- Increased job satisfaction

My life has been filled with terrible misfortune,
most of which never happened.

MICHEL DE MONTAIGNE

STEP 2. NOURISH YOUR BODY: Trying to execute without maintaining a healthy body is like a truck driver pulling his rig with a dilapidated cab that won't shift out of the lower gears. If your mind is willing, but your body is weak, you'll find yourself falling short of your destination. Legendary football coach Vince Lombardi was right when he declared that fatigue makes cowards of us all. Here are several ideas to keep your motor running throughout the day:

- **Exercise regularly:** A little daily exercise will do wonders for your attitude and weight. You don't have to become an Olympian. Top performers stay fit by doing something aerobic regularly, even if it's a quick power walk. One mile burns about 125 calories, whether you walk it in 20 minutes or run it in ten. There are 3,500 calories in one pound. Thus, if you walk one mile a day (at lunch) for 28 days, you lose one pound. A mile a day melts the pounds away and keeps you refreshed throughout the day.
- **Sleep well:** What happens to you if you only get five hours of sleep? Patti Milligan, director of nutrition at Tignum, summarized a sleep study that measured the effects of five hours of sleep per night for seven days on blood-glucose metabolism in healthy men.[10] Results showed that during the one-week study, metabolic changes occurred consistent with increased insulin resistance. Insulin resistance is associated with increased risk of diabetes, cognitive decline, joint deterioration, and other degenerative diseases. Milligan also pointed out that there's evidence that among those who suffer from impaired glucose metabolism, lifespan is reduced by eight to ten years. What happens if you only deprive yourself of sleep once in a while? Milligan cites studies demonstrating that healthy individuals deprived of a single night's sleep have a 30% drop in their immune system activity, while the emotional centers of the brain become 60% more reactive in those who extend their sleep deprivation to 36 hours.
- **Eat right:** A few weeks ago, my cycling buddy Jim and I were sweating our way up the Santa Monica Mountains in Malibu. As we reached the top of the 6.7-mile (8% grade) mountain road, Jim asked if I wanted to bike down the opposite side of the mountain and come up another canyon road. He wanted to do what we called a double. I said sure. We had done hundreds of doubles together. Unfortunately, on the second half of the climb on that second mountain, I bonked — an abrupt drop in energy. The stress of the second mountain depleted me of fuel needed to do the work, and I was unable to perform well. As I struggled up the mountain, I realized why this climb was so different from the many others Jim and I had undertaken. This was a very rare spontaneous double — I had not planned to bike for three hours in the mountains. Therefore, I didn't eat or drink properly in preparation. When I finally reached Jim, who was waiting for me at the top, I asked him if he had prepared for a double. "I

always prepare for a double, Dave." We laughed all the way down the mountain about my lesson—we perform only as well as we eat.

The stress of today's work environment requires that we all prepare for a double every day. Make sure you have the fuel in your body to avoid the leader's bonk. Here are a few additional tips to help you execute with passion and courage by managing your energy:

- Keep your blood sugar levels steady: It is nearly impossible to execute consistently if you experience a drop in your energy during the day. Most of these low-energy dips are the result of a decrease in blood glucose. To keep your energy up, experts[11] recommend that you eat:
  - Several small meals instead of three supersized meals
  - Strategic snacks (nuts, seeds, energy bars) instead of junk food
  - Complex carbohydrates (whole grains, fruits, vegetables) instead of simple carbohydrates (white flours, cakes, sweets)
  - Protein foods (fish, eggs, yogurt, beans) in combination with your complex carbohydrates

Also, eat slowly and mindfully. It takes 20 minutes for your digestive system to detect that you are eating. If you eat too fast, you'll eat too much before realizing you are full.

- Maintain adequate hydration throughout the day: Drink several glasses of water a day. Avoid drinking too many beverages that have a diuretic effect, such as alcohol and caffeine. The best way to assess whether you are well hydrated is to not e the color of your urine. If your urine is colorless or slightly yellow, you're adequately hydrated.
- Forget about dieting: If you go *on* a diet, you'll go *off* it. The first three letters of the word "diet" tell you all you need to know. Instead, modify your eating habits and follow the recommendations as outlined here. Stay current on the latest health developments by reading *The UC Berkeley Wellness Newsletter* (www.wellnessletter.com) or *WebMD.com.*

Adapt—don't adopt—these steps to your system

The director of communications for a large healthcare firm told me that he did not want to incorporate a self-management module in the leadership class I was customizing for his team. When asked why, he said that the last time-management course his executives attended was not received well because the facilitator pushed his company's products (personal digital assistants, software, calendars) as the key to implementing the ideas presented.

My philosophy, I assured him, was the exact opposite. This last step in my six-step process of daily execution is all about taking what he and his team learned from me and combining it with what they were currently doing.

This last step invites you to adapt these self-management principles to your current approach to time management. When you combine old habits (your current practices) with new tools (the self-management tactics you want to try from this chapter), implementation is much easier.

For example, I have had executives schedule a recurring appointment in Microsoft Outlook that reminds them to use a few of these ideas. Another executive told me that he spent the first few minutes every morning writing and prioritizing a short to-do list on paper, which he keeps in the center of his desk. A third leader e-mailed me that she now starts her team meetings with the team's quarterly goals to keep her team focused on A and B priorities.

You cannot manage time — but you can manage yourself. If you want to execute with more passion and courage, I encourage you to adapt this six-step process to do just that.

Make progress on your priorities

Leaders, at all levels of the organization, march boldly in the direction of their dreams by making progress on their priorities. At higher levels of leadership, the creation and execution of the organization's strategic plan are the priority. Unfortunately, the failure to translate a strategic plan into desired outcomes is an epidemic in most organizations. According to a survey of 1,526 global executives by the American Management Association (AMA),[12] only 3% of respondents said their companies are "very successful" at strategic implementation.

In this same report, the AMA reported that an analysis of 197 global companies by researchers at Marakon Associates found that those failing to bridge this strategy-to-performance gap realized only 63% of their strategy's potential value.

Take the assessment in Table 17.2 to identify your organization's strengths and weaknesses in implementing strategy; then, we'll discuss how you can execute your strategic plan.

TABLE 17.2

The Strategy Implementation Assessment

Use this 1 to 5 scale as a guide in answering ten questions.

Never or to a Very Small Extent	To a Small Extent	To a Moderate Extent	To a Large Extent	Always or to a Very Great Extent
1	2	3	4	5

To what extent does my organization:

1. Create a focused strategy with SMART goals while minimizing conflicting priorities?
2. Develop strategic action plans with specific resources and accountabilities clearly defined?
3. Ensure senior leaders are engaged visibly and fully throughout strategic implementation?
4. Empower first-line supervisors and middle managers to do what it takes to execute strategy?
5. Update performance goals for individuals and units to support strategic implementation?
6. Frequently use a variety of two-way communication tools to explain and evaluate execution?
7. Implement an adaptive organizational structure that facilitates cross-functional collaboration?
8. Align performance measures, incentives, and consequences to strategic implementation?
9. Build new workforce competencies to support the strategic implementation requirements?
10. Fill the talent pipeline by assessing, training, and recruiting leaders capable of execution?

Add scores to determine your assessment results:

40–50 = High likelihood of successfully implementing strategy

30–39 = Moderate likelihood of successfully implementing strategy

20–29 = Low likelihood of successfully implementing strategy

Scores less than 20 = The strategic plan is gathering dust on the shelf.

How well did you do on this assessment? Buddha taught that the first step of change is to wake up—to increase our awareness of what is. Now that you are aware of the ten keys to strategic implementation (that's really what the assessment is), you can do something about it.[13] Share the Strategy Implementation Assessment with your team members. Invite each of them to take the assessment individually and then discuss the implications collectively.

During these discussions, identify those statements that received the lowest scores and brainstorm tactics to address them. Because the ten statements in the assessment are also the keys for successful implementation, you can use the low-scoring statements as a springboard for your conversations. For example, if statement number 5 received a low score, brainstorm possible approaches to update performance goals to support strategic implementation. Lead a discussion about how to make progress on your priorities.

What is to give light must endure burning.

VIKTOR FRANKL

HOW TO TAKE CALCULATED RISKS

The heat is greatest at the tip of a rocket. When executives choose to be out front, they will take heat. Enron didn't fail just because of a few greedy executives at the top; it also failed because numerous leaders throughout the organization were afraid to speak up. They didn't want to feel the heat if they questioned their dysfunctional culture.

Executives who execute with passion and courage, on the other hand, are not afraid to take a stand on important issues. They'll take the heat— but only after calculating risks. Consider the sales manager who refuses to sell outdated products, the accountant who writes the memo about the "irregularities" she sees on the books, the supervisor who challenges his boss with difficult questions, the researcher who publishes a paper contradicting her co-worker's findings, or the manager who holds his team members accountable for their performance (unlike Greg, the executive in this chapter's opening story).

These acts of everyday courage illustrate what it means to execute with passion and courage by taking calculated risks.

Professor Kathleen Reardon of the University of Southern California discovered that the heart of courage in organizations is risk calculation when she interviewed more than 200 courageous leaders.[14] Risk calculation is different from the courage we see when firefighters rush into burning buildings or a neighbor leaps into a raging river to save a drowning child. Reardon showed that extraordinary business leaders execute bold moves by assessing and ameliorating risk using a six-step decision-making methodology:

1. Clarify goals.
2. Evaluate goal importance.
3. Build support.
4. Weigh the risks and benefits.
5. Select the right time.
6. Develop contingency plans.

Clarify goals

When you're considering a risky situation, answer these questions:

- What do I hope to achieve realistically?
- What will success in this scenario look like?
- What is my ideal outcome?

I once coached an executive who was distraught that one of his colleagues, Chris, might be fired. He felt the CEO was acting on false information about Chris. When I asked him what he hoped to achieve, realistically, he realized he needed a better understanding of Chris's performance from other perspectives before talking to the CEO.

In our follow-up conversations, he told me that his colleagues had information about Chris's poor performance that he did not have. Furthermore, once he asked questions about his own motives, he realized that rescuing others had been a pattern all his life, probably due to alcoholism in his family. Although he thought "saving" others was always altruistic, he now knew that it was often self-serving—and at times risky.

Evaluate goal importance

Do you know people who always speak up in opposition regardless of the issue? They fail to pick their battles carefully. They do not consider the value of the goal when deciding to present a contrary, and perhaps risky, point of view. They fail to ask the fundamental questions:

- How important is this issue?
- If no one says or does anything, who might get hurt?

Many executives find it helpful to categorize issues according to importance when they are deciding if they should speak up. Use these levels to help pick your battles:

- Of the lowest level of importance are issues that you don't feel strongly about, although you may have a preference regarding the outcome.
- On the second level are issues that you feel strongly about, even though they don't involve core values.

- The third level Reardon calls "spear in the sand" issues: You feel strongly about them and they involve values worth fighting for.

Build support

Everybody loves the solitary hero who takes risks. Hollywood sells us Spider-Man, Iron Man, and Wonder Woman. We place business leaders like Jack Welch, Steve Jobs, and Oprah high on their pedestals. But in reality, leaders who take risks successfully are not out there by themselves; they build support among their constituencies.

In the early 1980s, our research team at UC San Diego Medical Center used a method for calculating the heart's blood volume developed at UCSD by our cardiology colleagues. One late night in the laboratory, I observed great variations in blood volumes from the same patients. During the next several weeks, I confirmed my initial observations: The technique for calculating blood volumes, invented by people I was working with, was unreliable.

Before presenting this data to the director of our lab, I shared the information with a few of my trusted team members in one-on-one, confidential conversations. I asked their opinions regarding the data, our techniques, and biological variability. It was soon clear to us that the technique developed and published by our colleagues did not work. I then took our data to Vic, my boss—the director of our research project. He arranged for us to present our findings in front of the entire cardiology department, including those who had published reports that the technique did work.

My presentation went well because I minimized my risk by building support. (The primary investigator who developed this technique refused to visit our laboratory despite numerous invitations before my presentation.) Eventually, we published our findings in a peer-reviewed journal that refuted our colleagues' earlier work.[15]

Weigh the risks and benefits of different approaches

The fourth step in taking calculated risks involves trade-offs.

- Who stands to win?
- Who stands to lose?
- What are the pros and cons of the alternatives?
- What is the probability that your actions will affect a solution or your possible promotion?

Imagine that you are a mid-level sales manager for a $100 million manufacturer. During one of your all-hands meetings at a trade show, the vice president of engineering announces a forthcoming software release. One of your top salespeople asks to talk to you privately after the announcement. She is upset about a particular feature that will be included as part of this software release. She tells you that the manner in which they are going to display pictures will be very unpopular with customers.

You know that this young, bright salesperson knows what she is talking about because, before joining your team, she spent years working with experts at MIT on how to display these pictures. Unfortunately, you also understand that in your very hierarchical, silo-oriented company, the engineers do not like being told how to do their job. In addition, the senior leadership in your company does not take kindly to salespeople "interfering" with product development.

So, what would you do if you were the sales manager? In this true story, the sales manager told the saleswoman that it was too risky because her suggestions would fall on deaf ears. The company released the software, customers rejected it, and sales went into a tailspin.

Did the saleswoman and her manager do the right thing? Probably not. Because the sales manager did not weigh the risks and the benefits of various options, he did not take the appropriate risks—he failed to execute with passion and courage. A normally well-rounded leader became a lopsided leader under pressure. He and his sales colleague could have quietly surveyed their customers regarding display preferences. Maybe a few other salespeople would have agreed to survey their customers. Armed with data, the manager could have called one of his friends in engineering or marketing and asked how to best disseminate the findings. Remember—measurement minimizes argument. Had they considered the pros and cons of the various alternatives, they might have executed with more passion and courage.

Select the right time

Risky decisions have unique gestation periods. Some situations demand quick thinking and action. Other times, the prudent path is deliberate and thoughtful calculation. Answer questions such as:

- What are the pluses and minuses of taking my time?
- Am I emotionally prepared to take this risk now?
- Can I take a few small steps now that would lead to courageous action later?

Develop contingency plans

Let's say that one of your key customers calls, warning you that he has not been happy with your company's service lately. You think about asking Shannon, one of your star managers, to meet with the customer (who is also a manager) and handle the situation. After all, he is Shannon's customer. You wonder if Shannon is up to the task, and whether the customer will be upset that he's not dealing with you, a higher-level executive. It's a bit risky to give it to Shannon. What would you do?

When this situation arose with a leader I was coaching, I encouraged the leader to coach Shannon to handle a face-to-face meeting with the customer. When the executive stated it was too risky, I asked him about possible backup plans if the meeting started to move in an undesirable direction. He discussed his concerns with Shannon, and then they brainstormed options.

They decided that they both should attend the meeting, although Shannon would lead it. They also determined that the executive could intervene if the meeting started veering in the wrong direction. Their contingency plans included the executive asking more questions, calling for a break, or gently taking over the meeting.

In a follow-up coaching call, the executive told me that the meeting went well because he and Shannon developed contingency plans that enabled them to take a calculated risk—coaching one of his high-performers to handle a strategic customer's difficult issue.

The Famous Father Who Took a Big Risk

By 1786, George Washington was convinced that the United States was reeling toward disunion. Congress failed to retaliate when the British did not give over their outposts in the Northwest Territories to the United States, as mandated by the terms of the peace treaty. Foreign powers refused to allow American ships in the ports of the West Indies. Neither local governments nor America's national government was able to cope when the people of western Massachusetts broke out in rebellion. To save the union (again), George Washington pondered a great risk.

Washington understood that eight years of bloody battles, ending with the liberation of America from the mighty British Empire, had cemented his untarnished reputation and high honor in history. He felt that if he now associated himself with a feeble government that proved unworthy or incapable of sustaining independence, his reputation would be hammered into oblivion.

As Washington calculated this risk, he clarified the importance of the goal, contemplated the support of the nation, and weighed the risks and benefits of taking action. He understood that it was time to act and that his only contingency plan, should he fail, would be to limp home to his Mount Vernon plantation.

In the end, Washington concluded "the good of my country requires my reputation to be put at risk."[16] He marched off to Philadelphia (Washington, DC had yet to be built) at the invitation of Congress, which promptly and unanimously voted him the first president of the United States. Washington's calculated risk saved our fledgling democracy. It is one of the reasons presidential scholars continue to assign Washington the highest leadership scores of any president in America's history and refer to him as the father of the country.

How to confront difficult issues

Harry Stonecipher, former CEO of Boeing, interrupted my executive retreat at the Boeing Leadership Center several years ago. He said he needed to talk with his executives about difficult issues. The essence of his message was that these senior executives needed to communicate more directly when dealing with difficult issues such as layoffs, budget allocations, succession planning, and conflict. He reminded them that organizations pay high-level executives to tackle thorny problems—not to worry about being liked or criticized. He concluded by urging them to lead with courage, candor, and conviction.

To execute with passion and courage, commanding leaders not only manage themselves and take calculated risks, they deal directly with difficult issues and conflict.

Carol Bartz, former CEO of Yahoo, would agree with Harry Stonecipher. She tells the story of a friend who needed to take a six-month assignment far from home.[17] Unfortunately, her friend had an old, ailing dog that could not go with her. Other friends recommended that she board the dying animal at great expense. Carol told her kindly that putting the animal to sleep was better than putting the sick dog in a strange environment for six months. Carol's friend was furious at her suggestion and chose to board the dog. Six months later, she returned home to find the dog at death's door, and she put the animal to sleep. Soon thereafter, the friend thanked Carol for being the only one who cared enough to confront her with the truth.

How well do you deal with difficult issues and confront others with the truth? Here are several tips to help you and your team handle these situations well, and consistently:

1. Identify your "spear in the sand" issues.
2. Use your tombstone as a stepping-stone.
3. Start small.
4. Involve others.
5. Respond promptly.
6. Communicate the what, why, and how.
7. Confront the right conflict.

Identify your "spear in the sand" issues

To stand up for what you believe, you must be clear about what you believe. Write answers to these questions:

- What is most important to me?
- What are my highest values and ideals?
- What is worth fighting for?

Use your tombstone as a stepping-stone

Your legacy is not a name on a building or street. A lasting legacy echoes through time with the actions of others who have been inspired by your ideas and behaviors. I encourage you to write your own obituary to gain clarity on what you want people to think, say, and do because of your time on this planet.

Your life is the dash between two dates on your tombstone. That dash is made up of thousands of dots, representing how you choose to live your life every day. Understanding that your life is a brief dash between birth and death puts values and difficult issues in perspective. Use this view to access the courage needed when your convictions are tested.

Start small

If you shrink from standing tall on difficult issues, practice in small, safe environments first. Speak up when friends are having a political debate. Challenge someone who cuts in line. Disagree with colleagues at a meeting without being disagreeable. State your opinion without apology.

Involve others

If you need to make a tough decision, invite others to the table after you have gathered data, analyzed the alternatives, and selected a few options.

Ask your direct reports, peers, boss, and perhaps even your customers for their perspectives. You gain the benefit of their counsel and a greater probability that they will support your final decision.

Respond promptly

Notice I didn't say to react promptly. The difference between a reaction and a response is reflection. Leaders who react promptly communicate that issues control them. Leaders who *respond* promptly communicate that they understand that there is an issue, and that they are reflecting on the best course of action.

Communicate the what, why, and how

After you make a difficult decision, make sure others know why and how you made the decision. The *why* behind any decision is the steam — the MOTORvation — behind *what* needs to be done. People will be fired up to follow through if they understand why you chose a particular course of action. The *how* shows the process you went through in making the decision. Remember, if people don't believe in the process, they won't commit to the outcome of the process.

Confront the right conflict

Harry Stonecipher struck me as a leader who was willing to tackle any conflict head-on. How about you? Do you always address conflicts directly? When should you avoid it? How can you use conflict to achieve positive outcomes? The next section answers these questions as it describes how to put conflict to work for you.

Does your conflict hurt or help?

Randy was under pressure as the product manager for a medical supply company. His team needed to design and deliver a new bedside monitor within 12 months. Unfortunately, his design team felt that the marketing group hadn't provided adequate information to design the monitor. His manufacturing colleagues were angry that his design team was taking too long to select lead wires. Project meetings, which often began with minor disagreements about specifications, usually degenerated into personal attacks.

Three months into the project, Randy knew his project and reputation were in trouble.

"The absence of conflict is not harmony, it's apathy."[18] Managing conflict well begins by understanding that the word "conflict" derives from the Latin *conflictus* — a striking together. Thus, when two people have a conflict, they can chose to strike each other by butting heads like a couple of rams on a mountain, or they can strike the source of the conflict together, like two basketball players double-teaming the opposing team's high scorer.

The problem with Randy's team wasn't that they had conflict; rather, it was that they didn't distinguish hurtful from helpful conflict—emotional from cognitive conflict.

Emotional conflict involves personal friction, clashing styles, or relationships problems. It focuses on personalities and therefore hurts decision-making and decreases a team's willingness to collaborate. You've seen this type of conflict at home and at work, haven't you? It's not very productive, is it?

Cognitive conflict, on the other hand, arises when there are disagreements about tasks and issues. Cognitive conflict focuses on what needs to get done to move things forward. When team members feel free to express differences openly and challenge each other's assumptions, they identify flawed thinking, flag weaknesses, and contribute creative ideas. This is why cognitive conflict facilitates decision-making and goal achievement.

In summarizing ten years of research on "how management teams can have a good fight," Professor Kathleen Eisenhardt reports that the most successful companies use six tactics for discouraging emotional conflict while encouraging cognitive conflict.[19]

- Gather data and focus on the facts.
- Brainstorm alternatives to enrich dialogue and debate.
- Discuss, agree on, and share common goals.
- Inject humor in decision-making.
- Maintain a balance of power.
- Resolve issues without forcing consensus.

Gather data and focus on the facts

Years ago, as 15-time All-Star Shaquille O'Neal stepped to the free-throw line in overtime, the announcers said, "Although Shaq is only a 50% lifetime free-throw shooter, he usually makes them when it counts." I turned to my wife and complained, "These announcers always say that." But I had never heard any of them cite statistics regarding his free-throw shooting percentage in the final minutes of games.

Have you seen variations of this theme at work? Leaders who argue positions without facts make a lot of noise, but seldom bring substance to issues.

An empty barrel makes the most noise.

PROVERB

Professor Eisenhardt points out that at one high-tech company, the top management team examines a wide variety of operating measures on a monthly, weekly, and daily basis. For example, every week they focus on bookings, backlogs, margins, engineering milestones, cash, scrap, and work in process. Armed with facts, conflicts are data-driven instead of personality clashes.

If you want to minimize emotional conflict, gather and discuss data.

Brainstorm alternatives to enrich dialogue and debate

Executives often tell me that they want their teams to make a decision and move on. This can be a mistake if it forces team members to make quick black-and-white choices that ignore the paradoxes of leadership, with little room to shift positions or engage in cognitive conflict.

When you're dealing with strategic issues, you might instead want to require multiple alternatives. Consider the electronics company that faced a cash-flow crisis caused by explosive growth. The CEO assigned a team of executives to look at numerous alternative solutions. The team explored a buffet of options such as extending the company's line of credit, selling stock, outsourcing, and strategic partnering.

Generating several options actually energized these executives and led to creative discussions about how to combine elements of each, which is what they eventually did. Commitment to executing their plan was much higher because they discussed and considered numerous alternatives.

Discuss, agree on, and share common goals

A project manager at CDG, a Boeing subsidiary, complained during a training class that his team had too many emotional debates during project meetings. I suggested that he insert the project goal as a header on all his project documents, including meeting agendas and minutes. I also encouraged him to start each meeting by stating the overall goal of the project. If team members started to become emotional, I suggested that he remind them of the project's goal and then ask them to focus on facts and the task at hand.

People marching in the same direction seldom point fingers at each other.

Inject humor in decision-making

Humor is the shock absorber of conflict. As you and your team travel down the bumpy road of work, your ride will be smoother if you use humor. Teams that handle conflict well relieve the tension of work with the joy of laughter. Notice that I said humor helps handle — not avoid — conflict. I once conducted a retreat with a group of executives who laughed a lot. During the retreat, however, it became clear to them that their over-the-top humor was actually hurting their efforts to productively and proactively deal with difficult issues.

To use humor to manage conflict instead of masking it, one computer manufacturer starts its meetings with jokes and encourages employees to dress up for every conceivable holiday, from April Fool's Day to Halloween. The executives at this company point out that their attempts to act like humor beings, rather than human beings, may seem silly. Yet they have found it creates an environment that minimizes emotional conflict, promotes cognitive conflict, and relieves stress. (These executives contend that it is difficult to have an emotional argument with someone who has a fake arrow sticking through his head.)

Interestingly, science says having a sense of humor is more important than laughing. Researchers in Norway surveyed 54,000 people to gauge how easily they found humor in real-life situations and enjoyed being with those who had a sense of humor. They defined a sense of humor as "a particular playful perspective on everyday life."[20] Seven years later, those who scored in the top quarter for humor appreciation were 35% more likely to be living than those in the bottom quarter. Participants who had a cancer diagnosis at the beginning of the study were 75% more likely to be alive if they scored higher in the "appreciation of humor" group. If you want to cushion your team from the emotional bumps of conflict, invite them to dream up ways to make their work more playFULL.

Maintain a balance of power

My first leader at Holiday Ridge Day Camp was Larry — a laissez faire, hands-off counselor. Our team was disorganized and late to events; we performed poorly when we got there and argued among ourselves a lot. On the other end of the spectrum were groups led by autocratic leaders like Joel. I stayed away from those kids because they were hostile during games and bullied others in the camp's many shadows.

At the tender age of ten, I realized that the best leaders were like another camp counselor, Rusty. He was organized, positive, disciplined, and involved his kids in decision-making. Although they didn't always win the games, Rusty's teams always seemed to have the most fun. I had discovered that the best counselors balanced power.

What was true at Holiday Ridge many years ago is true for you today. If you want to minimize emotional conflict, you need to manage the tension between being too controlling (like Joel) and too hands-off (like Larry). To be more like Rusty, evaluate your decision-making process by surveying your team members. Ask them how engaged they are with team decisions. If they feel engaged and perceive that your process is fair, they'll support your decisions and execute well. If they feel the process is not fair, they may subtly and subconsciously sabotage implementation.

A fair decision-making process includes:

- Defined roles, responsibilities, and authority
- Written norms for decision-making
- Opportunities for genuine input before the boss's biases are aired

Resolve issues without forcing consensus

On New Year's Day in 1777, General Charles Cornwallis arrived at the British camp in Princeton, New Jersey. He was not a happy camper. George Washington's army had turned the tide of the American Revolution by crossing the Delaware River and attacking British troops on Christmas. Cornwallis called a meeting of his generals "not to ask what should be done as Washington did, but to tell his subordinates what he meant to do."[21]

Therein lies the difference between the men's methods of resolving issues. Cornwallis made all the major decisions by himself and rejected contrary advice from his officers. Washington had an improvisational and inclusive approach to command. He met frequently with his generals and encouraged the free exchange of views. He created a community of inclusion without forcing consensus. Washington's style worked well with America's less stratified society and ideas of liberty and freedom. It led to skillful collaboration and minimized emotional conflict.

It will do the same for you with today's diverse workforce.

Of course, having too much input from too many people can bog down decision-making process and create emotional conflict. The most effective leaders, like Washington, resolve difficult conflict by first discussing the issue and trying to reach consensus with others. If they succeed, the decision is settled. If they don't reach consensus, these effective leaders make the decision with input—but no consensus—from the group.

Have a good fight

At a meeting in San Francisco, the leader of a not-for-profit organization was encouraging her managers to define the norms for their team meetings. One manager suggested that one norm be "to make sure that our meetings minimize conflict." I explained the difference between emotional and cognitive conflict, and then encouraged them to create norms that minimized emotional conflict but would allow for cognitive conflict. Here are a few ideas we discussed that you can adapt:

- Encourage diversity: A single point of view is no way to see the world. I asked the group to look around and assess the diversity of the room. They saw mostly white males. But diversity is not limited to ethnicity or gender. It includes age, backgrounds, culture, opinions, educational and occupational experiences, industry expertise, leadership styles, and other variables. Diversity improves decision-making if team members recognize that different perspectives and open minds yield better results.
- Meet regularly: Team members that know each other understand the various positions people take on certain issues. Thus, they know how to present their ideas in ways that are more compelling and acceptable to others. Frequent interaction builds the confidence that disagreements and dissent will not damage the relationship. Instead of one long monthly meeting, try shorter meetings every other week.
- Support role variety: Ask team members to play and rotate various roles at your meetings, such as the devil's advocate, stay-on-task master, creative visionary, customer advocate, and timer.
- Treat apathy: If disagreements are resolved too quickly, you often end up with groupthink and subtle discontent. Don't mistake quick agreement or silence for consensus. If you see people jump to agreement too quickly or sit too quietly, ask probing questions to make sure they are not just collapsing into consensus.

In the opening story of this chapter, Greg lost his job because he became a lopsided leader under pressure. He did not execute the CEO's new strategies. He failed to realize that the leader's job is to unleash the energy of people toward worthy goals every day. This requires the ability to execute—to get things done with and through others—especially when the heat is on.

You now have several tools to help you execute with passion and courage regardless of the temperature. Refer to the questions in Table 17.3 to further improve your ability to master this competency of commanding leadership.

TABLE 17.3

Tips for Executing with Passion and Courage

- What can you do to become more bottom-line/results-oriented?
- How might you and your team use a "Not To Do" list?
- How can you make sure that your unit meets its goals and objectives?
- Where are the bottlenecks, redundancies, policies, and procedures that bog you down?
- How can you increase your clarity about what is most important to you?
- Do you need to increase your ability to confront difficult issues head-on?
- How might you improve your eating, sleeping, or exercise habits to increase your energy?
- How can you and your team better manage the stress and strain of work?
- How well do you challenge senior management?
- How willing are you can make bold moves?
- How often do you celebrate independent thinking with your team members?

WaMu's CEO, Kerry Killinger, certainly asked himself many of these questions. Reportedly, however, he never had the courage to doubt his answers. He also excluded those executives who dared to question his answers. Under the best circumstances, that's a recipe for disaster; under the circumstances of the financial collapse preceding the Great Recession, it amplified WaMu's disaster globally.

That much is clear. In retrospect, things often are clear—unlike when looking into the future. And, as the next chapter reveals, when the future is foggy the best initial response is not to execute but to camp.

CHAPTER 18

When the Future Is Foggy—Camp!

Neurosis is the inability to tolerate ambiguity.

SIGMUND FREUD

EMBRACE AMBIGUITY AND PARADOX

"Which of these rivers was the Missouri?" That was the question Lewis wrote in his journal and discussed with Clark in June 1805. Lewis and Clark had been following President Jefferson's explicit orders for more than a year: "The object of your mission is to explore the Missouri River."

Now their arrival at a fork in the river left them stumped. They measured the size of the two rivers, detailed the characteristics of the water flowing in each, and sent scouts to explore the terrain into which each of the rivers flowed. They remained unsure which fork was the Missouri.

Faced with ambiguity, these leaders did what all great executives do: They camped...and conducted an experiment.

Lewis wrote in his journal:

> Captain Clark and myself concluded to set out early the next morning with a small party each, and ascend these rivers until we could perfectly satisfy ourselves. It was agreed that I should ascend the right hand fork and he the left. We agreed to go up those rivers one and a half day's march, or further if it should appear necessary to satisfy us more fully of the point in question.[1]

Captain Clark was much relieved when Captain Lewis finally arrived back in camp, two days late. The captains discussed their incomplete findings, pored over their faulty maps, and finally agreed that the south fork was the Missouri River.

The next morning, Lewis tried to convince the men of the expedition that the south fork was in fact the Missouri. The men didn't buy it. Every one of these seasoned veterans was convinced that the north fork was the way to go. Lewis listened to their arguments, but did not put the matter up for vote. The captains had camped, explored, and made their decision.

It turns out the captains were correct, perhaps because they had successfully demonstrated the second of the four core competencies of commanding leaders:

1. Execute with passion and courage.
2. EMBRACE AMBIGUITY AND PARADOX.
3. Regulate the emotions.
4. Choose responsibly.

THE FOG OF WORK

Executives often find it easy to act. Yet they seldom think about how to act when the future is uncertain. Because we have defined leadership as the process of unleashing the energy of others toward worthy goals, it's critical to apply a process (the how) that works well when the terrain is not well known. The story of Lewis and Clark, who spent nearly three years charting America's unknown territory west of the Mississippi River in the early 1800s, introduces us to a process of addressing these foggy issues.

Foggy leadership issues are those that have numerous interpretations and consequences. They are not black-and-white but gray. In business, they are matters that require contemplation before decisive action:

- How do we handle this new technology?
- What's the best way to deal with a complicated personnel issue?
- When and how should we enter this emerging market?

These decisions leave us feeling a bit unsteady, even lost, at least for a short time. What does it mean to be lost, even temporarily? Lost is when the map in your head doesn't match your terrain.

Wilderness experts tell us that when people become lost, the Rambo types are the first to die.[2] The ambiguity button in their mind is pushed, the emotional child who is afraid of the dark takes over, and a self-imposed nightmare unfolds because they act too quickly.

If Lewis and Clark made a quick decision (let's choose a route and march quickly) that turned out to be wrong, they would have lost considerable time wandering around instead of marching toward the Pacific Ocean. Haven't you seen leaders fail because they executed plans that no longer matched the terrain? Certainty, without flexibility, becomes rigidity.

On the other hand, if Lewis and Clark were too slow deciding (let's camp until we have all the information we want), they would have been trapped in the mountains during the forthcoming winter. Haven't you also seen leaders slowed down because they wanted piles of data and mountains of information when they faced uncertainty?

Either extreme—acting too fast or too slow in the face of a foggy issue—could have jeopardized their mission. One of the reasons Lewis and Clark were effective leaders was their ability to make good decisions in unfamiliar territory.

What's your process of decision-making when you face the fog of work?

Leading by managing ambiguity is essential because 90% of the issues leaders confront have several possible meanings or interpretations—according to the AMA's survey of 1,573 global corporations.[3] Yet few executives are skilled in thinking this way.

In our own analysis of 77 CEOs and executive team members, who were rated by 376 of their peers and direct reports using the XLM, we discovered that the leadership competency "embrace ambiguity and paradox" correlated highly with leadership effectiveness, but was the lowest-scoring of the 16 XLM leadership competencies. (See Appendix C.)

As one executive declared, "You mean we're least competent in a critical competency?"

Precisely.

My experience coaching and teaching thousands of leaders tells me that leaders who don't pause to reflect on how to decide when the future is foggy fail faster than you can say, "Bay of Pigs."

President John F. Kennedy authorized military assistance for the Bay of Pigs invasion in the spring of 1961. This was an attempt by 1,400 Cuban exiles to overthrow Castro with U.S. support. Within three days of landing, Castro's forces killed or captured most of them. By all accounts, the invasion was a complete military and political disaster.

In the wake of this catastrophe, Kennedy had the wisdom to ask how he and his best and brightest could have made such a terrible decision. He concluded that his flawed decision flowed from a flawed decision-making process. Kennedy came to realize that he needed to think differently in the face of foggy issues. Like Lewis and Clark, he learned how to embrace ambiguity and paradox, which he then put into practice to lead America successfully through his next challenge—the Cuban missile crisis.[4]

You can adapt many lessons from Lewis and Clark, President Kennedy, and other leaders to facilitate how you think about strategic yet ambiguous issues. A process is outlined in the remainder of this chapter. You don't need to use this process for all your decisions, just those that involve important action in unfamiliar territory. (Chapter 21 discusses further how to improve your general problem-solving and decision-making skills.)

The map is not the territory.
ALFRED KORZYBSKI

How to embrace ambiguity

There are a dozen techniques you can apply when confronted by ambiguous issues or challenges.

Create unstructured discussions

President Kennedy abandoned the structured, formal meetings that inhibited candid conversations during the Bay of Pigs in favor of informal conversations that ignored the etiquette of hierarchies. In other words, dropping rank at the door. Are you strong enough to leave your title outside the meeting room?

Invite the rank and file

Author Stephen Ambrose observed that we knew more about the surface of the moon in 1969 than Lewis and Clark knew about the territory they were exploring in 1805. Whenever they were uncertain, Lewis and Clarke asked all 35 men of the Corps of Discovery (and later their Shoshone companion Sacajawea) for input. After carefully considering the various perspectives, the captains made the decision.

Assign a devil's advocate

President Kennedy divided his Cuban missile crisis team into two subgroups and charged them with developing alternative approaches. In addition, Kennedy assigned the role of devil's advocate to make sure that he and his team surfaced and debated every assumption and risk.

Analyze probable causes of the problem

Generate a list of the possible causes. Use a rating scale of 1 to 5, with 1 being a slight possibility and 5 being a highly probable cause. In a column next to your ratings, write what you must do to investigate the cause further.

Then, rate how much effort is required to conduct the investigation. Again, use a scale from 1 to 5, with 1 being minimal effort and 5 being tremendous effort.

Finally, weigh the probability of the cause and the amount of time required to investigate further and determine how you will proceed.

Review your analysis with the rank and file and those who might disagree with your findings.

Minimize unnecessary data collection

Do you ever find yourself collecting data just because it's going to make you feel better? If so, ask yourself these questions:

- Is what I'm collecting absolutely necessary?
- How much value does it really add?

Just being conscious of how much is enough will help limit the amount of unnecessary information that crosses your desk. Recognize that you may not have all the information you would like when you make a decision in the fog.

Think big and act small

To increase your comfort with uncertainty, keep your overall vision in mind as you take small steps. By shuffling along slowly when it's dark, you minimize the risk of stubbing your toe. Bart Becht, CEO of global consumer-goods giant Reckitt Benckiser, points out that when he has two leaders who passionately disagree, he invites these two mavericks to conduct small-scale experiments. This is exactly how the company conducted its most successful project launch in history, the Air Wick Freshmatic.[5]

Prioritize and organize

When your cup is full, carry it even. It's easy to become distracted when dealing with uncertainty. Review your priorities with your boss. Set aside a specific time to work uninterrupted on your strategic yet ambiguous priorities. Focus on those fundamental few issues that matter most, not the meaningless many activities.

Once you think you have clear direction, expect things to change. With ambiguous issues, you probably won't be disappointed.

Accept criticism as learning

Executives who are adept at managing ambiguity learn from mistakes. They adopt the attitude that there is no failure — only feedback. You fail only when you choose not to learn from the experience. When (not if) you are being criticized by others, choose to interpret the criticism as learning for the future.

Reflect on past success

When have you successfully dealt with a previous ambiguous situation? As you recall a specific incident, consider what you were thinking at the time. How did you decide to manage that uncertainty? What decision-making process did you employ? How did it help? What did others say and do after you succeeded? How might you adapt the past actions to inform today's decision?

Model the best

Identify someone you know who is an "eye of the storm" type of an executive. These individuals maintain calmness despite the swirling winds that howl around them. Ask them how they maintain their composure when dealing with uncertainty. I once asked a neighborhood mom who raised several children, worked a part-time job, and managed an alcoholic husband how she handled the whirling dervish she called home. Whenever things became difficult, she said, she imagined that she was on an ocean liner throwing overboard anything that distracted her from the task at hand.

You may also want to watch classic (or soon-to-be classic) movies that demonstrate commanding skills during tenuous times: *Gentleman's Agreement, High Noon, The Fog of War, Exodus, The Lives of Others, All Quiet on the Western Front, Gettysburg, A Man for All Seasons, It's a Wonderful Life, Elizabeth I, The King's Speech, Lincoln,* and *Gandhi.*

Participate in ambiguous situations

Volunteer to join working committees or task forces on which you won't have much authority. As a volunteer member on the board of directors of an association, I find myself in situations when the president's direction is unclear and others are not open to my counsel. My comfort with uncertainty has increased and attachment to outcomes decreased. I am learning to be open to most things, attached to few.

When you stop learning,
you stop developing and you stop growing.
That's the end of the leader.

A. G. Lafley[6]

Traveling to a foreign country where you don't know the culture or language also helps embrace ambiguity. P&G CEO A.G. Lafley stretched his capacity to lead by managing uncertainty when, early in his career, he was assigned to India. He demonstrated "curious eyes" by immediately "going into somebody's house to watch how they live." Adopting a learning orientation was also found to be the most common habit among 250 executives who flourished in their overseas assignments.[7]

Teach others what you don't know well

It's easy to help others on topics at which you excel. However, if you want to increase your ability to manage ambiguous situations, teach others skills at which you don't feel you are an expert. This helps you become a faster learner and more secure with your insecurity.

He that leaveth nothing to chance will do few things ill,
but he will do very few things.

George Savile

Paradox in the White House

"They were born to hate each other."[8] Thomas Jefferson was an American aristocrat from the agricultural state of Virginia. He was a sloppily dressed visionary philosopher who advocated states' rights. Alexander Hamilton was a bastard immigrant from the West Indies who dressed meticulously, thought rationally, and argued for a strong federal government.

George Washington, the first president of America, appointed both of them to his cabinet, managed the tension between these two opposing personalities, and gave birth to a Confederation of United States.

Washington's ability to embrace paradox was central to his leadership genius. How prevalent is it in yours?

Paradox defined

Washington's history lesson reminds us that today's whitewater work environment requires leaders to manage paradoxical tensions.[9] As discussed in Chapter 1, a paradox is a statement that seems self-contradictory but in reality expresses a possible truth.

A leadership paradox involves contradictory yet interrelated elements that exist simultaneously.[10] Unlike a simple black-and-white (either/or) choice, a paradox is a dilemma that pulls in opposite directions at the same time. Specifically, it consists of two elements (often described as issues, sides, or poles) that put leaders at RISC because the elements are:

1. Recurrent: They keep coming back.
2. Interrelated: They need each other over time.
3. Simultaneous: They appear at the same time.
4. Contradictory: They pull in opposite directions.

Leading paradox at work

Researchers tell us that the ability to embrace both/and (paradoxical) thinking is a rare yet highly effective leadership skill.[11] Unlike Washington, many leaders over-focus on one element in a paradox instead of expanding their mindset to embrace both simultaneously.

For example, at a session with a group of marketing managers in a large insurance company (we'll call it Flex, Inc.), I pointed out that the managers' willingness to take on so many projects and agree to numerous project changes was overwhelming their employees.

The vice president of marketing objected; he believed that saying no to projects or freezing scope requirements would limit his team's ability to respond to executive mandates and environmental changes. He defended his company's "flexible" approach by pointing out that they had just acquired a former competitor (we'll call it Clear Corp.) that had been very clear about strategy but lacked flexibility.

I asked him if there was any downside to Clear Corp.'s sharp focus on a clear strategy.

He shot back, "Of course—it was their rigidity that actually sunk them. They couldn't adapt fast enough to a changing market. At Flex, Inc., we can!"

What would you say to this vice president and his team? Was he right? Of course, he was correct...and incomplete. Here's what I did during class: I invited the group to share any negative consequences that flowed from Flex, Inc.'s proclivity toward malleability. The managers lamented that over-focusing on being super-responsive to every demand was creating a chaotic environment, resentment, burnout, and turnover. I then suggested that because there were negative consequences of being both too flexible and too focused, they consider managing the tension between these two interdependent issues and avoid the either/or trap.

We fall into the either/or trap when we pick one side of a paradox in lieu of embracing both sides. In the previous example, the VP initially thought I was suggesting that he reject his company's flexible approach to embrace the purchased company's clear focus. In fact, I was inviting him to be a both/and thinker by embracing flexibility *and* clarity — both elements of his paradoxical dilemma.

Jim Collins and Jerry Porras interviewed 165 CEOs as part of their research for their groundbreaking book *Built to Last: Successful Habits of Visionary Companies*.[12] In a subsequent article, Collins pointed out that executives often "get caught up in what we call 'the Tyranny of the OR,' the belief that you cannot live with two seemingly contradictory ideas at the same time. . . ." It is the belief that you can't have change *and* stability, you can't be conservative *and* bold, you can't have low costs *and* high quality.[13]

The tragedy of either/or thinking reared its head at Xerox when CEO Richard Thoman, newly recruited from IBM, embarked on an overly aggressive, global strategy. Mismanaging the change and stability paradox doomed the strategy, and his brief tenure put the company in the intensive care unit. Fortunately, Anne Mulcahy managed these tensions well and built a team that rehabilitated Xerox. It's one of the reasons she was selected CEO of the Year by *Chief Executive* magazine.

> *In formal logic, a contradiction is the sign of defeat:*
> *but in the evolution of real knowledge,*
> *it marks the first step in progress toward victory.*
>
> Alfred North Whitehead

How to lead by thinking paradoxically

How would you describe the best executives you saw at work? Professor Robert Quinn of the University of Michigan's Ross School of Business asked 295 MBA students to answer this question by completing his competing values assessment.[14] He found that he could categorize only 5% of the executives as "masters."

Masters are mentors *and* directors, innovators *and* coordinators, facilitators *and* producers. Quinn concluded that "perhaps effectiveness is the result of maintaining a creative tension between contrasting demands." Masters, in other words, are leaders who manage the tension of paradoxical roles.

Maintaining a creative tension between contrasting demands endows leaders with the agility to respond to the dynamic demands of a changing environment. Like a lion stalking its prey on the African plains, executives who think paradoxically are highly skilled at changing gears quickly. One minute they may have philosophical discussions about the future, the next they pounce on the details of a project plan.

Professor Wendy Smith and her colleagues' analysis of 132 executives on 12 top teams found that embracing paradox is a competitive advantage "as our world becomes more global, fast paced, and hypercompetitive."[15]

In another study, researchers surveyed 520 business organizations in 17 countries. They reported that "when the CEO makes it a priority to balance the concerns of customers, employees, and the community while also taking environmental impact into account, employees perceived [the CEO] as visionary and participatory." This perception leads employees to work harder, thereby improving corporate profits.[16]

Sustainability is not only about saving the environment; it is about meeting the competing demands of conflicting stakeholders. Developing paradoxical thinking skills helps executives manage today's whitewater environment while at the same time creating conditions to thrive tomorrow.

Embracing paradox is how CEO Gardner Kent was thinking when he came up with his competitive strategy. Kent's bus company, Green Tortoise, was having difficulty competing with the Greyhound and Gray Rabbit until Kent started thinking in opposites. Instead of competing on speed with his bus competitors, Kent decided to add extra days and make bus trips more fun. These fun trips led to an entire new market and profit center.[17]

Professor Donald Conlon of Michigan State University's Broad College of Business and his colleagues confirmed the importance of contrarian thinking when they studied 20 British string quartets and discovered that the most successful groups recognized and managed paradoxes in their work.[18] Professor Nic Beech of the University of St. Andrews School of Management found what works for musicians also applies to managers when he studied 400 middle managers in the United Kingdom. He concluded that merely raising awareness of the paradoxical tensions leaders feel at work enhanced their ability to manage these opposing demands.[19]

The research tells us that the most effective executives *supplement* their traditional either/or approach to problem-solving with both/and paradoxical thinking. They don't replace one with the other.

Harvard Business School's Gautam Mukunda supports our earlier conclusion that Abraham Lincoln embraced a critical paradox as he led the United States through its darkest days. Lincoln, he wrote, "uniquely combined the highest levels of two seemingly antagonistic traits. Lincoln was both supremely confident and supremely humble."[20]

Lincoln's naval commanders might have recognized this next analogy: Managing a paradox is like to sailing a small boat on a windy day. When the wind grabs your sails and starts tipping you over, you don't let the wind have its way with you. Instead, you scramble to the other side of the boat and hang over the edge while holding the ropes. You get where you want to go by managing the tension between your strong hands and the wind in the sails (the two elements of this paradox). Harnessing the tension keeps you moving toward your destination.

Here are ten tools to help expand your paradoxical thinking when you need to harness the tension of opposites.

Look through other windows

Understand that how we perceive our business challenge and environment in the present moment is not reality. It is our view of reality. Our reality is filtered by our limited mental model — our narrow and biased view of the world.

Our view is shaped by our landscape.

Embrace paradoxical thinking when you have an issue to deal with by pretending you are on the outside of a house looking through one window into one room. Assume you do not know what is going on throughout the room. You can't see behind the couch or into two of the corners, much less the rooms on the opposite side of the house.

This is how Isadore Sharp was thinking as he developed the Four Seasons hotel chain in the early 1970s. He was the first to see that hotels did not need to fall into two simple categories: the large, luxury hotel that caters to the business traveler or the small, family-friendly hotel with modest amenities. Instead of choosing one of the existing models, Sharp believed that there was something else to see by using his opposable mind. He "combined the best of the small hotel with the best of a large hotel."[21] He was a both/and thinker in an either/or world.

Invite the loyal opposition to your table

Welcome conflicting models, styles, and opinions. A closed mind is a wonderful thing to lose. Effective leaders such as Analog Device founder and former CEO Ray Stata invite contrary views. This "opposition as resource" style of thinking was behind Stata's decision to build a soundproof room next to his office, where he engaged in heated debates with his detail-oriented chief operating officer, Jerry Fishman.[22] He was strong and smart enough to doubt his own opinion, which allowed him to invite those with conflicting views to lively debates.

"We are asking the people to be able to pat their head and rub their stomach at the same times, and not only continue to be the drivers of technology and product excellence in their product silos, but also be contributors at the enterprise level...to the solutions business. And it's confusing," Stata said.[23] "It's this, what we call ambidexterity, that's required. It [takes] a much higher level of sophistication in terms of management skills and business processes to pull that off."

Fail fast and small—and learn

Executives who embrace contrarian thinking conduct little experiments to test assumptions and address challenging issues. When he built his third hotel, the Four Seasons in London, with only 220 rooms, Sharp proved that intimacy and luxury could coexist happily and profitably.

When Lori, a mid-level manager, complained that one of her colleagues was probably not committed to Lori's critical project, and thus shouldn't be given any tasks related to it, I invited her to test her assumption by giving her colleague a smaller task. She did. Her colleague failed, and Lori took her off the project before she could do further damage.

Bill Sahlman of Harvard Business School observes that the "remarkable increase in the degree of entrepreneurial experimentation" in the world is because the Internet dramatically lowers the cost of starting many businesses.[24] Today's internal and external entrepreneurs realize that, to paraphrase Henry Ford, failure is merely feedback that allows them to try again more intelligently. Entrepreneurial-thinking executives capture feedback by emphasizing learning at multiple levels. IBM created its Strategic Leadership Forum to ensure that leaders from across the enterprise "debate and integrate paradoxical strategies."[25]

Make the abstract concrete

Paradoxical thinkers are not dreamers disconnected from reality. They are paradoxical thinkers giving birth to a new model of reality, as Kent did with Green Tortoise bus line and Sharp did with Four Seasons hotels. They imagine broadly *as* they monitor closely. They are possibility *and* probability thinkers. Like kite flyers, they let their dreams fly high *while* tethered to the ground.

Appreciate the arduous journey from complexity to simplicity

In the search for opposites, leaders risk getting lost in a convoluted maze of complexity. Yet messiness doesn't frighten the opposable mind.

Sharp's experiment in London identified a messy problem called profits. He discovered that his new hotel model (deliver intimacy and luxury) would not provide adequate profits unless he was able to charge a premium price for the experience. To understand what customers would actually pay for, his team dove into the complexity of the customer experience. Through extensive interviews and surveys, they were the first to document that high-end travelers want an at-home feeling. That's why they became the first hotel chain to offer shampoo in the shower, makeup mirrors, hair dryers, 24-hour room service, overnight shoe shines, and dry cleaning. Their journey from complexity to simplicity took them through the swamp of ambiguity.

I would not give a fig for the simplicity this side of complexity, but I would give my life for the simplicity on the other side of complexity.

OLIVER WENDELL HOLMES, SR.

Practice shifting gears

To stretch your mind, change the rhythm of your work. Arrange your schedule so that you spend time contemplating innovative growth strategies, followed by focusing on operational efficiency. Conduct a motivating team meeting after counseling an underperformer. Fast-transition activities teach the mind agility. In nature, sports, and leadership, it is not the strongest who thrive—it is the most agile.

Harold Goddijn, CEO of the navigation-device maker TomTom, understands the importance of agility when he reminds leaders to negotiate their immediate storms while navigating toward their long-term vision. "Your short-term management is about cash, working capital, all those things that keep you going—while at the same time you have to keep an eye on the future and keep investing long term. That's extremely challenging in the current environment."[26]

Agility is the ability to respond flexibly to a rapidly changing environment. And paradoxical thinking is an essential element of agility.

Adopt the beginner's mind

Zen teacher Suzuki wrote that "in the beginner's mind there are many possibilities, in the expert's mind there are few." Avoid the arrogance of excellence by spending a few minutes every morning pretending you don't know anything about what you're doing. Assume that your window is fogged as you stand outside your own house looking in:

- How can you see through other windows?
- Who might have different perceptions?
- What other ways are there to discover what's going on inside?
- Where might you go for more info?

Peter Norton applied the beginner's mind when he created the famous Norton Utilities software (sold to Symantec years later). One of the first innovative, paradoxical utilities that he brought to market was Undelete, which allowed computer users to recover files they might have erased accidentally. Perhaps the years he spent as a Zen Buddhist helped him see the utility of paradoxical thinking: doing by undoing—the yin and yang of life in a simple computer program.

Yin is loosely translated as "shady place," while yang means "sunny place." We can think of yin and yang in terms of how the sunlight illuminates the mountains and valleys. As the world turns, the sun appears to move across the sky, and yin and yang trade places. What was once in darkness is now seen and that which was seen is now in darkness. The beginner's mind embraces the wisdom of both.

Lead with your strengths and manage your weaknesses

We do best what we enjoy most. That's why we should spend the majority of our time working in those areas that access our strengths. However, as we learned in Chapter 4, just as a bodybuilder who pumps iron but refuses to stretch becomes inflexible, executives who overuse their strengths often become strong to a fault.

To expand your paradoxical thinking, spend 20 minutes every day working on a weaker competency. In my coaching, I have found that the executives who improve the most are those who select a competency that is 1) important to their work and 2) opposite one of their strengths. So, if you excel at clarifying objectives and expectations, consider improving your ability to adapt strategies to meet your goals, if you scored relatively low in that competency. If engaging others is your strength, executing with passion and courage may need your attention.

Working outside your comfort zone exercises the agility muscles required to adapt in a competitive global environment.

Support the opposition after the battle

Not long ago, I reminded the president of an association that I disagreed with a decision she and the board of directors made. I also affirmed that because the decision had been made, I would support it.

When your management makes a final decision that you disagree with, support it wholeheartedly. When it's time to surrender, demonstrate your commitment to management's decision. Let your team know that you now support the decision and expect them to execute it. CEOs such as Bart Becht want "80% alignment, followed by 100% agreement to implement."

Listen to the extreme

When I was young, we had only three television stations to watch, a few radio stations to listen to, and one local newspaper to read. Today, we can easily multiply these few alternatives by a hundred or more to understand how fragmented our world has become. We have many more choices now; unfortunately, one of the side effects of increased fragmentation is that it becomes easier to insulate ourselves from those we disagree with. Comfortably numb in our cocoon, we tweet and text only our inner circle. Our worldview becomes our mental blinders.

A politically liberal friend once told me that she listens to conservative talk radio regularly. When I asked why she paid attention to the extreme opposite views, she said, "It helps me stretch." She taught me to listen to both extremes. I also now read *The Week* and *The Economist* magazines because of their balanced approach to reporting the news. How are you stretching your views and finding the middle ground?

Extraordinary leaders such as George Washington are masters of paradox. Washington longed to be seen as a great leader *and* reluctantly accepted his appointment to lead the Continental Army during the American Revolution. He was ambitious *and* had to be persuaded to accept a second term as president of the United States. He was a commanding leader who shot deserters *and* an empowering person who wept at the tragedy of war. Washington's ability to hold two opposing ideas in his mind at the same time enhanced his ability to lead.

The ten tools we've just examined will help you do the same. Adapt them to find your version of what Aristotle called the golden mean — the middle road. The mean between the extreme is always worth contemplating, although it is not *always* the road worth taking. (Ironically, always taking the middle road would be extreme!)

Table 18.1 presents a series of questions to help you and your team expand your thinking by embracing ambiguity and paradox. Use paradoxical thinking as another arrow in your quiver. It should complement your black-or-white (either/or) approach to leadership issues—not replace it.

Excellence is a paradoxical phenomenon that emerges under conditions of uncertainty and creative tension.

ROBERT E. QUINN

TABLE 18.1

Tips for Embracing Ambiguity and Paradox

- How can you free yourself from the need to have all the data before deciding?
- What small steps can you and your team take when faced with uncertainty?
- What do you need to let go of and hold on to in order to embrace change?
- How can you build the platform of stability to help others deal with constant change?
- Where can you use flowcharts or storyboards to visualize complex processes or issues?
- When should you ask more "why" questions to decrease ambiguity?
- Do you need to applaud progress to decrease attachment to perfectionism?
- How often do you solicit opposing views when making difficult decisions?
- To whom can you turn for contrary evidence?
- What new tasks or responsibilities should you take on to stretch your comfort zone?
- Where can you add variety to your work?
- How can you become more comfortable with the complexity needed to embrace paradox?
- In what situations do you need to exhibit more flexibility?

• • •

WaMu's executives failed to embrace ambiguity and paradox: They, like many executives in the financial services sector of our global economy, failed to manage the tension between profit and risk. WaMu leaders counted on constantly increasing residential property values to hide the fact that the vast majority of the bank's customers hadn't the foggiest idea what an unconventional loan was or how it worked—or that most of them had negative equity in their properties. WaMu executives over-focused on one side of a paradox (profits), ignored the other side (risks), and everyone suffered the negative consequences of their failure to stretch when they were pulled.

The effective executives discussed in this chapter—figures from history (Washington, Lincoln, Kennedy) and business (Isadore Sharp, Gardner Kent, even middle-manager Lori) did not snap when they felt pulled. Their ability to embrace ambiguity and paradox was facilitated by another commanding competency—their capacity to regulate their emotions—that is the focus of the next chapter.

CHAPTER 19

Marry Head and Heart

Any person capable of angering you becomes your master.

EPICTETUS

The executive marched into the spacious meeting room. Two hundred journalists and editors waited anxiously for him to deliver the news. He confirmed their worst fears: Despite Herculean efforts, the company was closing their entire news division. All the journalists and editors were losing their jobs.

It was hard to take. The executive who delivered this devastating blow was even harder to take. His brusque style and contentious mood triggered a nasty reaction from the crowd. He needed security to usher him from the enraged mob.

Another executive visited this same group of reporters and editors on the next day. He took a respectful and somber approach to these wounded professionals. He shared stories about the importance of journalism in society, his own career struggles, and the layoffs he had endured. He closed by telling them that despite the struggles he too had faced, he had remained dedicated to the profession. He wished them well.

This second executive did not need a security escort; he left with applause and cheers ringing in his ears.[1]

Regulate the Emotions

How do you leave your employees after a staff meeting, one-on-one session, or all-hands meeting? Do you disregard the emotions of the moment and plow ahead with your agenda, leaving a flood of negative feelings to wash over them upon your departure...like the first executive? Or do you marry your rational and emotional skills to achieve a more desirable outcome...like the second executive? Stories like these illustrate the importance of regulating the emotions — the fourth essential skill of emotional intelligence (EI), and the third competency of commanding leaders:

1. Execute with passion and courage.
2. Embrace ambiguity and paradox.
3. REGULATE THE EMOTIONS.
4. Choose responsibly.

As discussed in earlier chapters, emotionally intelligent executives perform better, get promoted faster, and have lower turnover compared to those who are less emotionally intelligent. In addition, according to a study of more than 100,000 executives, EI is a better predictor of performance than technical skill or experience.[2] As a quick reminder, let's touch on the first three skills of EI before we dive into skill number four, which marries the head and heart.

Perceive emotions

Are you in touch? Emotions contain data. They are signals telling us that something is going on that needs our attention. If we are not aware of this data, we miss an enormous amount of feedback necessary for effective leadership. Thus, the first step in being an emotionally intelligent executive is to identify what emotions we, and those around us, feel. In the opening story, the first executive who spoke to employees either failed to detect the emotional smoke signals in others or he ignored them.

Use emotions

Do you have emotions or do they have you? How we feel affects how we think. In fact, our emotions are always influencing our thinking. The only question is, How? Emotionally intelligent executives use their emotions to facilitate their thinking. They have emotions, but their emotions do not have them.

If the first executive had thought about what emotions would best direct his attention to the problem of "communicating the bad news" about layoffs, he might have been able to deliver the news better. For instance, if he had used a relaxation technique to calm down, it might have been easier for him to focus on what others needed from him, which might have led to a more empathetic approach than the one he took.

Understand emotions

Can you forecast the emotional future? One of the reasons we need to grow our emotional intelligence is to be able to perform better—to produce outcomes that are more desirable. This requires a general knowledge of where our emotions come from, and a robust vocabulary to describe them.

These proficiencies allow us to conduct a quick what-if analysis. If the first executive had understood that anger is frequently caused by feelings of being treated unfairly, and that the elevator to anger begins in the lobby of annoyance, he could have asked himself questions such as:

- What might happen if I take a somber tone to my presentation?
- What's the probable outcome if I share a story of my own struggles?
- Will it help matters if I let these employees know I believe in our profession?

Of course, this is not the process the first executive used; he didn't think about how different approaches might create different emotional outcomes. What process do you use?

How's your marriage...between head and heart?

Though we don't know for sure, the second executive probably employed the first three skills of an EI leader—perceiving, using, and understanding emotions—thereby enabling him to regulate his emotions, which is the fourth skill. Leaders who regulate their emotions exercise self-control and think clearly even when they are experiencing strong emotions. They maintain their cool when situations get hot. You seldom see them become defensive or lose their composure under pressure.

They also can "psych themselves up" (and others, too) or be a calming influence. Their James Bond demeanor does not mean they don't have passionate feelings—only that they temper passion with reason. They understand that masking emotions is not managing emotions. They make better decisions because they marry their heart and their head.

Executives who regulate their emotions create environments of greater trust, fairness, integrity, and openness to change.[3] That's because politics, infighting, and resistance to change decrease when employees know that they can speak their mind and share their concerns without the boss losing his or her temper.

A group of researchers at the University of Amsterdam tested the effects of a leader displaying anger versus happiness on 140 graduate students under stress. Their conclusion: "Our findings suggest that leaders who were capable of accurately diagnosing their subordinates and the situation, and of regulating their emotions accordingly, will be more successful in effectively managing group processes and stimulating performance."[4]

Witness is the greatest science for an inward revolution.

OSHO

A senior vice president grumbled that his team did not come to him with bad news. I told him that they were afraid of his emotional outbursts. "But I never shoot the messenger," was his quick retort.

"I know, but unless you learn to regulate your emotions, the messengers will never even come knocking," was my reply.

Here are some best practices you can use to keep calm when you feel the heat.

Stay open to your emotions

Because emotions contain information, closing ourselves off to certain emotions decreases essential feedback. We seldom shut out positive emotions. Yet all emotions contain information. If you find that you typically shut down when uncomfortable situations arise, practice this technique:

1. Determine which emotion you would like to work on.
2. List the various situations tending to cause that emotion.
3. List the situations from the least to the most emotionally intense.
4. Use your imagination to relax (focusing on deep breathing, progressive muscle relaxation, calmness).
5. Generate a calm and pleasant mood.
6. Picture the least intense emotional situation.
7. When you find yourself becoming tense, go back to the relaxing step (4) and then generate a calm mood (5).

The goal is to visualize the emotional situation and stay open to the emotion. You begin with the easiest situations and progress slowly toward the more difficult ones. (If your emotions are too painful or difficult, please see a health professional.)

Change your emotion

Do you ever wish you could change your emotion in a split-second – wouldn't that be a great skill?

Guess what? You already do it.

What about the time you were really upset and then the phone rang and—because of who was calling—you had to answer pleasantly?

See, you already exercise this skill. Perhaps not consciously, but you do it. If you want to do it consciously and consistently, try the following steps:

1. Determine which emotion you would like to change.
2. Choose a situation that causes this emotion.

3. Use your imagination to picture that situation. Make the experience as real as possible.
4. Bring the emotion that you want to change into the situation you have imagined.
5. Think of an interruption that could occur realistically in that situation, such as a phone call, a knock on the door, an instant message or tweet, someone yelling your name, your pet rubbing your leg, etc.
6. As the interruption occurs, watch the scene unfold without judgment. Pretend you are observing yourself on the movie screen. Don't criticize what you see, just be aware of what you see and feel as you watch yourself on the screen.
7. Replay the sequence until the emotion's intensity diminishes under your detached gaze.

Reason with emotions

Do you ever bring the office home? Something negative happens at work and it spills into your home life—it happens to all of us. We fail to regulate emotions when we allow the emotions to extend into other areas of our lives. You can minimize this problem by reasoning with emotions. Here's how:

1. Determine which emotion you tend to take home.
2. Think of a recent, specific situation in which this emotion was aroused.
3. Write answers to these questions or use Morning Pages to address them:
   - Was it reasonable to feel this way in this situation?
   - Do you often feel this way when this situation happens?
   - Why do you feel this way?
   - What truly caused the feeling?
   - Would you like to change the way you feel about it?
   - How would a leader you admire interpret the situation?
   - Would it be beneficial if you chose to think of this situation differently?
   - How could you think of this situation and the emotion differently?

Hug your reptilian brain

Emotions flow from the neurotransmitters of your brain's limbic system, sometimes referred to in evolutionary terms as your reptilian brain. It's the seat of feelings, impulses, and drives. It's home to your fight-or-flight mechanism. Your limbic system hijacks your brain under stress. Your copilot, the analytical neocortex—the rational thinking portion of your brain—is often gagged and bound when the heat is on. That's why thinking clearly under pressure is often difficult.

To improve your capacity to regulate your emotions, engage your reptilian brain in training. Listening to a lecture or reading a book (including this one), which is how most leadership training is delivered, doesn't enhance emotional intelligence because the learning doesn't involve the limbic system. Furthermore, practice does not make perfect—progressive practice, in simulated conditions of reality, makes perfect.

For example, not long ago I interviewed the CEO of a billion-dollar company about the emotional growth of one of his executives, whom I had been coaching for the last four months. The CEO stated that his executive was "a different guy" because of the dramatic improvements he had made in a very short period. The CEO asked me how I did it.

Of course, my ego wanted to tell him that my weekly coaching sessions made a big difference. Instead, I told him that I had recruited people (a few peers and direct reports) that the executive surrounded himself with and invited them to be part of my 360-coaching process. Thus, the executive's own circle of influence provided timely, frequent, and accurate feedback from the trenches.

Leadership coaching is most successful when coaches involve the limbic system in progressive practice under real conditions. That's how executives learn to hug their reptilian brain when stressed.

Here are key questions to help you hug your reptilian brain by marrying your head and heart during taxing circumstances:

- What are you feeling physically?
- What are you feeling emotionally?
- What does it make you want to do?
- What will happen if you do that?
- Where is that feeling coming from... really?
- What is the ideal outcome you desire?
- What options might lead you toward that outcome?

Say your ABCs

Here are a few other quick tips to help you keep your cool as soon as you start feeling the heat. I call them the ABCs of composure:

- Accept the feeling.
  Don't deny your emotion. Accept and observe the feeling. Don't judge it, either. See and feel it for what it is—a feeling.
- Breathe to relieve.
  Inhale all the negativity that swirls around this feeling. Take this deep, slow breath from your belly and let it all in. As the air slowly enters

your lungs, imagine that all your positive energy envelops this negative situation. Like a bright sunrise, let the core of your real self surround the feeling and situation. Then, as you slowly exhale, allow your powerful, positive light to flow out as your gift. Imagine this illuminating light of calm spreading out in all directions from the heart of who you really are — from your best self. One executive says he imagines the light coming from his heart as sunlight lifting the fog.

- Command your body.
  As you release the tension through breathing, show it in your face and speak it in your voice. Let your cheeks relax and smile, if it's appropriate. Slow your speech and lower your voice. Act as if you feel relaxed and you become more relaxed.

How would you coach Charlie?

Let's summarize all four emotional intelligence abilities (perceive, use, understand, regulate) with an exercise where you coach Charlie, the director of operations in your organization. Imagine Charlie is one of your direct reports, and he shares this particular challenge with you...

The IT department was added to Charlie's responsibilities as part of a reorganization that occurred six months earlier. Bob, the long-time manager of IT who is nearing the end of his career, now has Charlie as his new manager. Charlie and Bob had been colleagues for the last five years.

Since the reorganization, Bob hasn't been much of a team player: He's slow to return Charlie's calls and is barely delivering his projects on time. He's not contributing much to the important cross-functional teams to which Charlie assigned him. He also seems annoyed whenever Charlie asks for status reports.

Charlie's had a few informal conversations with Bob regarding how things are going, his role on the team, and the importance of his projects. Bob nodded, smiled, and said he was fine with everything. Although his work is still somewhat satisfactory, Charlie is concerned that Bob's negative attitude could become worse and/or infect others. Bob's performance review is coming up, and Charlie asks you if the review is an opportunity to address the issue more directly.

What would you recommend? Would you tell Charlie to have a direct "lay it on the line" conversation with Bob? Alternatively, would you suggest that Charlie invite Bob to the restaurant they frequented as colleagues to have a gentler dialogue over lunch?

There are no guarantees that a single approach will always work, but Charlie has a higher probability of achieving his desired outcome if you coach him to apply the four EI abilities.

Here's how I coached Charlie:

1. Realize that Bob is probably in an overall negative mood because Charlie was promoted to be his boss (perceive emotions).
2. Recognize that Bob's negativity might limit his receptivity to any explanation or suggestion Charlie may offer, at least early on in the conversation (use emotion).
3. Understand that Bob's feeling of being annoyed could be caused by his belief that he was not treated fairly because the reorganization process was never explained. In addition, appreciate that this annoyance might escalate to anger, if matters are not handled well (understand).
4. Regulate Charlie's emotion by not reacting to any of Bob's negativity or passive-aggressive behavior during the performance review. Instead, lead Bob to a better outcome by having a direct and difficult conversation during the performance review.

Here's how the conversation went, according to Charlie:

CHARLIE: It's been six months since the reorganization. Before we talk about your performance, I want to know how you feel about us. How are you and I are doing?

BOB: I think we're doing just fine.

CHARLIE: Really? I'm surprised to hear you say that. I've felt that there has been a little tension between us since the reorganization. I've noticed that it takes a while for you to return my calls. You also seem not to be fully engaged in a few of our projects. So, I'm guessing I'm not doing something right.

BOB: Well, I've been really busy.

CHARLIE: Bob, I'm not sure how the executive team decided who went where in the reorganization; they've never explained their thinking behind the reorganization. For all I know, it could have been either one of us who ended up in my position, but they put me here. And I need your help and your experience to make this new organization effective. What can I do to improve my communication with you and/or our overall relationship?

According to Charlie, Bob's entire appearance changed when he took this "I need you to help me" approach. Bob relaxed, smiled with his eyes (a real smile) for the first time in a long time, and opened up in ways he never had before. Although Bob didn't have any specific suggestions for Charlie, Charlie told me that the performance issues he had with Bob disappeared. Six months later, Bob and his team are still performing well. Charlie believes things got better because he became a better emotionally intelligent executive.

Here are some questions to help you grow your and your team's emotional intelligence:

- Which situations tend to affect you and your team members emotionally?
- Could your internal state be caused by lack of sleep, poor nutrition, or stress?
- Do you need to decrease how often you jump into conversations?
- In what situations do you need to use your emotions, rather than allowing them to use you?
- How might you arrange a time-out session when you are feeling emotional?
- Do you take a few moments to clarify your intention before every communication?
- Where might you find other daily, healthy outlets for your emotional release?
- What breathing exercises or relaxation techniques might help you regulate your emotions?
- What questions might you ask to better reason with emotion?
- Do you recognize the difference between what happens and your story about what happens?
- How well do you access your free will to choose your response to emotional issues?
- Who might provide ongoing feedback to help you regulate your emotions better?
- What techniques could you practice to maintain poise and composure in the face of interpersonal threats or challenges?
- How might you decrease defensiveness during difficult situations?

These questions are good reminders of how emotions influence the ability to apply commanding leadership competencies, especially when the heat is on. When Washington Mutual experienced a dramatic loss in profits in 2004, the board appointed President and Chief Operating Officer

Steve Rotella to turn the company around. Rotella was quick to dismiss the importance of EI. Of WaMu's five corporate values—fair, caring, human, dynamic, and driven—he disregarded the first three and emphasized only the last two.[5] Within two years, employee turnover in customer-focused positions increased to 50%, consumer complaints skyrocketed, and WaMu's rapid decline accelerated.

One of the lessons we can learn from WaMu's demise is that ignoring emotions at work makes it hard to make good choices—the topic of the next and final chapter about the competencies of the commanding leadership style.

CHAPTER 20

The Jungle Is Neutral

Between stimulus and response is a space called choice.

STEPHEN COVEY

The gods condemned the mythological Greek Sisyphus to spend eternity rolling a rock up a mountain, only to see it roll down again. In the final chapter of his philosophical essay *The Myth of Sisyphus,* Albert Camus compares the absurd nature of human life to Sisyphus's predicament. Yet his essay concludes, "The struggle itself...is enough to fill a man's heart. One must imagine Sisyphus happy."

How could endlessly rolling a rock up a mountain culminate in happiness? Camus must be crazy, right?

Perhaps.

But what if the story is a metaphor about choosing to make meaning out of difficulty? How much more effective would we be if we refused to fall victim to the destructive "woe is we" mentality, instead choosing to interpret adversity constructively?

CHOOSE RESPONSIBLY

My first act of free will shall be to believe in free will.

WILLIAM JAMES

To choose responsibly is the final competency of the commanding leadership style:

1. Execute with passion and courage.
2. Embrace ambiguity and paradox.
3. Regulate the emotions.
4. CHOOSE RESPONSIBLY.

Decades of research shows that "influencing followers' perceptions, attitudes, and beliefs can strengthen their commitment to their organization's goals, spurring them to embark on new directions with enthusiasm instead of resistance."[1] That's why making sense of the environment by "making meaning" for followers is critical.

Executives are ineffective when, like former President Richard Nixon during the Watergate scandal, they blame others when they fall. You can't help others make sense of difficult circumstances if you are wasting time blaming others for those circumstances. Effective leaders, like former president John F. Kennedy, take responsibility for their choices when they fail (Bay of Pigs), choose to act on what they learn (Cuban missile crisis), and inspire others to take action.

Choosing to roll the rock responsibly is important when leaders fail during their workday (experience a short-term setback) and when their career hits an obstacle (confront longer-term adversity).

Failure is only the opportunity to begin again more intelligently.

HENRY FORD

FAIL SUCCESSFULLY EVERY DAY

Robert Shapiro, former CEO of Monsanto, was troubled to find that the company's organizational culture had conditioned employees to view unsuccessful products or projects as personal failures.[2] He knew this narrow view of failure was choking his innovation pipeline. To encourage an experimentation mindset in their everyday approach to work, Shapiro employed a number of tactics. Adapt his techniques so you and your team can learn how to fail successfully every day, too.

Distinguish between excusable and inexcusable failure

Employees must know that executives encourage learning from excusable failure, but won't tolerate sloppy work. You can make this distinction clear by implementing after-action reviews (AARs) in your organization. Answer these probing questions after any failure:

- What were the desired outcomes?
- What outcomes actually were achieved?
- Why did the failure occur?
- How well was the effort organized and monitored?
- Did the leader collaborate and consult with the right people?
- How was risk assessed?
- How will the lessons learned be disseminated?

Don't praise too much

Professor Richard Farson and his colleagues (cited originally in Chapter 2) found that creativity decreases with praise. Employees actually want their leaders to be more interested in their work and less focused on patting them on the back. Robert Pirsig, who wrote *Zen and the Art of Motorcycle Maintenance,* was correct when he reminded us that caring is the precursor of quality. When the leader takes a nonjudgmental and caring interest in the work itself (and the ongoing learning), employees are more willing to tolerate failure. This is consistent with the research of Professor Carroll Dweck, as covered in Chapter 11.

Fess up when you mess up

Executives who candidly admit their own mistakes communicate their desire for their organization to experiment and learn. Former Coca-Cola CEO Roberto Goizueta took responsibility, and years of ribbing, for the New Coke fiasco that occurred during his time at the helm. Admitting his mistake taught employees that tolerance of mistakes was the norm. Hundreds of memos and speeches could not have communicated as well.

John Antioco, former CEO of Blockbuster, was also quick to fess up to a few "do differently next time," in an interview in *Harvard Business Review.*[3] (The entire issue was actually dedicated to failure.)

Share the wealth of information

Sharing information is a critical step in any transformation. Post-it notes might not be here today if 3M's Spencer Silver had decided to sit on information regarding the failed adhesive he invented. He promoted the concept within 3M without much success until a colleague, Art Fry, imagined using it to anchor his bookmark in his hymnbook.[4] 3M profited from its culture of rewarding information exchange.

When you distribute information—even when it doesn't make you look good—employees learn to collaborate across boundaries, and internal silos melt like snow forts on a warm winter day.

The fastest way to succeed is to double your failure rate.

IBM founder Thomas Watson, Sr.

Benedict Arnold was a brilliant, highly decorated leader in the Continental Army during America's war for independence... until he was blindsided by injury and insult (being passed over for promotion and colleagues claiming credit for his victories). General Arnold chose to handle his career setbacks by turning his back on his country. In America, his name is now synonymous with traitor.

Contrast his failure to manage career adversity with how former U.S. President Jimmy Carter recovered from his 1980 reelection loss to Ronald Reagan. Carter chose to dedicate his life to the alleviation of human suffering, built The Carter Center, and later won the Nobel Peace Prize "for his decades of untiring effort to find peaceful solutions to international conflicts, to advance democracy and human rights, and to promote economic and social development."[5]

Why do some executives make poor choices when smacked by career adversity while others handle this hardship like a rubber ball? Diane Coutu, a senior editor at *Harvard Business Review,* studied resilient business leaders, Holocaust survivors, and children.[6] She discovered that the most resilient individuals chose to:

1. Accept reality.
2. Improvise.
3. Value meaning.

Accept reality

When leadership researcher and author Jim Collins interviewed Vice Admiral James Stockdale, held prisoner and tortured by the Vietcong for eight years, he asked Stockdale, "Who didn't make it out of the prisoner camps?"

The leader responded, "Oh, that's easy, the optimists. They were the ones who said we are going to be out by Christmas. And then they said we'd be out by Easter, then the Fourth of July, then by Thanksgiving, and then it was Christmas again." Then Stockdale added, "They died of a broken heart."[7]

Commanding leaders choose responsibly by seeing reality the way it is *and* having faith that it will get better. That's what Collins calls the Stockdale paradox. The sun will come out, but maybe not tomorrow.

This is the approach Jamie Dimon chose to take when he was fired as president of Citigroup by then-chairman Sandy Weill following 16 years of collaboration. Dimon scanned the already-prepared press release and understood that the board of directors agreed with Weill. He saw reality staring him in the face and walked out. A year and a half later, he took the job of CEO at Bank One. He subsequently took the top job at JPMorgan Chase, which later bought Bank One. Dimon took a play out of former GE CEO Jack Welch's playbook: Welch taught reality as a value by cautioning leaders to "see the world as it is, not just the way you want it to be."

Improvise

The logistics company UPS considers service a core value. Executives empower their drivers to do whatever it takes (including improvise) to deliver packages on time. This is exactly what they did one day after Hurricane Andrew devastated southeast Florida. People were living in shelters and cars because the storm had reduced their homes to rubble. Yet the hurricane didn't stop the UPS drivers from delivering critical packages to desperate customers. UPS quickly provided service by setting up diversion sites to sort packages amid the carnage.

How well do you improvise when you hit a stumbling block?

I spoke with a recently promoted executive, Marsha, who is struggling with her new responsibilities. Marsha feels she is not managing her transition well because she hasn't found ways to handle the obstacles that accompany her new position. Much like you might improvise a dinner today from yesterday's leftovers, Marsha and I are now producing a flexible plan that leads with her strengths and manages her weaknesses.

Value meaning

Effective leaders make sense out of their struggles by searching for meaning based on their values. Values offer a way to interpret what is going on and where to go. Values are the North Star during an executive's "dark night of the soul." The self-serving values of Benedict Arnold (arrogant, prideful, victim mindset) contrast sharply with the servant leader values of Jimmy Carter (caring, compassionate, humanitarian).

Nelson Mandela is another example of a leader using values to make meaning out of adversity. To avert a civil war in South Africa (after spending 27 years in prison), Mandela felt he needed to assuage the fears of whites before addressing the many grievances of blacks. Because he placed a high value on unity, he chose to symbolize unity by focusing the nation on rugby, a sport usually ignored by blacks.

Despite great internal opposition, Mandela persisted in using rugby as a powerful metaphor to make unity meaningful for all his people. In the end, South Africa won the Rugby World Cup, and millions of black and white fans sang the team song in harmony. The nation marched down the path of reconciliation, not retaliation, because a leader chose to make meaning out of difficulty by focusing on the value of unity.[8]

What values are you living that can rally your team in tough times?

> *We must not let our differences blind us from the unity that binds us.*
>
> HUSTON SMITH

Mandela's story also illustrates the importance of choosing to lead by managing meaning, not just information. We no longer live in the information age; we drown in the information *overload* age. Employees flounder in a flood of e-mails, instant messages, and Internet and intranet news. Effective executives help their managers focus on what is most important in this torrent of information, especially during stressful times.[9]

STAY FOCUSED DURING TOUGH TIMES

Answer the following questions to help interpret information in a meaningful way when you're faced with hard decisions:

- What are the relevant facts?
- What's the ideal outcome?
- How does this ideal outcome relate to our vision and core values?
- With whom should we brainstorm options?
- What options create the greatest good for the greatest number?
- How will we express our core values as we take action?

Choosing to answer these questions will help you see the light during your dark night. Choice steers your thinking, thereby determining how well you navigate everyday failure and career adversity. A wise elder once related this story:

> One evening an old Cherokee leader told his grandson about a battle that goes on inside all people. He said, "My son, the battle is between two wolves inside us all. One is Bad. It is envy, jealousy, regret, greed, arrogance, self-pity, guilt, resentment, inferiority, lies, false pride, superiority, and ego. The other is Good. It is joy, peace, love, hope, serenity, humility, kindness, benevolence, empathy, generosity, truth, compassion and faith."
>
> The grandson thought about it for a minute and then asked his grandfather, "Which wolf wins?"
>
> The old Cherokee replied, "The one you feed."

Everybody has a rock to roll—and a wolf to feed. How you choose to push your rock and which wolf to feed throughout your day and career is up to you. I encourage you to use the tools in this chapter to make the right choices. If you do, I imagine that you, too, may end up like Sisyphus: happy.

Choosing responsibly lifts us from "woe is me" to "WOW, it's up to me."

Exercise your commanding competencies

In Section V, we have described the commanding leader as an individual who executes with passion and courage, embraces ambiguity and paradox, regulates the emotions, and chooses responsibly. Reflect for a moment on historical, business, or military leaders who are strong in the commanding style. Who comes to mind? Do names like former British Prime Minister Margaret Thatcher, George Washington, Steve Jobs, or Jack Welch surface?

How does this style relate to your world? In this space below, please make a quick list of responsibilities you have that require accessing your commanding leadership competencies:

____

____

____

____

Specific duties that leaders from our classes have identified as requiring commanding competencies style are listed in Table 20.1.

TABLE 20.1

Duties Requiring Commanding Leader Competencies

- Terminating an employee
- Standing up to your boss
- Asserting your own ideas, even if they are unpopular with your team
- Having a difficult or uncomfortable conversation
- Delivering bad news to your boss or team
- Taking small steps when dealing with ambiguous issues
- Inviting those who disagree with you to the table for honest dialogue
- Holding team members accountable for their attitudes during change
- Helping others make sense of, and interpret, difficult events or experiences
- Refusing to play the victim when unpopular initiatives, policies, or procedures are adopted
- Driving for results, despite obstacles

Table 20.2 lists several questions to help you think about how to grow the four competencies of the commanding leader and address many of the duties listed in Table 20.1. Each question is also a practical tactic that can help you expand your commanding skills. You may also want to discuss them with your team members.

TABLE 20.2

10 Questions to Help You Choose Responsibly

1. How well do you distinguish between excusable and inexcusable failure?
2. What can your team do to decrease the fear-of-failure mindset?
3. What can your team do to increase the experimental mindset?
4. How well do you advertise your mistakes?
5. How do you and your team choose to perceive failure?
6. Are there situations where you do not see or accept reality?
7. Are you clear about the core values that drive your choices?
8. How can you be more optimistic during tough times?
9. How might you involve your team in choosing to make meaning out of adversity?
10. What small, daily actions could you choose to take to be more positive?

What you resist persists

In Chapter 17, you read about Greg, an empowering leader who lacked some of the key competencies of the commanding style. He failed to execute with passion and courage by refusing to address the poor performance among his team members. He also ignored the swelling signs of discontent among his colleagues, who were upset at the poor service that their teams were receiving from Greg's managers.

I worked with Greg and some of his team members on their leadership issues. After a two-day workshop, I told Greg that his three poor-performing managers were the ones most resistant to the leadership tools presented in class. I recommended that he employ his organization's progressive discipline policy with them and that he and I enter a coaching relationship.

Greg showed great discomfort at the thought of holding his non-performers accountable and developing other commanding competencies. He said it was "not his style to confront people." What he was really saying was that he did not want to learn how to manage the tension required to access the commanding leadership skills — his relative weakness — while still holding on to his empowering leadership style — his relative strength. In other words, Greg did not want to stretch when he felt pulled.

That's what got him fired.

What got Kerry Killinger fired wasn't actually too different, even if the scale was orders of magnitude greater. He pushed WaMu into riskier and riskier portfolios of unconventional loans even as his risk management and compliance teams repeatedly told him it was an irresponsible choice. Instead of stretching when he felt pulled, Killinger systematically removed the source of the tension—the executives at WaMu who questioned him.

Failing to manage the tensions of leadership derails many leaders. Don't let it hurt your growth. The management of tension is the essence of growth.

• • •

We have discussed the two ways you can grow your leadership effectiveness, especially when you are pulled by opposing demands.

First, you can develop the weaker competencies that cause you to be a lopsided leader under pressure. That's been the focus of chapters 5 through 20—to provide you with powerful, practical tools for expanding your XLM. By developing a bigger and more well-rounded XLM, you gain the agility to respond flexibly to your dynamic environment. Instead of snapping, you stretch when you're pulled.

The second way to grow your leadership effectiveness is to improve the quality and consistency of your daily decision-making and problem-solving. Employing the XLM to do this is the focus of the next chapter.

Section VI

Use It, Don't Lose It—
How to Apply What You Learn

This final section contains only two chapters. The first will help you apply the XLM as a daily decision-making and problem-solving tool. The second will help you implement the best ideas you gleaned from the book into actual practice.

CHAPTER 21

Quality Decision-Making and Problem-Solving

The most serious mistakes are not being made as a result of wrong answers. The truly dangerous thing is asking the wrong questions.

PETER DRUCKER

THE PROBLEM WITH PROBLEMS

If you had all the time and money in the world whenever you had a decision to make, could you make quality decisions every time? Maybe. But that's the problem with problems, isn't it? You don't have all the time or money in the world to solve them. As you decide how to address any issue, you are — whether you know it or not — weighing a trade-off between effort and accuracy.[1]

Failure to find the right balance between effort and accuracy is caused by what Professor John Hammond and his colleagues call "the hidden traps in decision-making."[2] Like sand traps to a golfer, these decision traps influence our thinking, thereby affecting our decisions, which impact our actions, thus governing our outcomes. Better outcomes begin with better thinking about decisions and problems.

You've read about my million-dollar idea, the interactive CD-ROM *Strategy* that automated medical marketing. I spent two years and a truckload of money creating and marketing this innovative product when I started my own company many years ago. It failed miserably because, back then, I didn't know about these decision-making traps or how to avoid them. This chapter will help you understand and circumvent them.

Does it surprise you to read there are only seven decision-making traps? When we're facing difficult choices, it can seem as if the traps are innumerable, like playing golf on the beach. But in reality, these seven are the most common causes of poor decision-making.

Anchoring

Let me ask you a couple of quick questions:

- Do you think that the population of Malaysia is greater than 100 million?
- What is your best estimate of the population of California?

If you're like most people, the information embedded in the first question influenced your answer to the second question. This is an example of the anchoring trap — our tendency to give a disproportionate weight to the first information we receive. As Professor Hammond and his colleagues reported in the *Harvard Business Review,* "Initial impressions, estimates, or data anchor subsequent thoughts and judgments."[3]

When do you fall into this trap? How about when creating forecasts? Do you rely too heavily on past data? The trap is also frequent during negotiations (opening positions), the hiring process (first impressions), and performance evaluations (review last year's evaluation).

Much of the misery from the Great Recession is attributable to financial leaders who believed the housing market would continue its meteoric rise. One reason they mismanaged the paradoxical tension between risk and profit is because they thought information embedded in past housing profits accurately predicted future housing profits. Executives who answer today's challenges with yesterday's thinking also fall into this trap.

Avoid the anchoring bias by remembering that although the past may *predict* the future, it does not *equal* the future. When you review numbers to develop a forecast, question where the numbers come from and the motivations of those who provided them. Learn from the past without being seduced by it. (By the way, the population of Malaysia is 28.7 million; California's is 37.2 million.)

It's okay to look at the past, just don't stare.

BENJAMIN DOVER

Status quo

Please complete this sentence: An object in motion tends to ____________.

If you answered "stay in motion," you get a gold star. And remember, the flip-side of this physics law is that an object at rest tends to stay at rest.

This law is also at work when we make decisions. We have a tendency to stick to the status quo—to leave well enough alone and go with the flow. To get along we learn to go along. Just as it's always easier to swim downriver, when making decisions it feels safer not to try something new. Often, that's because our organizational cultures have conditioned us not to rock the boat. It's less risky to do what is conventional in most organizations because, as Hammond and his colleagues say, "Sins of commission (doing something) tend to be punished much more severely than sins of omission (doing nothing)."

Climb out of status quo trap by answering three questions:

1. How would I approach this decision if I were starting from scratch?
2. What if I acted as if the culture supported an experimental ("let's try it") mindset?
3. Is there a way to test the idea without a major investment?

Sunk costs

Kelley Knutson, executive vice president of global services for credit card processor TSYS, shared one of his painful leadership lessons several years ago when I was working with his team in the U.K. He said he was not hurt as much by the "good" employees that got away as he was by the "bad" (poor performers) he allowed to stay too long. Kelley learned how the concept of sunk costs applied to decisions.

How about you?

Did you ever spend too much time trying to improve the performance of an employee you should have fired? Did you ever continue investing in a project that you (or one of your direct reports) should have canceled long ago? Have you heard about bankers who continued to lend money to a failing business? Or a gambler who kept playing because he hoped his luck would change?

These scenarios are all examples of the sunk costs trap—"the tendency to continue an endeavor once an investment in money, effort, or time has been made."[4] The primary reason I threw good money after bad with my CD-ROM project was that I was reluctant to admit errors to myself or others. Don't let this happen to you.

You can step around this trap by asking yourself, If I had not spent any time or money on this activity, would I do so now?

Framing

Which of the two middle circles, surrounded by different size circles, is larger?

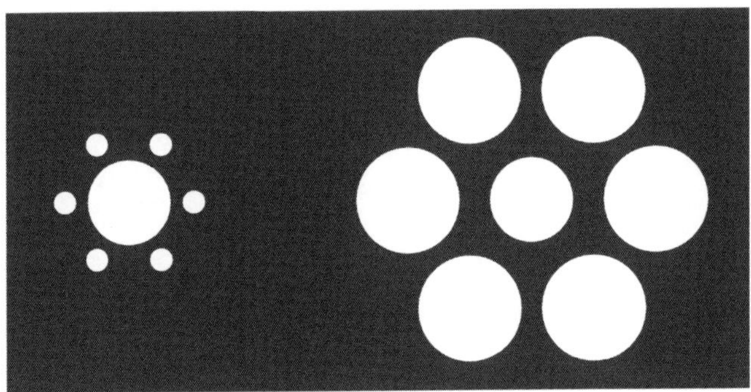

Although it appears that the left-middle circle is larger, both the left-middle and right-middle circles are the same size. The left looks bigger because it's surrounded by smaller circles, thus providing different reference points. Context matters because it influences perception.

In decision-making, this is called the framing trap, which we can also illustrate by answering two questions:

> Would you accept a 50-50 chance of either losing $300 or winning $500?

What if, instead, I asked:

> Would you prefer to keep your checking account balance of $2,000 or to accept a 50-50 chance of having either $1,700 or $2,500 in your account?

If you actually had $2,000 in your checking account, these two questions would pose the same problem and risk. From a rational perspective, your decision should be the same. However, numerous studies have shown that many people would decide to refuse the 50-50 chance in the first question, but accept it in the second. This is because of their different reference points. The first question emphasizes absolute gains and losses, which triggers the thought of losing money. The second question, with its reference point of $2,000, frames the decision in a different perspective by emphasizing the relatively minor financial impact of losing money when you already have $2,000.

While executives are seldom skilled at framing an issue, politicians usually are. Al Gore was able to frame a global warming issue with his book titled *An Inconvenient Truth*. The title says that although the truth may be inconvenient, and it may not be what you want to hear, it is the truth and you should listen. Gore also framed the issue as a "moral imperative." By linking the issue to people's lives and values, he mobilized the environmentalist movement and the mass media.

You also see the same principle apply in stem cell debates. Pro-life politicians frame stem cell research as murder because it destroys human embryos. Stem cell advocates fight back by framing the research as our best hope of attacking debilitating diseases affecting millions of Americans. Advocates know that it is difficult to call an influential spokesperson like actor Michael J. Fox a murderer.

False assumptions

Professors Robert Cross and Susan Brodt tell the story of a Fortune 100 company that made a major investment to manufacture and distribute a core product in Asia.[5] They reported that the project's champion knew very little about Asia, but was convinced he could succeed in Asia just as he had in the United States. He held fast to his assumptions despite financial, operational, and strategic information that contradicted his views. After it became an utter fiasco, the project manager and senior executives realized that their poor decision rested on their false assumptions.

Assumptions are the hidden foundations on which we build decisions. If the assumptions are shaky, the decisions seldom hold up and the house of cards collapses. Avoid this trap by asking your team to surface assumptions in a brainstorming session. Write this simple statement—*I assume*—on a whiteboard and ask everyone to complete the sentence as it relates to a specific decision. Don't discuss any responses just yet. Just write what your team is telling you. Ask the team to continue surfacing these assumptions until you have a long list.

Then review and discuss those assumptions that are most likely to affect the decision most negatively. Make sure you discuss possible false assumptions related to overestimating the value of consensus, undervaluing objective assessments, and closing the door on constructive feedback. These three false assumptions often lead to poor decisions.

Missed signals

In the mid-1990s, one of England's oldest merchant banks went bankrupt after losing a billion dollars on unauthorized trades by a single trader. A government report on the collapse of this bank concluded that "a number of warning signs were present, but that individuals in a number of different departments failed to face up to, or follow up on, identified problems."[6]

How often do you miss the signals? How can you set up a simple system to track important signals as you pursue your strategic goals?

Competition

The emotional urge to win during a competitive challenge often leads to costly decision errors. The medical device company Boston Scientific fell into this trap during its acquisition of the medical device maker Guidant. First, Johnson & Johnson announced plans to acquire Guidant. Soon thereafter, J&J threatened to pull out and lowered its purchase price offer because of Guidant's pacemaker recall. That's when Boston Scientific—J&J's rival—offered to buy Guidant. The bidding war was on.

Boston Scientific's final and "winning" offer of $27.2 billion was $1.8 billion more than J&J's initial bid. Most financial analysts believe that this was a disastrous acquisition by Boston Scientific, demonstrated by the drop in its share price. How could smart individuals make such a costly error? The emotion of competition played a role in overriding sound decision-making.[7]

Any one of these seven decision-making traps can drag us down. As a quick recap, let's see which ones I fell into during my CD-ROM disaster:

- I based my early profit projections on optimistic market penetration, thus subjecting myself to the perils of the anchoring trap.
- The status quo trap reared its ugly head when I refused to kill the project when I realized the project was in deep trouble.
- Sunk costs almost buried me because my ego encouraged me to throw good money after bad.
- I fell into the framing trap by comparing my relatively minor losses to the millions of dollars that Silicon Valley entrepreneurs were losing.
- I also made a number of false assumptions, including the belief that users would spend time entering data and that physicians cared about marketing.
- I missed many signals, including hints from friends in medicine who were not enthusiastic about my product.
- My ego was so attached to winning that persistence morphed into obstinancy.

Now let's learn how to use four simple questions—questions that encompass the four styles of the XLM—to steer clear of these traps and make better and more consistent daily decisions.

Four questions that improve decision-making and problem-solving

Think of a challenge confronting you or your team. We are going to use that challenge to discuss a fundamental approach to making decisions. Remember, better thinking leads to better decisions; these decisions determine your actions, thereby producing your results. Thus, the precursor to quality leadership results is quality leadership thinking.

The XLM is shown in Figure 21.1, with the four fundamental questions that can help you make better decisions when confronting everyday challenges.

FIGURE 21.1

Four Fundamental Questions That Lead to Better Decisions

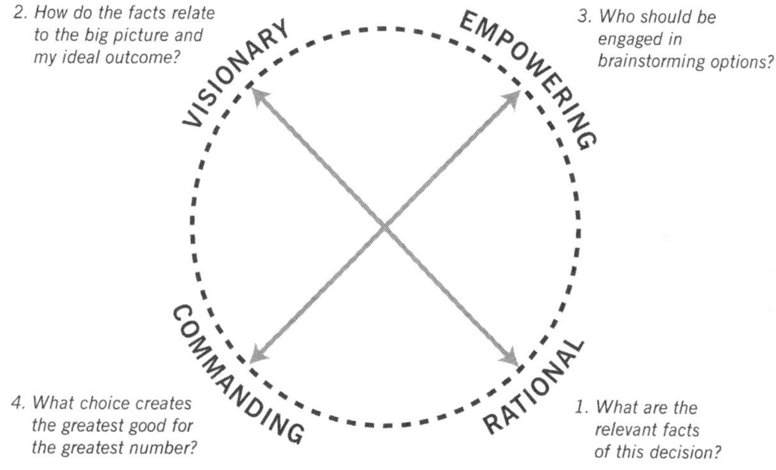

When you choose to ask these questions, you are actually drawing on the wisdom of the ages. That's because these four questions are rooted in philosophy.

Epistemology

This is the branch of philosophy that investigates the study of knowledge—how we know what we know. In decision-making, the first question we must ask ourselves is, "What are the relevant facts of this decision?"

This is a rational thinking question because it relates to monitoring our environment closely and being in touch with the facts.

For example, when confronted by poor-performing employees, do you gather all the facts related to their performance before beginning a counseling session?

Metaphysics

This branch of philosophy deals with universal truths and ultimate questions—how it all relates to the big picture. In decision-making, the second question we ask ourselves is, "How does the challenge relate to the big picture and our ideal outcome?"

This is a visionary thinking question because it invites contemplation of a broad perspective, strategic implications, and long-term consequences.

For example, when you are deciding how to handle an employee who made a mistake, do you take the time to look at the mistake in the context of the employee's overall, long-term performance? Have you considered what the best outcome could be?

Ethics

This branch of philosophy is concerned with the moral code and values we use when interacting with others—how decisions affect others. In decision-making, the third question we ask is, "Who should be engaged in brainstorming options and alternatives?"

This is an empowering question because it focuses our attention on involving and serving those we lead.

For example, the president of an association, Michelle, was hiring a senior executive. She preferred to offer the position to an internal candidate, Bill. Unfortunately, Bill was weak in the core competency of communicating trust and empathy. Michelle had talked about this weakness with Bill a few times, but hadn't seen much growth. I invited Michelle to engage Bill by asking him to create a detailed plan to improve the competency. Michelle did just that, and subsequently hired Bill, who is now making great strides in his weaker competency and performing well in his new position.

How could you engage stakeholders more fully when you make decisions?

Existentialism

The last major branch of our philosophical tree reminds us that human beings have free will and therefore are responsible for their actions. It leads us to the final decision-making question based on utilitarianism: "What choice creates the greatest good for the greatest number?"

This commanding question compels us to refuse victim thinking and accept responsibility for our choices and their consequences.

Answer these four simple XLM questions and you can avoid falling into daily decision-making traps. As evidence, here's an e-mail I received from one CEO:

> Dear Dave,
>
> Thank you for coaching me to use the XLM as a decision-making tool. This simple and powerful approach clarified our current situation and provided direction in making a decision that resulted in a savings of $147,000. I now use the XLM as I make decisions throughout the day.
>
> Thanks again,
>
> Jim

As you go about making your daily decisions, I encourage you to keep the XLM in front of you and ask the four key questions in Figure 21.1. Use it at your meetings by asking your team to brainstorm answers to these questions. Although this process won't tell you what to do, it will help frame the discussion.

How surprised will you be when you find yourself making better decisions because you seldom stumble into the seven decision-making traps?

Leaders don't tell others what to think.
They teach them how to think.

Deep questions for difficult challenges

When important challenges become more difficult, ambiguous, or complex, you can also use the XLM as a guide for asking deeper questions. Let's outline a series of questions, categorized by leadership style, that can improve your decision-making and problem-solving when confronting these especially difficult challenges.

Rational questions

In deciding how to address a complex challenge, the rational style invites you to be aware of the external and internal framework of your decision by asking:

- Have I defined the problem well?
- Do I have the correct information to meet this challenge?
- What is my backup plan?
- What assumptions am I making?
- How will I monitor the implementation of this decision?

Visionary questions

While rational thinking is related to gathering the facts about your challenge, visionary thinking considers those facts in a much broader context.

Ironically, moving closer to a concrete solution requires that you step back and reflect on the big picture. This means evaluating your challenge in the context of your overall strategy by answering such questions as:

- How does this challenge relate to the organization's direction?
- Is this a problem worth investing resources to solve?
- Have I imagined the downstream negative consequences?
- When do I really need to decide?
- Imagine that I am looking back on this decision from the future and it has turned out poorly. What went wrong?
- What might I think when I'm sitting in a rocking chair and reflecting on this issue during retirement?
- Am I too invested in the status quo?
- How is my ego affected by this situation?

Empowering questions

The third key to meeting a difficult challenge is to think about it from an empowering perspective, which requires that you consider such questions as:

- Who are the key stakeholders affected by this decision?
- How might we engage these stakeholders in exploring alternatives?
- Have we considered the opinions of those with whom I often disagree?
- Do we have options that express our core values?

Commanding questions

Eventually you must choose what to do, or what not to do. Here are a few more questions that will help you think critically as you access your free will responsibly:

- How risky are my alternatives?
- Can I test the alternatives on a small scale before I decide?
- If everyone in this organization had to do exactly what I am contemplating doing, what type of organization would we have?
- What is the best thing to do for the greatest number of people without violating individual rights?

A vice president I've been coaching reported that he was very pleased with the work that his direct reports were now bringing to him. He had coached them to apply the XLM to their decision-making, as I had coached him. His managers no longer brought him problems; instead, they brought well-thought-out options—what he considers completed staff work.

The vice president understood that leadership is the process of unleashing the energy of people toward worthy goals. He also realized that the essence of leadership is decision-making and problem-solving. His management team is now using the XLM as a process to improve the quality and consistency of decision-making and problem-solving. You can too.

As Peter Drucker reminds us, leadership used to be about having the right answers. Now, it's about asking the right questions. I encourage you and your team to use the XLM to ask the fundamental questions in this chapter.

• • •

Knowledge is not power; applied knowledge is power. Our next and concluding chapter shows you how to apply the best ideas you gleaned from this book into a simple, yet powerful development plan. It is the most important chapter because the purpose of the book is to help you expand your leadership capacity so you can make a bigger and better difference in people's lives.

CHAPTER 22
The Most Important Part of This Book

If your actions inspire others to dream more, learn more, do more, and become more, you are a leader.

JOHN QUINCY ADAMS

VELCRO...OR TEFLON?

The world-renowned research cardiologist at UC San Diego marched into my office many years ago and announced, "Dave, congratulations! Your abstract was accepted and you're going to present our research at the scientific conference."

I gulped, "Okay, Vic." I had finished graduate school only three months before and was completing my internship. This was going to be the first scientific meeting I'd ever attended, much less presented at.

Vic continued, "We also have a rule here that if you go to a conference, you have to teach what you learn to the rest of us when you get back."

"Do you mind if I ask why you have that rule?"

"Dave, the only reason to go to any meeting or conference is to improve things after the meeting." Vic smiled. "If you have to teach us what you learn, there's a greater chance that the learning will stick."

Ever since that conversation 33 years ago, I have continued to refine a powerful process to increase the chance that my learning and teaching sticks like Velcro. This process is based on my philosophy that the most important part of any learning is what happens *after* you learn it, what my colleagues at Emory call WISDOM—What I Shall Do On Monday! That's why I think this chapter in the most important part of the book.

The following section describes the process to help you avoid Teflon learning by having a Velcro experience. Many executives discover that using this seven-step system delivers the greatest return on their training buck. So, feel free to share it.

Brainstorm challenges and strategies

Begin by answering this question: What major challenges am I facing at work?

Let your ideas flow and keep your pen moving as you brainstorm the answers to this question. You might also want to reflect on your goals, your organization's strategy, and the paradoxical challenges described in Chapter 1.

Write a SMART goal

Based on your business challenges, professional goals, and your organization's strategic imperatives, write a goal for your executive development plan that is:

- Specific
- Measurable
- Attainable
- Responsible
- Timed

What skill or competency do you want to improve? For example, one executive stated her goal as follows: Improve my coaching skills by mid-year to help my direct reports develop professionally.

Meet with your leader

Meet with your boss for a few minutes to discuss your goal. Ask how well you have aligned your development goal with your boss's and the organization's overall strategy.

Create an insights, ideas, and behaviors page

What insights, ideas, and behaviors (IIBs) did you gain from the book? If you don't have any, go back and review the table of contents and create a list of your favorite ideas from the chapter headings. You may also find it helpful to review and adapt the following IIBs, which come from leaders who have attended my classes over the years:

- Use the XLM for personal and team development: Ask team members to assess their XLM (http://xlmassessment.com/). Then develop ways to leverage the team's talents and hold each other accountable for stretching. Meet every two weeks to measure progress and celebrate successes.

- Work on a weaker competency: Select a weaker XLM competency to work on independent from my team. Adapt a few of the tools (in the chapter describing that competency) to strengthen this competency.
- Improve emotional intelligence: Use the ideas (in the chapters on EI) to help regulate emotions.
- Focus on what's important to team members: Meet individually with one team member every day for five minutes to discuss individual concerns, clarify expectations, and applaud small successes.
- Increase two-way communication: Speak last at meetings, ask more questions, listen better, and remember that broadcasting is not communicating.
- Conduct after-action reviews: Coach others by delegating small portions of a job, and then ask these five questions after completion:
  1. What results did we expect and achieve?
  2. Why the difference?
  3. What lessons were learned?
  4. How will we use these lessons in the future?
  5. Who else might benefit from these lessons?
- Make better decisions using the XLM: Access all four leadership styles (rational, visionary, empowering, commanding) when making decisions. Use this process to encourage direct reports to submit completed staff work and recommendations.
- Manage anxiety: When stressed, ask the team, How can we view this problem or situation differently? Remind them that anxiety is the essence of growth, and that great companies approach difficulties as opportunities grow.
- Understand concerns and focus on influence: Use Stephen Covey's circle of concern and influence to encourage everyone on the team to choose responsibly.

Review your favorite IIBs with a partner

Review your list of IIBs with a partner or colleague. Focus your discussion on a few IIBs that will help you reach your goal. For example: "I will coach my direct reports by scheduling one five-minute meeting every day with one of them."

Link your new behaviors with an old habit

One of the best ways to remind yourself to practice your new behaviors is to link those new behaviors to an existing habit or system (old habit

+ new behavior = new habit). For example: Linking Outlook scheduling (old habit) and coaching (new behavior) will help create the new habit of coaching your direct reports. At a retreat with political leaders, one leader indicated that she was going to use her old habit of taking notes in meetings with her new behavior of asking more questions by writing a question mark at the top of her notepad every time she asked questions. Another executive said that sticking Post-it notes on her phone would be a great reminder to practice her new behavior.

Review and celebrate progress

Solicit feedback from a colleague or your manager regarding your implementation of these behaviors. Ask them to help you monitor your progress. Once a week, report the progress and challenges you are experiencing as you use your new behaviors. Make sure you also celebrate your small successes.

My first scientific presentation many years ago didn't go very well, but my debrief to my colleagues back at UCSD about what I learned at the meeting did. In fact, after that meeting, Vic hired me and I spent the next five years as a researcher...and learning how to make learning stick like Velcro.

How about you?

A closing story about you

The sun danced on the stainless steel rails of the hospital bed as the late-afternoon sun filtered through the blinds. The orderly, a petite Latina in her mid-50s, placed her polishing cloth in the blue plastic bucket. Then, she calmed the sheets on the empty bed with long, slow, smooth strokes. She picked up her blue bucket and a clipboard, checked a few items off her list, and then turned to speak with the bald patient in the other bed.

I heard them both laugh as I watched from the hallway. The orderly then walked out of the patient's room into the noisy corridor and came face-to-face with me.

"Excuse me, ma'am," I said. "May I ask you a question?"

"Yes," she said, "of course."

"You do such a wonderful job here. What are you thinking as you work?"

A broad smile spread across her face and lit up her big brown eyes. Her machine-gun response with a heavy accent came straight at me. "Our department leader told us a long time ago to clean the patient's room thinking that the next patient going to be in the bed would be our mothers."

"Thank you," I said, "for making a difference to all the patients in this hospital and their families."

She startled me by asking, "How do you know I make a difference to patients?"

"Because the woman dying of lung cancer in the other bed is my mother. And Mom has told me all about you. She looks forward to your visits. You mean more to my mom than many of the doctors and nurses here." I smiled. "But don't tell them, OK?"

She thanked me for making her day and floated down the hall, about an inch off the ground.

The leader's job is to unleash the energy of others toward worthy goals. The orderly's department leader did just that, and it meant the world to my mother and me. I close with this story because it illustrates the impact that executives like you have on people's lives every single day. This story is really about the huge difference you make.

As you lead your team, your family, and your life, my hope is that *The Executive's Paradox* helps you stretch when you're pulled, so you make an even bigger difference.

Thank you.

Appendices

APPENDIX A

Desperately Seeking Someone

I am convinced that nothing we do is more important than hiring and developing people. At the end of the day you bet on people, not on strategies.

LARRY BOSSIDY

LINCOLN'S WAR FOR TALENT

When asked why he filled his top three cabinet posts with his opponents from the 1860 Republican presidential nomination, Abraham Lincoln responded, "I had looked the party over and concluded these were the very strongest men."[1]

Lincoln understood that his performance depended greatly on the team he put together. He also knew there was a huge cost if he didn't hire the strongest people for the job.

Do you know your costs of hiring the wrong people?

CALCULATE THE COSTS OF TURNOVER

A Watson Wyatt survey estimated the total costs of turnover for a typical employee to be between 48% and 61% of the person's annual salary.[2] The report pointed out that hiring costs have three components:

1. Hard dollar costs (e.g., recruiting)
2. Lost productivity (before leaving, during recruitment, and throughout the on-boarding of the new hire)
3. Other losses (e.g., lower morale, changing priorities to handle other employees' work)

For a firm with 10,000 employees earning an average salary of $50,000 per year (including benefits), a 15% annual turnover rate would cost $36 million to $45.75 million annually.

What are your costs?

Another way to look at the financial implications of hiring decisions is to multiply the average number of years employees stay in your organization times their salary. For example, if you are hiring a mid-level manager with a salary of $100,000 per year and your managers stay for an average of ten years, every mid-level manager hiring decision you make is a $1 million decision.

It pays to hire right.

Finding top talent

How easy is it for you to find good employees to hire? Depending on the position and availability of the talent pool for that position, finding good employees may be relatively easy (store clerk in a slow economy) to extraordinarily difficult (mid-level IT manager in a growing segment of the industry).

One reason it is difficult to find excellent employees is related to the law of averages, as illustrated by the IQ bell curve in Figure A.1. The normal bell curve distribution tells us that 34% of the population is a little above and a little below (one standard deviation of) the average performers in most qualities that you might hire for (e.g., intelligence, people skills, work habits, personality characteristics). If you want to hire top talent, you are searching for them in the right-most portion of the curve (i.e., way above average). This means that there are very, very few top performers (2.1%) in your candidate pool.

The left portion of the curve also tells us that there are some poor performers out there. So, you'd better have excellent interviewing skills to weed out these low performers.

FIGURE A.1
The Bell Curve of Talent

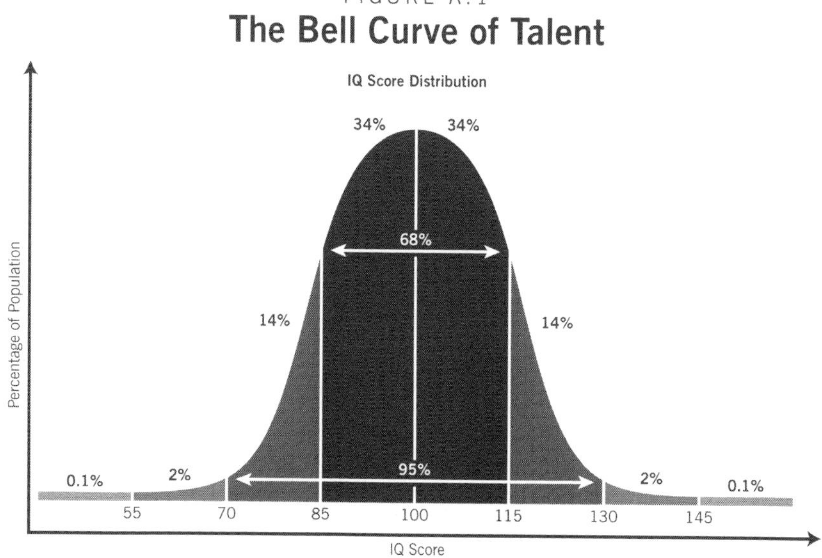

How well do you interview others?

How good are leaders at interviewing and hiring the best?

The University of Texas Medical School helped answer this question when its leaders interviewed and scored 800 applicants in an effort to admit only the best.[3] These ratings played an important role in the selection of the students, along with grades and the quality of the undergraduate schools the students attended. Thus, the medical school admitted only students who ranked high.

In an unexpected twist, the Texas legislature required the medical school to admit another 50 students. Because competing schools had already admitted all the other top candidates, the University of Texas Medical School was forced to admit 50 poorly ranked medical students.

The good news was that no one at the school (except a few researchers) knew there was a high-ranking and low-ranking group. The startling news was that, four years later, there was no performance difference between these two groups. Graduation rates, honors received, and grades were all the same. In addition, both groups performed equally well during the first year of residency.

So much for the interviewing strategies of top medical schools—and the same can be said for most organizations!

Researchers George Hollenbeck and Robert Eichinger of the Lominger group remind us that executives in most organizations, commit six common mistakes during the interview process:[4]

MISTAKE 1. LACK OF PREPARATION: You can't hit a target if you do not aim for it. Yet that's exactly what executives do when they conduct an interview without clearly defining the nature of the responsibilities and competencies needed to fulfill a specific job.

MISTAKE 2. FIRST-IMPRESSION BIAS: Many executives reach their hiring decision within the first three minutes of the interview, often subconsciously. They then spend the rest of the interview confirming their initial impression.

MISTAKE 3. LIMITED NOTE-TAKING: Failure to take notes during the interview makes it difficult to discuss the candidates with colleagues after all interviews conclude.

MISTAKE 4. FOCUSING ON IRRELEVANT BEHAVIORS: Spending too much time discussing intriguing but irrelevant behaviors decreases the amount of time one can spend understanding specific behaviors required to perform essential job functions.

Mistake 5. Leading questions: Often, interviewers spend too much time providing information or asking questions that inadvertently tell candidates what is most important to the interviewer.

Mistake 6. Unstructured evaluation process: Failing to establish or adhere to clear evaluation criteria to compare candidates also hurts decision-making.

Across all industries, about 50% of new employees leave within the first seven months. Which of these six mistakes contribute to turnover among your new hires? What are your strategies for avoiding these very costly mistakes?

Your success as an executive is determined greatly by whether you win your war for top talent. The battle begins by framing this process as a prediction issue. In other words, base everything you do in the hiring process on what probably predicts success on the job. For example, when you ask specific questions, you should do so because you have evidence that their answers predict job performance. The XLM can help you frame your entire hiring process as a prediction issue, thereby increasing the probability that you will your war for talent.

Use the XLM to win your war for talent

The XLM is a weapon to help you win your war. Use it to structure your interviewing process. The XLM approach has several advantages compared to an informal or unstructured process because it helps you:

- Specify the critical behavior and core competencies required for the job.
- Increase the involvement from those who will work with the new hire.
- Facilitate the evaluation and selection of candidates.
- Provide better legal validity than an unstructured, conversational interview.

Because the XLM approach to interviewing and hiring top talent is based on research, I predict you will probably get the results you want (better hires, higher productivity, lower turnover and costs) as you adapt it to suit your environment.

FIGURE A.2

Apply the XLM to Interview and Hire Top Talent

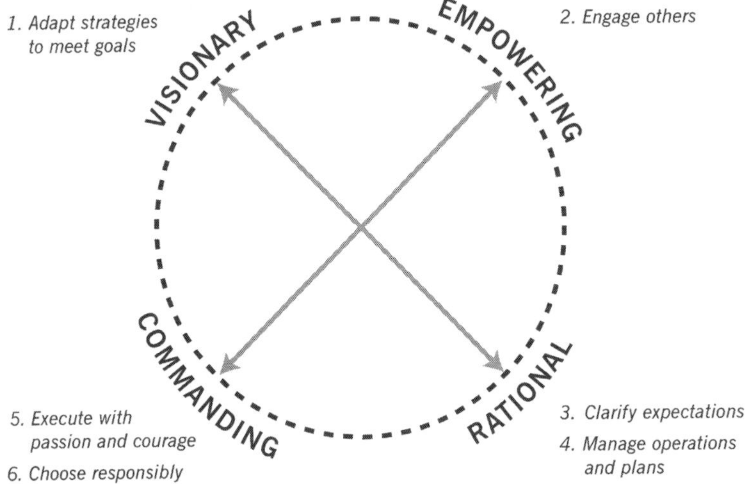

Adapt strategies to meet goals

How does this position relate to our strategy? This is the first question to ask when you have an open position. Do you really need that position at this time? If so, how do the duties relate to your big picture? Too often, leaders hire just because the position is open.

I suggest that you reposition your open position by thinking strategically. Answer these SWOT (strengths, weaknesses, opportunities, threats) questions with key members of your hiring team:

- What are our strategic goals?
- What are our biggest challenges and threats to achieving these goals?
- What are the critical objectives the person in this position must accomplish?
- For someone to accomplish these objectives, what skills and competencies must the person have?
- What weaknesses are unacceptable?

Engage others

The people who understand what skills are necessary to fill the open position are those who are in contact with that position. It is logical and desirable, therefore, to engage them as you define and refine the competencies of the position. Here are two methods for obtaining fast and effective 360-feedback for your job analysis.

1. The five-minute, one-on-one meeting: Ask several team members who surround the open position to meet with you, one-on-one, for five minutes. These team members should include colleagues (those who do a job similar to the one you are hiring for), subordinates (those who report to that position), and supervisors (those who manage employees in the position you're hiring for).

Begin this brief meeting by reminding them how valuable their contribution is to the hiring process. Then, ask each person, individually, to help you hire the best person for the open position by writing the answers to these questions:

- Now that ______________________________ (name of the person who left the open position) is gone and the position is open, what competencies would you like to see in the new hire?
- What do you think are the keys to success in that job?
- What weaknesses would cause the biggest problems for a person in that position?
- Six months from now, if we hired someone great, what behaviors would you see in this person at work?
- Is there anything else I should know to hire the best person for the job?

2. The two-minute drill: Conduct this drill as an agenda item during a meeting with people who understand the open position. These people may include team members (including people selected for a one-on-one, five-minute meeting), as well as the HR and the recruiting team. Explain that you need their input on this critical hire. Inform them that one important predictor of retention and employee satisfaction is "fit," which is why you have devised the following exercise:

- Distribute a blank sheet of paper.
- Ask people to draw a one-inch diameter circle in the middle of the page, and to print the word FIT in the middle of the circle.
- Tell them that you will give a prize to the person who writes the most answers to a question. They have only two minutes to write as many answers as possible. Remind them that quantity, not quality, is what counts. Ask them to answer this question: What skills, qualities, and competencies must a person have to be a great fit for this position?
- At the end of two minutes, have each person count the number of answers, and then give a prize for the person with the most.

- Collect the individual sheets and tell people you'll process their answers later. (You may also choose to debrief the exercise during the meeting.) Make sure you inform people at a future meeting how you used their input.
- Analyze the input. Identify which skills, qualities, and competencies best fit the open position.

Clarify expectations

The job description is the target you are aiming for during the hiring process. Update the job description by reviewing your job analysis (i.e., strategic analysis, team input from the previous exercises, and feedback from your HR department). Make sure that the job description clearly identifies a few critical competencies — essential job functions — that relate to specific results.

Manage operations and plans

Many leaders feel that they can just wing it when it comes to the interview process. Of course, they *can*—anyone can. The problem is that poorly structured interviews fail to weed out poor performers, and good candidates often refuse job offers if they feel that the interview process has gone poorly.

Research clearly shows that a well-planned interview is far superior to an informal, unstructured interviewing process.[5] In addition to leading to better hires, a structured interview increases the confidence of interviewers, facilitates standardization, and improves defensibility in court.

Plan a structured interview by following these steps:

1. Identify the five to seven key competencies required to perform the job, based on the updated job description.
2. Create a scoring sheet to assess the candidates' responses based on these competencies.
3. Schedule the time needed for the interview (approximately ten minutes for each competency) and select a neutral location.
4. Review the candidates' background information by scanning their resumes.
5. Prepare a list of questions that target the key competencies. The nature of the questions should be consistent with an in-depth job interview, as explained below.

Execute with passion and courage

The outcome of the previous steps yields a clear picture of the ideal candidate and prepares you to conduct what I call a "depth interview." The depth interview has six simple steps, and most leaders execute the first five well. We'll outline these five briefly and spend the majority of this subsection discussing the last critical interview step for predicting success on the job.

1. Introduce yourself: Meet the candidate on neutral ground, preferably not your office. Your initial goal is to help the other person feel relaxed. If you do need to meet in your office, pull your chair around from behind your desk so that you are on "their side."

2. Explain the process: Inform the candidate what the process is. Briefly explain the format you would like to follow.

3. Establish rapport: Offer to get the candidate coffee or something to drink. People will usually say no, unless you indicate that you are getting something for yourself. Some interviewers like to take the candidate on a brief tour. This works well if your facility has some special attraction.

4. Give a quick overview: Let the candidate know what your organization is about and how the position the person is applying for fits into the mission of the organization. This is the time to sell your organization, but it should be a "quick overview." I've cringed as executives babble on about their organization for 15 minutes. That's 25% of the time allocated to most interviews. You are not learning anything when you're talking. So keep it brief.

5. Ask a transition question: After the early chit-chat, ask a transition question, such as, "Before we get started, can you tell me...."

- Why are you interested in this position?
- How did you hear about the open position?
- What do you know about our organization?

6. Interview for depth: Your primary job during the interview is to determine if the person who shows up for the interview is probably going to be the same person who shows up for the job. Your focus, therefore, must be to penetrate the candidate's veneer and ascertain who is beneath the surface, because that is who is going arrive at work every day.

These guidelines for interviewing for depth do just that:

- Focus on fit questions: The number-one cause of employee turnover in the first year is lack of fit. If they don't fit, they're going to quit. Fit relates to the skills needed to perform the duties and the employee's ability to fit into the culture of your organization. Your job, during the interview, is to ask questions relevant to these two domains. Specifically, focus on the fundamental few areas that target those essential job functions that you uncovered when you engaged others in refining the job description.
- Keep it simple and short (KISS): The candidate should speak 80% of the time. Ask brief questions that you prepared in advance.
- Ask open-ended questions: To keep the job candidate talking, ask mostly open-ended questions that someone cannot answer with one word. For example, instead of asking if teamwork is important to the candidate (close-ended), ask the person to tell you about a time when she created teamwork to accomplish a difficult goal (open-ended).
- Ask broad questions in the beginning and narrow questions at the end: For example, if performing under pressure at crunch time is an essential skill, ask what qualities the person feels are important in performing the duties (a general question). If the candidate does not bring up performing under pressure, you have learned that this skill is not at the forefront of his mind. On the other hand, if you ask specifically about performing under pressure early in the interview, you've just told the candidate that crunch time is important to performing this job well. For the rest of the interview, the candidate may try to convince you that his nickname is "Captain Crunch." I'm not suggesting that you avoid asking this question altogether; rather, I am inviting you to ask about what is most important to you nearer the end of the interview.
- Ask layered questions: Obviously, candidates try to impress everyone they meet during the interview. Asking layered questions is one way to see beneath appearances and uncover the real candidate. Layered questions get to the heart of any topic by reaching the soul of any candidate. I'm referring to three important questions:
    1. Tell me...
    2. Why?
    3. How?

1. *Tell me questions* ask the candidate to tell you about a past experience (behavior-based) or a future situation (situational), or to role-play. Because the past usually forecasts the future, I encourage you to ask more questions related to the past. For example, if you are interviewing a candidate to manage your rapidly growing shipping department, you might ask "collaboration" questions such as these:
   - Tell me about the process you went through the last time you purchased capital equipment for your shipping department. (Behavior-based)
   - Tell me how you would evaluate a vendor partnership if you were going to make a major equipment purchase. (Situational)
   - Imagine I am your purchasing department, calling you because I'm unhappy that we have not been kept up-to-date regarding the purchase of new equipment. Tell me how you would handle this situation. (Role-play)
2. *Why questions* are follow-up questions, specifically targeted to the candidates response to your *tell me* questions. Using the previous examples, you might ask the following why questions:
   - Why would you take that approach to purchasing?
   - Why do you feel your strategy would actually work with vendors?
   - That was a great role-play. Why did you take that approach to resolve the issue?
3. *How questions* ask the candidate to project his previous answers to your environment. These questions assess whether the candidate really understands how this skill applies in new situations. They also provide excellent insight into an important general competency called *learning agility*. Learning agility is the will and skill to learn from experience. It is highly correlated with performance ratings, promotions, and success after promotions.[6] Continuing with our previous examples, you could follow up the candidate's answers to your why questions with these questions:
   - How might that purchasing approach be adapted to our team-oriented environment?
   - How would you ensure great vendor relationships if you worked in a government-regulated environment?
   - If you worked here, how would you make sure that people in purchasing felt included in the process, yet didn't slow down your equipment purchase?

Do you see what happens during the layered questions? You start with the easy, surface questions. Then you drill down. Many candidates will answer the first *tell me* question easily. However, as you ask follow-up questions that drill deeper, weaker candidates start floundering like fish out of water because they are out of their element in the area you are probing. Layered questions allow you to sort out candidates with depth from those who have none.

You should focus the majority of your interview on layered questions related to fit. I suggest you rate the candidate using a scoring sheet as you finish each line of questioning. It will make it much easier for you to compare the candidates objectively when all the interviews conclude. If you don't document and score your interviews, you are more likely to hire the last candidate interviewed, regardless of the person's fit. In hiring, this decision-making trap is called the "recency effect," and it is similar to the anchoring trap (discussed in Chapter 21).

Choose responsibly

Near the end of the interview, close strong by taking these final, critical steps:

1. Ask the candidates if they have any questions, or if there is something they would like to say.
2. Explain the next steps so the candidates know what to expect and when they'll hear back from you.
3. Ask them this question right before they walk out your door: If we offer you this position, what would cause you to take it? This question lets you know exactly what it will take to hire your top candidates.

As the door hits the candidate in the hindquarters, quantify the candidate according to the essential job functions. Use a simple spreadsheet and evaluate all your candidates on a one-to-five scale. Some interviewers find it more accurate to grade candidates during the interview process, but at the very least you need to score your candidates immediately after the interview concludes.

Hiring top talent is critical to executive and organizational success. Table A.1 summarizes ten hiring practices outlined by the XLM process. I urge you to work with your HR team to adapt them to fit your environment, so you win your war for talent.

TABLE A.1

XLM-Based Best Practices for Hiring Top Talent

1. Understand the costs of hiring poorly.
2. Update the job description with input from those who truly know the position.
3. Avoid confirmation bias. It occurs when the interviewer forms an early opinion of the candidate and subsequently searches to confirm that opinion, consciously or unconsciously, throughout the interview.
4. Structure your interviews using the depth approach.
5. Take notes during the interview.
6. Interview for the few skills that produce results, based on the job analysis.
7. Train those who conduct the interviews.
8. Evaluate the candidates using a behavior-based scoring sheet.
9. Avoid panel interviewers, unless the position requires communicating under pressure in front of others.[7]
10. Conduct pre-screening on those competencies that research confirms truly make a difference in performance (conscientiousness, emotional intelligence, IQ, learning agility).

• • •

Lincoln understood that his performance depended on his team. He also knew there was a huge cost if he didn't hire the best and the brightest. The same is true for you. Appendix A has given you guidelines for hiring top talent.

Lincoln also appreciated that his talented team of rivals would, at times, fail to meet his high expectations. What to do when good employees perform poorly? Executives have been asking this question for decades. Even if you hire the best fit for the job, your good employees will make mistakes. Appendix B ensures that you'll know how to keep them on the job when they do.

APPENDIX B

How to Counsel Underperformers

Treat people as if they were what they ought to be, and you help them to become what they are capable of being.

GOETHE

POSITIVE RESULTS FROM DIFFICULT CONVERSATIONS

How would you handle these scenarios?

- The team productivity from a good manager has dropped below acceptable levels for the third time in the past year.
- An increasing number of projects that you are responsible for have not been completed on time or within budget. Your boss tells you to find out why your project managers are starting to fail and fix the problem.

What do these two scenarios have in common? They require a conversation that might be difficult or — at least to some degree — uncomfortable for many executives. Of course, the desired outcome of these counseling sessions is to produce better results after the conversations. While this may sound obvious, leaders often tell me that their goal in a counseling session is to get the person to understand — or get the employee to do his job.

Leaders forget that the entire focus of feedback should be on improving performance after the sessions. How much improvement do you see *after* you've had a counseling session?

There is good news and bad news in answering that question:

- The good news is that a meta-analysis by Professors Avraham Kluger and Angelo DeNisi, encompassing 23,663 observations, demonstrated that there is an overall average gain in performance following feedback interventions.[1]
- The bad news is that more than one-third of the feedback sessions actually *decrease* performance.

This problem of poor counseling sessions is exacerbated by ineffective performance management systems in the vast majority of organizations. The Institute for Corporate Productivity (formerly known as the Human Resource Institute) analyzed data on 1,031 respondents and found that only 8% indicated that their internal performance management system contributed significantly to individual performance improvement.[2]

Mistakes when counseling underperformers

Why do many counseling sessions fail to accomplish their primary objective? Usually, it's because the executive commits one or more of the seven deadly sins people make when giving feedback. These include:

- Providing vague feedback. Telling a manager that he is not performing well or needs to improve his presentations does not identify the specific behaviors that need improvement.
- Judging the individual instead of the behavior: Telling someone she was too harsh or needs to be a better communicator is a judgment of the individual that puts her on the defensive.
- Talking too much: If an executive is uncomfortable during a counseling session, he may talk too much. Don't spend too much time giving advice, talking about your own experience, or spending excessive time on problem-solving.
- Misusing the sandwich technique: Providing criticism in between two compliments sounds like a good idea, but it is rarely executed properly. The employee often perceives the approach as manipulative.
- Exaggerating: Terms such as "never" or "always" are loaded with emotional baggage. When a manager hears you using absolutes, he imagines all the times when he didn't do what you claim that he did.
- Using passive-aggressive humor: Telling someone you are glad she could make it when she's five minutes late to your meeting is indirect, ineffective, and passive-aggressive.
- Concluding without a plan: Ending a counseling session without gaining agreement to a step-by-step follow-up plan is like trying to drive to a good restaurant in a strange city without directions. You'll end up somewhere, but it probably won't be where you want to be, and the outcome won't be fulfilling.

Use the XLM to avoid mistakes

The XLM can help you avoid these common mistakes and conduct effective counseling sessions. The systematic approach to managing these conversations is illustrated in Figure B.1. Because leadership is the process of unleashing the energy of others toward worthy goals, I encourage you to share this process with your direct reports to help them conduct effective counseling sessions with their employees.

FIGURE B.1

Use the XLM to Counsel Underperformers

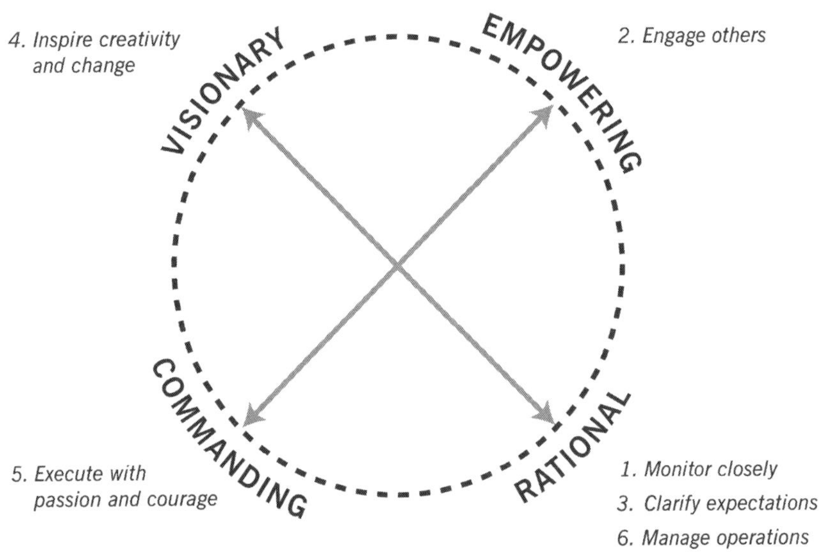

Monitor closely

Have you ever counseled employees who challenged your "facts" early in a conversation? If so, you know how difficult it is to get them back on track. This is why the first key to having a successful counseling session is to prepare for that meeting.

Consider answering the following questions to monitor the environment thoroughly in advance of your meeting:

- How often has this behavior occurred?
- Who can give you an accurate assessment of the facts?
- What does this individual's personnel file or previous performance review teach you?

- What are the performance standards and expectations described by the job description and employee handbook?
- What specific actions need to be taken, or behaviors improved, to meet the desired expectations?

A study of 87 small groups done by Professor Blaine Gaddis and his colleagues at the University of Oklahoma demonstrated that when leaders deliver feedback with negative emotions (via verbal and nonverbal signals), subordinates perceive the leader negatively and perform poorly after the feedback.[3]

Interestingly, leaders were perceived least favorably when negative facial expressions accompanied positive feedback and most favorably when both facial expressions and feedback were positive. So, make sure you pause and set a positive intention.

This research teaches us that to monitor closely also means being in touch with our own emotions and motivations. If we are too emotional about a particular incident or employee behavior, we need to take a time-out. By definition, it is difficult to be rational when we are emotional. Grandma was right: When upset count to ten, and when very upset count to a thousand.

Engage others

Meet the individual in neutral territory if possible, such as a conference room or vacant office. If you summon one of your managers to your office, his defensive routines may begin to kick in. If you must meet in your office, sit next to the employee, not behind your desk.

Begin your conversation by pointing out the value the employee brings to the organization. Identify specific instances when he met or exceeded the expectations of the job. Then, transition to the performance issue by asking him to help you understand the contrast between past acceptable performance and the recent drop in performance.

As you implement these steps, avoid the perils of the sandwich, or hamburger, technique of starting with positive comments, getting to the meat of the matter — the performance issue — and ending with positive comments. Employees see it as manipulative. I have found the best way to avoid the perils of the hamburger technique is to ask questions about the contrast between past good performance and the present drop in performance. Contrast is how we see.

Here are a few examples, using the power of contrast, to describe performance or another situation during a counseling session:

- "Cameron, last month your team's production numbers were above the industry average. Help me understand why we have seen a drop of 22% this month?"
- "Normally, Whitney, you're very even-tempered. That's why I need you to help me fathom what happened yesterday after lunch. What was going on when you were arguing on the loading dock?"
- "Jody, you usually follow the chain of command closely. Why you were talking to Kelly about the shipments this morning?"

Notice that the question is about a very specific situation and performance indicator (or behavior) that is in contrast to past good performance. This is no time to be vague. You must describe the exact situation and behavior that needs correction. At the same time, you are also engaging the employee by asking for help and clarification.

Continue the dialogue by focusing on understanding the manager's perspective and issues. Even when employees start blaming others or presenting excuses for their behavior, keep them engaged by using excellent communication skills such as reflective and active listening.

End this part of the conversation by summarizing the manager's point of view to *his* satisfaction. You do not need to agree with him, but he must feel heard if you are going to break through the defensive walls that often obstruct the achievement of your desired outcomes.

To be heard, listen well.

Clarify expectations

After the manager agrees that your summary of his explanation for his poor performance is accurate, show him a copy of his last performance review, his job description, or the employee handbook. That's right—pull out the job description and show him exactly what's expected. This is why I encourage you to prepare in advance; you should take time to review the job description and employee handbook during the first step in this process.

Explain that all the employees in his position are required to perform to a specific standard. As you talk, point to the performance standard or behaviors in his job description that he has not met. This sends two subtle and important messages to your employee:

1. You're treating him as you would anyone in his position.
2. You're pointing your finger at a performance standard, not at him.

To clarify expectations during a counseling session, make statements such as these:

- "Cameron, in our employee handbook, it clearly states that we need our supervisors to build teamwork and create an atmosphere of cooperation."
- "Whitney, we need all our production managers to meet these requirements."
- "Jody, the chain of command is laid out clearly in the sales manager's job description."

Inspire creativity and change

Invite the employee to be creative in helping you come up with a way to change his behavior. Tell him that together, you must come up with specific action steps to help him reach a specific performance standard. Ask him to take a few days to brainstorm a number of possible actions that will serve as the beginning of a performance improvement plan.

Here are a few examples of what you can say to clarify expectations during a counseling session:

- "Cameron, how about you take a few days to come up with a few ways to build teamwork and create a more cooperative atmosphere."
- "Whitney, I would like you to take some time to brainstorm possible action steps to meet these production requirements consistently."
- "Jody, what do you think we need to do to ensure that you follow the chain of command?"

Execute with passion and courage

You may need to access your commanding style as you encourage the employee to be involved in creating an improvement plan. How firm you need to be at this point often depends on how much responsibility the manager accepts for his poor performance and your skill in applying the first four steps (monitor, engage, clarify, inspire) of this process.

If the manager resists, let him know that you would rather have him follow a plan that you both created together, rather than one you have to dictate. Be firm and fair. You will have to manage the tension between your commanding and empowering leadership styles. As one executive put it, use an "iron fist in a velvet glove."

Manage operations

Gain agreement from the manager to implement a step-by-step plan to improve his performance. This step is a lot easier if he participated in the creation of this plan (as explained previously). How extensive the plan is depends on the nature of the behavior that must improve. For example, building teamwork and creating a more cooperative atmosphere would require a more comprehensive plan than ensuring someone follows the chain of command.

An effective plan for performance improvement should include these eight elements:

1. SMART goals and objectives
2. List of benefits—to the underperformer and the organization—of achieving the goal
3. Possible obstacles to overcome and their solutions
4. Action steps to improve performance
5. Details on how to measure the action steps
6. Partners to work with on specific action steps
7. Dates to review specific milestones and progress
8. Signature line for the underperformer and leader

Finally, use all four of your XLM leadership styles to help the individual implement his performance improvement plan. For example:

- Rational: Is the manager accomplishing specific objectives and meeting your expectations? Has he put systems in place that operationalize his plan?
- Visionary: Are you inspiring him to change and create new ways of doing things? Are you discussing the contributions he is making to the overall organization?
- Empowering: Are you encouraging him, listening to his concerns, and providing quality and timely feedback?
- Commanding: Are you addressing any difficult issues that arise? Are you holding him accountable for improving and avoiding the victim mentality?

APPENDIX C

Executive Development: XLM Research at the Top

As part of my ongoing coaching and consulting with executives in the transit industry, I investigated the utility of THE EXPANSIVE LEADERSHIP MODEL™ (XLM) as a tool to help them address their workforce development challenges. Although this research was conducted with transit executives, the research findings apply to executives in most industries.

Major challenge

The American Public Transit Association (APTA) identified the coming wave of retiring top transit executives as an "irreplaceable loss of industry knowledge and experience."[1] APTA's Blue Ribbon Panel on Workforce Development identified this issue as a major challenge because:

1. One-third of all senior transit executives will retire within five years.
2. Preparing the next generation of leaders is the top priority of 80% of those surveyed.
3. Skill gaps exist at all leadership levels.
4. Training programs must be developed that follow best practices.

How to meet the challenge

The specific objectives were to:

1. Identify the top challenges transit executives face.
2. Discover which competencies are strongest and weakest (i.e., the skills gaps) among transit executives.
3. Determine how well these competencies correlate with leadership effectiveness.
4. Learn how well leaders actually manage paradoxical tensions.

Population

To better understand the industry's challenges, I interviewed 26 transit CEOs. These CEOs led small, medium, and large agencies in diverse geographic locations within the United States. After the interviews, we invited them and members of their top management team (TMT) to complete the XLM online (http://xlmassessment.com/).

A total of 77 executives (16 CEOs and 61 of their TMT members) completed the assessment. In addition, because the XLM is a 360-degree feedback instrument, these 77 executives invited others known as raters (e.g., their boss, peers, direct reports) to assess them. A total of 376 raters completed the XLM assessment of these 77 executives. Thus, an average of five raters (4.8) evaluated each executive.

Assessment

The XLM assessment evaluates four fundamental leadership styles (rational, visionary, empowering, and commanding). Each style consists of four core competencies. The XLM uses a 5-point Likert scale on 48 questions to calculate the score for each of the 16 competencies. Seven additional questions evaluate leadership effectiveness on a 5-point scale, including questions such as:

- To what extent would you rate this leader's overall leadership effectiveness as outstanding?
- To what extent would you say that this leader's GROUP or TEAM has a very positive impact on the organization?
- Compared to all other leaders you've known, how would you rate this leader's competency?

We averaged ratings on the seven leadership effectiveness questions to derive an overall leadership effectiveness score for each executive. We then conducted a correlational analysis to determine how well the 16 core competencies correlated with overall leadership effectiveness.

Results

Table C.1 presents the top 20 challenges derived from interviews with the 26 transit CEOs.

TABLE C.1

Top 20 Transit Challenges

1. Manage funding cuts.
2. Follow new mandates.
3. Engage/motivate employees.
4. Implement service reductions.
5. Meet short-term objectives.
6. Innovate for the long-term.
7. Get more done with less.
8. Take time to coach/mentor others.
9. Deliver legacy projects.
10. Meet community's real needs.
11. Maintain standard IT platforms.
12. Adapt software to address local needs.
13. Become a regional mobility manager.
14. Address each city's issue.
15. Manage generational and cultural differences.
16. Adhere to uniform policies and procedures.
17. Gain buy-in to the accelerated pace of change.
18. Build a platform of stability.
19. Meet the increasing demands of work.
20. Have a fulfilling home life.

The executives' average scores (from highest to lowest) on the 5-point Likert scale for each of 16 competencies is shown in Table C.2. The four lowest scores (weaknesses) are in bold. The scores ranged from 3.88 to 3.51.

TABLE C.2

The 16 Leadership Competencies Ranking and Scores

1. Serve ethically (3.88)
2. Choose responsibly (3.87)
3. Execute with passion and courage (3.85)
4. Imagine broadly (3.82)
5. Clarify objectives & expectations (3.81)
6. Motivate teamwork (3.78)
7. Inspire creativity and change (3.75)
8. Adapt strategies to meet goals (3.74)
9. Monitor closely (3.73)
10. Manage operations and plans (.3.70)
11. Communicate trust and empathy (3.70)
12. Engage others (3.70)
13. **Regulate the emotions (3.63)**
14. **Cultivate innovative growth (3.62)**
15. **Know thyself and others (3.55)**
16. **Embrace ambiguity and paradox (3.51)**

The correlations between each of the 16 competencies and the executives' overall leadership effectiveness score are shown in Table C.3. In this type of research, correlations greater than .30 are considered significant, while correlations greater than .50 are considered high. The correlations ranged from .43 to .63 — with the lowest four correlations in bold in the table. The fact that the lowest-scoring competency is "embrace ambiguity and paradox," and that it correlates well (.56) with overall leadership effectiveness, strongly suggests that transit leaders do not manage paradoxical tensions well.

TABLE C.3

Correlations Between the 16 Leadership Competencies and Overall Leadership Effectiveness

1. Serve ethically (.43)
2. Choose responsibly (.52)
3. Execute with passion and courage (.58)
4. Imagine broadly (.55)
5. Clarify objectives and expectations (.56)
6. Motivate teamwork (.58)
7. Inspire creativity and change (.54)
8. Adapt strategies to meet goals (.60)
9. Monitor closely (.60)
10. Manage operations and plans (.59)
11. Communicate trust and empathy (.47)
12. Engage others (.63)
13. **Regulate the emotions (.48)**
14. **Cultivate innovative growth (.59)**
15. **Know thyself and others (.57)**
16. **Embrace ambiguity and paradox (.56)**

Discussion and lessons learned

These results confirm the utility of the XLM as a tool to help transit executives meet their workforce development challenges in four ways. First, the challenges identified by the 26 transit CEOs are paradoxical. You can confirm this by re-reading the list of challenges in Table C.1 while adding the words *and at the same time* after every odd-numbered challenge — that is, read number one and number two together with the words *and at the same time* between them. Do the same with numbers three and four, five and six, and so forth.

What I discovered from the 26 interviews was that many of the challenges transit executives face are, in fact, paradoxes—they pull in opposite directions simultaneously. If we reformat the top 20 challenges into paradoxes, we can create the top 10 list in Table C.4. Notice that these challenges are similar to those found among executives in all industries, as discussed in Chapter 1 (Table 1.2).

TABLE C.4

Transit's Top 10 Paradoxical Challenges

1. Manage funding cuts *and* Follow new mandates.
2. Engage/motivate employees *and* Implement service reductions.
3. Meet short-term objectives *and* Innovate for long-term growth.
4. Get more done with less *and* Take time to coach/mentor others.
5. Deliver legacy projects *and* Meet the community's real needs.
6. Maintain standard IT platforms *and* Adapt software to address local needs.
7. Become a regional mobility manager *and* Address each city's issues.
8. Embrace generational/cultural diversity *and* Adhere to uniform policies.
9. Gain buy-in to the accelerated pace of change *and* Provide a platform of stability.
10. Meet the increasing demands of work *and* Have a fulfilling home life.

The second way this research confirms the utility of the XLM is that the analysis identified the four highest- and lowest-scoring competencies (strengths and weaknesses, respectively, shown in Table C.2) for the transit executives. The lower scores—indicating skills gaps—include two competencies related to emotional intelligence (regulate the emotions, know thyself and others), one related to innovation (cultivate innovative growth), and the lowest-scoring competency of all (embrace ambiguity and paradox). Although each executive must decide if performing relatively poorly in these competencies actually hurts his or her effectiveness, my experience working with leaders during the last decade is that skills gaps in emotional intelligence, innovation, and management of paradoxical issues create enormous problems in addressing today's workforce challenges.

For example, I'm helping one transit TMT rebuild trust damaged by mismanagement of the me-we paradox. TMT members tend to over-focus on their own unit (me) at the expense of the overall organization (we). A few of these executives think the answer is to focus on the organization, but I remind them that this is *not* the best approach. Instead, I'm coaching them to manage the tension between meeting their individual needs *and* those of the overall organization at the same time. They're learning to stretch when they're pulled by opposing demands.

The third confirmation of the XLM's usefulness is that the analysis validated that the 16 competencies correlate highly with transit leadership effectiveness. It's important to note that correlation does not equal causation. We must be careful not to overstate the significance of these findings; however, when we combine these findings with the fact that I selected these competencies after an exhaustive analysis of the leadership literature, and that I have been using this model successfully in the transit industry for many years, these high correlations are not surprising.

Finally, this research confirms the utility of the XLM as a tool to help transit executives meet their workforce development challenges because we discovered that transit leaders score most poorly in a critical competency: Although the leadership competency "embrace ambiguity and paradox" is highly correlated with leadership effectiveness (.56), it is the lowest-ranked of the 16 competencies assessed. As Mike Scanlon, past chair of APTA and CEO at SamTrans remarked, "Are you telling us that we are least effective in the most important competency—the one that can help in today's paradoxical environment?"

Precisely.

Transit leaders are not alone in their need to develop this low-scoring skill. In a study of 1,000 organizations during a 20-year period, researchers found that leaders mismanage paradoxes between 38% and 45% of the time, and suffer poor performance as a result.[2] The most common error was addressing one issue of a paradox independently of the other. The good news is that small improvements in managing paradoxical issues can significantly increase organizational performance.[3]

Competing stakeholders, resource constraints, and an accelerating pace of change are workplace trends that aren't going away, and they all conspire to pull leaders in opposite directions. When combined with another trend, the high retirement rate of senior transit executives in this case study, they create a major workforce development challenge. The XLM is a paradoxical model, as explained throughout this book, and therefore a useful tool to help all executives—transit and otherwise—meet the challenge.

References

CHAPTER 1: The Executive's Paradox

[1] Patrick Duignan, *Leaders Lead: Strengthening the Australian School Project,* address at the Carlton Crest Hotel, Parramatta, New South Wales, June 27, 2002.

[2] Dick Fuld, quoted in Stefan Stern, Strengths become weaknesses, *Financial Times,* September 21, 2009, http://www.ft.com/intl/cms/s/0/38d4d3a8-a6f4-11de-bd14-00144feabdc0.html#axzz2PVJJIf8E.

[3] Cinderella's Moment: A Special Report on Financial Risk, *The Economist,* February 13, 2010, 9-11.

[4] Toyota: Losing Its Shine, *The Economist,* December 1, 2009, 75-77.

[5] Nightmare Liner, *The Economist,* September 3, 2011, 63.

[6] Geoffrey A. Moore, To Succeed in the Long Term, Focus on the Middle Term, *Harvard Business Review,* July-August 2007, 84-90.

[7] Dominc Dodd and Ken Favaro, Managing the Right Tension, *Harvard Business Review,* December 2006, 62-74.

[8] Yves Morieux, Six Rules: Six Ways to Get People to Solve Problems Without You, *Harvard Business Review,* September 2011, 78-86.

[9] Adapted from Leadership Today and in the Future, *MWorld: Journal of the American Management Association,* Winter 2006, 21-26.

[10] Howard Slaatte, *The Pertinence of Paradox.* Humanities Press: New York, 1968.

[11] Wendy Smith and Marianne Lewis, Theory Development: Toward a Theory of Paradox: A Dynamic Equilibrium Model of Organizing, *Academy of Management Review* 36, no. 2 (2011), 381-403.

[12] Too Much Buzz, *Schumpeter* (blog), *The Economist,* December 31, 2011, 50.

[13] Marianne Lewis, Exploring Paradox: Toward a More Comprehensive Guide, *Academy of Management Review* 35, no. 4 (2000), 760-776.

[14] Dominic Dodd and Ken Favaro, Managing the Right Tension, *Harvard Business Review,* December 2006, 62-74.

[15] David Eagleman, The Mystery of Expertise, *The Week,* December 30, 2011, 48-49.

[16] Eddie Harmon-Jones, David Amodio, and Cindy Harmon-Jones, Action-Based Model of Dissonance: A Review, Integration, and Expansion of Conceptions of Cognitive Conflict, *Advances in Experimental Social Psychology* 41 (2009), 119-166.

[17] Jonathan Gosling and Henry Mintzberg, The Five Minds of the Manager, *Harvard Business Review,* November 2003, 54-63.

CHAPTER 2: The Power of Paradoxical Thinking

[1] These various researchers and their works are: Robert Quinn, *Beyond Rational Management: Mastering the Paradoxes in Competing Demands of High Performance.* Jossey-Bass: San Francisco, 1988; Peter Koestenbaum, *Leadership: The Inner Side of Greatness.* Jossey-Bass: San Francisco, 2002; Bob Kaplan and Rob Kaiser, *The Versatile Leader: Make the Most of Your Strengths Without Overdoing It.* Pfeiffer: San Francisco, 2006; Katherine A. Lawrence, Peter Lenk, and Robert E. Quinn, Behavioral Complexity in Leadership: The Psychometric Properties of a New Instrument to Measure Behavioral Repertoire, *The Leadership Quarterly* 20 (2009), 87-102.

[2] Richard Farson, *Management of the Absurd: Paradoxes in Leadership.* Simon & Schuster: New York, 1996.

CHAPTER 4: How the Most Agile Executives Stretch

[1] Edwin Locke, *The Prime Movers: Traits of the Great Wealth Creators.* AMACOM: New York, 2000, 49.

[2] Gary Yukl, *Leadership in Organizations.* Prentice Hall: Upper Saddle River, NJ, 2006, 6.

[3] AP Interview: Wal-Mart CEO talks leadership, lifehttp://www.winknews.com/mobile/index.php/mobile/article/AP-Interview-Wal-Mart-CEO-talks-leadership-life#ixzz1D0UHnoA2.

[4] Gerald Parshall, The Strategists of War, *U.S. News & World Report,* March 16, 1998, 50-80.

[5] Jim Collins, *Good to Great.* HarperCollins: New York, 2001.

CHAPTER 5: Knowing Where You're Going

[1] Peter Drucker, *Management: Tasks, Responsibilities,* Practices. Harper & Row: New York, 1974, 414.

[2] John H. Humphreys and Walter O. Einstein, Leadership and temperament congruence: extending the expectancy model of work motivation, *Journal of Leadership & Organizational Studies* 10, no. 4 (Spring 2004), 58-79.

[3] Timothy L. Keiningham et al., Linking Customer Loyalty to Growth, *MIT Sloan Management Review,* Summer 2008, 51-57.

[4] F.F. Reichheld, The One Number You Need to Grow, *Harvard Business Review,* December 2003, 46-54.

[5] Keiningham et al., Linking Customer Loyalty to Growth.

CHAPTER 6: Knowing Where You're Going Doesn't Get You There

[1] Edwin Locke and Gary Latham, *A Theory of Goal Setting and Task Performance.* Prentice Hall: Englewood Cliffs, NJ, 1990.

[2] B. Goldman et al., Goal-directedness and Personal Identity as Correlates of Life Outcomes, *Psychological Reports* 91 (2002), 153-166.

CHAPTER 7: Getting to Know All About You

[1] David Dunning, Chip Heath, and Jerry Suls, Flawed Self-Assessment: Implications for Health, Education, and the Workplace, *Psychological Sciences in the Public Interest* 5, no. 3 (2004), 69-106.

[2] Glenn Regehr and Kevin Eva, Self-assessment, Self-direction, and the Self-regulating Professional, *Clinical Orthopaedics and Related Research,* no. 449 (2006), 34-38.

[3] Kevin Dunbar, *How Scientists Really Reason: Scientific Reasoning in Real-World Laboratories, in Mechanisms of Insight,* ed. R.J. Sternberg and J. Davidson. MIT Press: Cambridge, MA, 1995, http://www.utsc.utoronto.ca/~dunbarlab/pubpdfs/DunbarStern.pdf.

[4] Robert Eichinger, Michael Lombardo, and David Ulrich, *100 Things You Need to Know.* Lominger: Minneapolis, 2006, 256-258.

[5] Daniel Goleman, Richard E. Boyatzis, and Annie McKee, *Primal Leadership: Realizing the Power of Emotional Intelligence,* Harvard Business School Press, Boston, 2002.

[6] Alicia Grandey, Emotion Regulation in the Workplace: A New Way to Conceptualize Emotional Labor, *Journal of Occupational Health Psychology* 5, no. 1 (2000), 95-110.

[7] John Mayer, Richard Roberts, and Sigal Barsade, Human Abilities: Emotional Intelligence, *Annual Review of Psychology* 59 (2008) 511.

[8] Mayer, Roberts, and Barsade, Human Abilities: Emotional Intelligence.

[9] Sigal Barsade and Donald Gibson, Why Does Affect Matter in Organizations? *Academy of Management Perspectives,* February 2007, 36-59.

[10] John Mayer, Peter Salovey, and David Caruso, Emotional Intelligence: New Ability or Eclectic Traits? *American Psychologist,* September 2008, 503-517.

[11] James Stengel, Andrea Dixon, and Cris Allen, Listening Begins at Home, *Harvard Business Review,* November 2003, 106-116.

[12] P&G Investor Relations archive, "A.G. Lafley, Chairman of the Board," July 2009, http://phx.corporate-ir.net/External.File?item=UGFyZW50SUQ9OTQzOHxDaGlsZElEPS0xfFR5cGU9Mw==&t=1.

[13] J. Cameron and M. Bryan, *The Artist's Way*. G.P. Putnam, New York, 1992.

[14] Sandra Blakeslee and Matthew Blakeslee, Where Mind and Body Meet, *Scientific American Mind,* August/September 2007, 44-50.

[15] Claire Ashton et al., Mimicry and Me: The Impact of Mimicry on Self-Construal, *Social Cognition* 25, no. 4 (2007), 518-535.

[16] Elizabeth King Humphrey, Be Sad and Succeed, *Scientific American Mind,* March/April 2010, 12.

[17] Joseph Forgas, When Sad Is Better Than Happy: Negative Affect Can Improve the Quality and Effectiveness of Persuasive Messages and Social Influence Strategies, *Journal of Experimental Social Psychology* 43 (2007), 513-528.

[18] Melinda Wenner, How Fantasies Affect Focus, *Scientific American Mind,* March/April 2010, 10.

[19] Barsade and Gibson, Why Does Affect Matter in Organizations?, 45.

[20] David Caruso and Peter Salovey, *The Emotionally Intelligent Manager: How to Develop and Use the Four Key Emotional Skills of Leadership.* Josse-Bass: San Francisco, 2004, 41-51.

[21] Giora Keinan, Decision-Making Under Stress: Scanning Both Alternatives Under Controllable and Uncontrollable Threats, *Journal of Personality and Social Psychology* 52, no. 3 (1987), 639-643.

[22] Caruso and Salovey, *The Emotionally Intelligent Manager.*

CHAPTER 8: Be Here Now

[1] Jesse Hempel, Why the Boss Really Had to Say Goodbye, *BusinessWeek,* July 4, 2005, 10.

[2] Kathleen Sutcliffe and Klaus Weber, The High Cost of Accurate Knowledge, *Harvard Business Review,* May 2003, 74-82.

[3] "The Toyota Way," http://www.toyota-forklifts.eu/en/company/Pages/The%20Toyota%20Way.aspx.

[4] Anthony Mayo and Nitin Nohria, Zeitgeist Leadership, *Harvard Business Review,* October 2005, 45-60.

[5] Gary Hamel and Liisa Välikangas, The Quest for Resilience, *Harvard Business Review,* September 2003, 52-63.

[6] Linda Stone, Living with Continuous Partial Attention, *Harvard Business Review,* February 2007.

[7] Stephen D. Reicher, Michael J. Platow, and S. Alexander Haslam, The New Psychology of Leadership, *Scientific American Mind,* August/September 2007, 22-29.

CHAPTER 9: Follow Which Yellow Brick Road?

[1] Sarah Kaplan and Eric Beinhocker, The Real Value of Strategic Planning, *MIT Sloan Management Review,* Winter 2003, 71-76.

[2] Robert Kaplan and David Norton, Mastering the Management System, *Harvard Business Review,* January 2008, 63-77.

[3] Towers Perrin 2005 survey, cited in American Management Association, *The Keys to Strategy Execution: A Global Study of Current Trends and Future Possibilities, 2006-2016,* http://www.enrollmentmarketing.org/research/AMA-keys-to-strategy-execution.pdf.

[4] Leadership through the crisis and after: McKinsey Global Survey results, http://www.mckinseyquarterly.com/Organization/Talent/Leadership_through_the_crisis_and_after_McKinsey_Global_Survey_results_2457.

[5] Ford protests GM Silverado Super Bowl ad, *Detroit Free Press,* February 6, 2012, http://www.usatoday.com/money/advertising/story/2012-02-06/ford-protests-GM-Silverado-Super-Bowl-ad/52988172/1.

[6] Benjamin Gomes-Casseres, Competing in Constellations: The Case of Fuji Xerox, *Strategy + Business,* first quarter 1997, 4-16, http://alliancestrategy.com/PDFs/BGC%20Fuji%20Xerox%20%20SnB97.pdf.

[7] Keith McFarland, Should You Build Strategy Like You Build Software? *MIT Sloan Management Review,* Spring 2008, 69-74.

[8] Rita Gunther McGrath, How the Growth Outliers Do It, *Harvard Business Review,* January- February 2012, 111-116.

[9] Chris Zook and James Allen, Growth Outside the Core, *Harvard Business Review,* December 2003, 66-73.

[10] W. Chan Kim and Renee Mauborgne, Blue Ocean Strategy, *Harvard Business Review,* October 2004, 76-84.

[11] http://en.wikipedia.org/wiki/Cirque_du_Soleil.

[12] Kim and Mauborgne, Blue Ocean Strategy.

[13] George S. Day and Paul J. H. Schoemaker, Scanning the Periphery, *Harvard Business Review,* November 2005, 135-148.

[14] Michael E. Porter, The Five Competitive Forces That Shape Strategy, *Harvard Business Review,* January 2008, 79-93.

[15] Chris Zook and James Allen, Growth Outside the Core, *Harvard Business Review,* December 2003, 67.

[16] Edwin Locke and Gary Latham, *A Theory of Goal Setting and Task Performance.* Prentice Hall: Englewood Cliffs, NJ, 1990.

[17] Chris Zook and James Allen, Growth Outside the Core, *Harvard Business Review,* December 2003, 67.

[18] Adapted from Jeanne M. Liedtka, Strategic Thinking: Can It Be Taught? *Long-Range Planning* 31 (1998), 120-129.

[19] Simplify and Repeat, *Schumpeter* (blog), *The Economist,* April 28, 2012, 76.

[20] Liedtka, Strategic Thinking: Can It Be Taught? *Long-Range Planning,* 126.

[21] Lee Fleming, Finding the organizational sources of technological breakthroughs: The story of Hewlett-Packard's thermal ink-jet, *Industrial and Corporate Change 11* (2002), 1059-1084.

[22] Ellen F. Goldman, Strategic Thinking at the Top, *MIT Sloan Management Review,* Summer 2007, 75-81.

CHAPTER 10: Elephants Dancing with the Stars

[1] Larry Yu, Measuring the Culture of Innovation, *MIT Sloan Management Review,* Summer 2007, 7.

[2] W. Chan Kim and Renee Mauborgne, Blue Ocean Strategy, *Harvard Business Review,* October 2004, 76-84.

[3] Rosabeth Moss Kanter, Block-by-Blockbuster Innovation, *Harvard Business Review,* May 2010, 38.

[4] Jeffrey Dyer, Hal Gregersen, and Clayton Christensen, The Innovator's DNA, *Harvard Business Review,* December 2009, 61-76.

[5] The World's 50 Most Innovative Companies, *BusinessWeek,* http://www.businessweek.com/interactive_reports/innovative_companies.html, and Boston Consulting Group (BCG) Report, Innovation 2010, http://tobiaslist.files.wordpress.com/2010/06/innovation-2010-bcg.pdf.

[6] Bala Iyer and Thomas Davenport, Reverse Engineering Google's Innovation Machine, *Harvard Business Review,* April 2008, 59-68, and BCG Report, Innovation 2010.

[7] Liz Warren, Ten years in: how Google raced ahead, *Computer Weekly,* http://www.computerweekly.com/feature/Ten-years-in-how-Google-raced-ahead.

[8] Ed Catmull, How Pixar Fosters Collective Creativity, *Harvard Business Review,* September 2008, 65-72.

[9] Cars Land at Disney California Adventure, *Theme Park Insider,* http://www.themeparkinsider.com/cars-land/.

[10] Jeffrey Dyer, Hal Gregersen, and Clayton Christensen, The Innovator's DNA, *Harvard Business Review,* December 2009, 61-76.

[11] Dyer, Gregersen, and Christensen, The Innovator's DNA, 63.

[12] Ibid.

[13] Honeywell International: From Bitter to Sweet, *The Economist,* April 14, 2012, 74-76.

[14] Dyer, Gregersen, and Christensen, The Innovator's DNA, 65.

[15] Van Wyck Brooks, *The Life of Emerson.* E.P. Dutton: New York, 1932, 270.

[16] Napoleon Hill, *Think and Grow Rich.* Fawcett Crest Book: New York, 1937.

[17] Harold Evans, Assaying Edison...and His Equals, *Strategy + Business,* no. 19 (2000), 32.

[18] Ken Auletta, "You've Got News," *The New Yorker,* January 24, 2011, http://www.newyorker.com/reporting/2011/01/24/110124fa_fact_auletta.

CHAPTER 11: Think Inside and Outside the Box

[1] Microsoft's Downfall: Inside the Executive E-mails and Cannibalistic Culture That Felled a Tech Giant, *Vanity Fair,* July 3, 2012, http://www.vanityfair.com/online/daily/2012/07/microsoft-downfall-emails-steve-ballmer.print.

[2] Teresa Amabile and Mukti Khaire, Creativity and the Role of the Leader, *Harvard Business Review,* October 2008, 101-109.

[3] Mariette DiChristina, Let Your Creativity Soar, *Scientific American Mind,* June/July 2008, 24-31.

[4] Kelly Lambert, Depressingly Easy, *Scientific American Mind,* August/September 2008, 30-37.

[5] Caroll Dweck, The Secret to Raising Smart Kids, *Scientific American Mind,* December 2007/January 2008, 36- 43.

[6] Geert Devos, Marc Buelens, and Dave Bouckenooghe, Contribution of Content, Context, and Process to Understanding Openness to Organizational Change: Two Experimental Simulation Studies, *The Journal of Social Psychology* 147, no. 6 (2007), 607-629; and Michael Beer and Nitin Nohria, Cracking the Code of Change, *Harvard Business Review,* May-June, 2000, 133-141.

[7] Harvey Robbins and Michael Finley, *Why Change Doesn't Work.* Texere Publishing: Oakland, CA, 2001.

[8] See, for example, J.P. Kotter and D.S. Cohen, *The Heart of Change: Real Life Stories of How People Change Their Organizations.* Harvard Business School Press, Boston, 2002.

[9] Cited in Gary Yukl, *Leadership in Organizations.* Prentice Hall, Upper Saddle River, NJ, 2006, 285; see also Dan Cohen, Building Strategic Agility, *MWorld: Journal of the American Management Association,* 2006, 12-15.

[10] Cited in Carolyn Aiken and Scott Keller, The CEO's role in leading transformation, *McKinsey Quarterly,* February 2007.

[11] Jeffrey Ford and Laurie Ford, Decoding Resistance to Change, *Harvard Business Review,* April 2009, 100.

[12] Kevin Maney, Mulcahy Traces Steps of Xerox's Comeback, *USA Today,* September 21, 2006, 4B.

[13] Edwin Locke, ed., *Handbook of Principles of Organizational Behavior.* Blackwell: Malden, MA, 2004, 377.

[14] John P. Kotter, Leading Change: Why Transformation Efforts Fail, *Harvard Business Review,* January 2007, 96-117.

[15] Ford and Ford, Decoding Resistance to Change, 99-103.

[16] David Gavin and Michael Roberto, Change Through Persuasion, *Harvard Business Review,* February 2005, 104-112.

[17] T.J. Larkin and Sandar Larkin, Reading and Changing Frontline Employees, *Harvard Business Review,* May-June 1996, 95-104.

[18] Alex Bryson and Michael White, Organizational Commitment: Do Workplace Practices Matter? Centre for Economic Performance, discussion paper, no. 881, July 2008.

[19] Chana Schoenberger, Should Bosses Rule by Consensus or Fiat? *Forbes,* September 6, 1999, 26.

[20] Stephen Covey, *The 7 Habits of Highly Effective People.* Simon & Schuster: New York, 1989, 47.

[21] Rob Goffee and Gareth Jones, What Holds the Modern Company Together, *Harvard Business Review,* November-December 1996, 133-148.

[22] David Wagner, Satisfaction Begins at Home, *MIT Sloan Management Review,* Spring 2006, 5.

[23] Richard Lepsinger, How Top-Performing Companies Get Ahead of the Pack and Stay There, *MWorld: Journal of the American Management Association,* Summer 2007, 3-4.

[24] Cohen, Building Strategic Agility, *MWorld,* 12-15.

[25] Locke, *Handbook of Principles of Organizational Behavior,* 371.

[26] Cohen, Building Strategic Agility, 13.

[27] Carolyn Aiken and Scott Keller, The CEO's role in leading transformation, *McKinsey Quarterly,* February 2007, 4.

[28] Seattle Children's Construction Updates, November 15, 2011, http://construction.seattlechildrens.org/2011/11/seattle-children%E2%80%99s-says-thank-you-and-farewell-to-ironworkers/.

[29] Conversations on health care reform: John Hammergren of McKesson, *McKinsey Quarterly,* May 2010, http://www.mckinseyquarterly.com/Conversations_on_health_care_reform_John_Hammergren_of_McKesson_2590.

[30] S.M. Kosslyn and S.T. Moulton, *Mental imagery and implicit memory, in Handbook of Imagination and Mental Simulation,* ed. K.D. Markman, W.M.P Klein, and J.A. Suhr. Hove: New York, 2009, 135-151.

[31] Daniel Kirschenbaum et al., Effects of Differential Self-Monitoring and Level of Mastery on Sports Performance: Brain Power Bowling, *Cognitive Therapy and Research* 6, no. 3 (1982), 335-342.

[32] T. Lawrence et al., The Underlying Structure of Continuous Change, *MIT Sloan Management Review* 47, no. 4 (2006), 59-66.

[33] Charles Handy, *The Age of Paradox.* Harvard Business School Press: Boston, 1994.

[34] Christopher Worley and Edward Lawler, Designing Organizations That Are Built to Change, *MIT Sloan Management Review,* Fall 2006, 19-23.

[35] *The Hero's Journey: Joseph Campbell on His Life and Work* (The Collected Works of Joseph Campbell), 3rd ed. New World Library: Novato, CA, 2003.

[36] Interview with Ray Stata, *Silicon Genius,* June 28, 2006, http://silicongenesis.stanford.edu/transcripts/stata.htm.

CHAPTER 12: Go Big or Go Home

[1] Timothy Hoff, How work context shapes physician approach to safety and error, *Quality Management in Health Care* 17, no. 2, 140-153.

[2] Thomas A. Stewart, Growth as a Process, *Harvard Business Review,* June 2006, 62-70.

[3] Ray Williams, Why Steve Jobs is not a leader to emulate, *Financial Post,* April 12, 2012, http://business.financialpost.com/2012/04/12/steve-jobs-is-not-a-leader-to-emulate/.

[4] Wesley Cohen and Daniel Levinthal, Absorptive Capacity: A New Perspective on Learning and Innovation, *Administrative Science Quarterly,* March 1990, 128-152.

[5] Grace Chua Beng Hui and Khairuddin Idris, What Makes Growth-Oriented Small Scale Companies Innovative? A Look at Absorptive Capacity, *Journal of Global Business Issues,* Spring 2009, 15-22.

[6] Bloomberg Businessweek Innovation & Design, http://www.businessweek.com/innovate/.

Section IV: How Empowering Executives Take Care

[1] Amory Lovins, "Soft Energy Paths for the 21st Century," Rocky Mountain Institute Publication E11-09, 2001, http://www.rmi.org/Knowledge-Center/Library/2011-09_GaikoSoftEnergyPaths.

CHAPTER 13: Love 'em or Lose 'em

[1] Edwin Locke, *Handbook of Principles of Organizational Behavior.* Blackwell: Malden, MA, 2004, 137-149.

[2] Towers Watson, 2012 Global Workforce Study, http://www.towerswatson.com/Insights/IC-Types/Survey-Research-Results/2012/07/2012-Towers-Watson-Global-Workforce-Study.

[3] Rodd Wagner and James Harter, The Heart of Great Managing, *Gallup Management Journal,* June 12, 2008.

[4] S. Bates, Getting Engaged, *HR Magazine* 49, no. 2, 2004.

[5] Towers Watson, 2012 Global Workforce Study.

[6] Wesley A. Scroggins, The Relationship Between Employee Fit Perceptions, Job Performance, and Retention: Implications of Perceived Fit, *Employee Responsibilities and Rights Journal* 20, no. 1 (March 2008), 57- 71.

[7] Locke, *Handbook of Principles of Organizational Behavior,* 76.

[8] Cynthia S. Miller, Meaningful Work Over the Life Course (dissertation, Fielding Graduate University, 2008, 22). Table 13.1 represents Professor Miller's modification of a model developed by N. Chalofsky, The humane workplace: Aligning of value-based organizational culture, meaningful work, and life balance. Chalofsky's presentation was delivered at the Organization Development Network Conference, Baltimore, October 23, 2007.

[9] Robert Morison, Tamara Erickson, and Ken Dychtwald, Managing Middlescence, *Harvard Business Review,* March 2006, 79-86.

[10] Suzy Wetlaufer; Perfecting Organizing for Empowerment: An Interview with AES's Roger Sant and Dennis Bakke, *Harvard Business Review,* January-February 1999, 111-123.

[11] Corporate Leadership Council, Driving Performance and Retention Through Employee Engagement, 2004, http://www.mckpeople.com.au/SiteMedia/w3svc161/Uploads/Documents/760af459-93b3-43c7-b52a-2a74e984c1a0.pdf.

CHAPTER 14: Can't We All Just Get Along?

[1] Steve Kozlowski and Daniel Ilgen, The Science of Team Success, *Scientific American Mind,* June/July 2007, 54-61.

[2] Vanessa Urch Druskat and Jane Wheeler, How to Lead a Self-Managing Team, *MIT Sloan Management Review,* Summer 2004, 65-71.

[3] *Agency for Healthcare Research and Quality,* January 2004, no. 281, 21.

[4] Adapted from the research by Vijay Govindarajan and Anil Gupta, Building an Effective Global Business Team, *MIT Sloan Management Review,* Summer 2001, 63-71.

[5] Frank LaFasto and Carl Larson, *When Teams Work Best.* Sage Publications: Thousand Oaks, CA, 2001.

[6] Deborah Ancona, Henrik Bresman, and Katrin Kaufer, The Comparative Advantage of X-Teams, *MIT Sloan Management Review,* Spring 2002, 33-39.

[7] Lee Fleming, Perfecting Cross-Pollination, *Harvard Business Review,* September 2004, 22-23.

[8] Ancona, Bresman, and Kaufer, Comparative Advantage of X-Teams.

[9] Stephen Ambrose, *Undaunted Courage.* Simon & Schuster: New York, 1996, 231.

[10] Ancona, Bresman, and Kaufer, Comparative Advantage of X-Teams.

[11] Ellen McGirt, Revolution in San Jose, *Fast Company,* December 2008/January 2009, 88-94 and 134-135.

[12] McGirt, Revolution in San Jose, 94.

[13] Govindarajan and Gupta, Building an Effective Global Business Team.

[14] Josh Hyatt, A Surprising Truth About Geographically Dispersed Teams, *MIT Sloan Management Review,* Summer 2008, 5-6.

[15] Charles O'Reilly et al., How Leadership Matters: The Effects of Leaders' Alignment on Strategy Implementation, *The Leadership Quarterly* 21 (2010), 104-113.

[16] Amy Edmondson, Michael Roberto, and Michael Watkins, A Dynamic Model of Top Management Effectiveness: Managing Unstructured Task Streams. *The Leadership Quarterly* 14 (2003), 297-325.

[17] Abraham Carmeli and John Schaubroeck, Top Management Team Behavioral Integration, Decision Quality, and Organizational Decline, *The Leadership Quarterly* 17 (2006), 441- 453.

[18] Nitin Nohria, Boris Groysberg, and Linda-Eling Lee, Employee Motivation: A Powerful New Model, *Harvard Business Review,* July-August 2008, 78-84.

[19] William Cohen, *A Class with Drucker: The Lost Lessons of the World's Greatest Management Teacher.* AMACOM: New York, 2008, 221.

CHAPTER 15: Trust Me

[1] Robert Galford and Anne Seiblod Drapeau, The Enemies of Trust, *Harvard Business Review,* February 2003, 89-95.

[2] Robert Hurley, The Decision to Trust, *Harvard Business Review,* September 2006, 55-62.

[3] WorkUSA 2002, Weathering the Storm: A Study of Employee Attitudes and Opinions, http://www.watsonwyatt.com/research/resrender.asp?id=W-557&page=1.

[4] Galford and Drapeau, The Enemies of Trust; see also Ingrid Smithey-Fulmer, Barry Gerhart, and Kimberly Scott, Are the 100 Best Better? An Empirical Investigation of the Relationship Between Being a "Great Place to Work" and Firm Performance, *Personnel Psychology* 56, no. 4 (Winter 2003), 965-993.

[5] Tony Simons and Randall Peterson, When to Let Them Duke It Out, *Harvard Business Review,* June 2006, 23-24.

[6] Kimberly Merriman, Low-Trust Teams Prefer Individualized Pay, *Harvard Business Review,* November 2008, 32.

[7] Dennis Reina and Michelle Reina, Building Sustainable Trust: Your Competitive Advantage, *MWorld: Journal of the American Management Association,* Summer 2006, 3-4.

[8] K. T. Dirks and D. L. Ferrin, Trust in Leadership: Meta-analytic Findings and Implications for Research and Practice, *Journal of Applied Psychology* 87 (2002), 611-628.

[9] Michael Pirson and Deepak Malhotra, The Secrets of Trust, *MIT Sloan Management Review* 49, no. 4 (Summer 2008), 43-50.

[10] Helen Coster, The 100 Most Trustworthy Companies, *Forbes,* http://www.forbes.com/2010/04/05/most-trustworthy-companies-leadership-governance-100.html.

[11] Thomas Philippe and Jerry W Koehler, Managerial actions that significantly affect employees' perceptions, *Journal of Academy of Business and Economics,* January 2005; and Laurence Prusak and Don Cohen, How to Invest in Social Capital, *Harvard Business Review,* June 2001, 86-93.

[12] Reina, Building Sustainable Trust, 4.

[13] Daniel Goleman and Richard Boyatzis, Social Intelligence and the Biology of Leadership, *Harvard Business Review,* September 2008, 74-81.

[14] Patrick Bawise and Sean Meehan, So You Think You're a Good Listener, *Harvard Business Review,* April 2008, 22.

[15] John Heritage et al., Reducing Patients' Unmet Concerns in Primary Care: The Difference One Word Can Make, *Journal of General Internal Medicine* 22, no. 10, (October 2007), 1429-1433.

CHAPTER 16: Do the Right Thing

[1] Katherine Sweetman, Employee Loyalty Around the Globe, *MIT Sloan Management Review,* Winter 2001, 16.

[2] Kim Cameron et al., Exploring the Relationships Between Organizational Virtuousness and Performance, *American Behavioral Scientist* 47, no. 6 (February 2004), 1-24.

[3] Daniel Kaufmann and Shang-Jin Wei, Does "Grease Money" Speed Up the Wheels of Commerce? http://siteresources.worldbank.org/INTWBIGOVANTCOR/Resources/grease.pdf.

[4] Cameron, Exploring the Relationships Between Organizational Virtuousness and Performance.

[5] Robert Cialdini et al., The Hidden Costs of Organizational Dishonesty, *MIT Sloan Management Review,* Spring 2004, 67-73.

[6] Ginger Graham, If You Want Honesty, Break Some Rules, *Harvard Business Review,* April 2002, 42-47.

[7] Dan Ariely, How Honest People Cheat, *Harvard Business Review,* February 2008, 24.

[8] Ariely, How Honest People Cheat.

[9] Larry Yu, Rational Cheaters Versus Intrinsic Motivators, *MIT Sloan Management Review,* Summer 2002, 10.

[10] Tony Simons, The High Cost of Lost Trust, *Harvard Business Review,* September 2002, 18-19.

[11] Darrell Rigby, Management Tools and Techniques: A Survey, *California Management Review* 43, no. 2 (2001), 139-159.

[12] Francesca Gino, Michael I. Norton, and Dan Ariely, The Counterfeit Self: The Deceptive Costs of Faking It, *Psychological Science* 21, no. 5 (May 2010), 712-720.

[13] Joel Brockner, Why It's So Hard to Be Fair, *Harvard Business Review,* March 2006, 122-129.

[14] J. S. Adams, Toward an Understanding of Inequity, *Journal of Abnormal and Social Psychology* 67, no. 5 (1963), 422-436.

[15] Felix Brodbeck et al., Cultural Variation of Leadership Prototypes Across 22 European Countries, *Journal of Occupational and Organizational Psychology* 73, no. 1 (March 2000), 1-29.

[16] Doris Kearns Goodwin, *Team of Rivals: The Political Genius of Abraham Lincoln.* Simon & Schuster: New York, 2005.

[17] Jim Collins, *Good to Great.* HarperCollins: New York, 2001, 20.

[18] Helen Kennedy, Former Merrill Lynch CEO John Thain resigns from Bank of America amid bonus scandal, *Daily News,* January 22, 2009, http://www.nydailynews.com/money/2009/01/22/2009-01-22_former_merrill_lynch_ceo_john_thain_resi.html.

[19] Justin Martin, Rise of the New Breed, *Chief Executive,* August 1, 2003.

Section V: How Commanding Executives Take Charge

[1] Moe Tkacik, I Like Big Bucks and I Cannot Lie, Slate.com, June 2, 2012, http://www.slate.com/articles/arts/books/2012/06/washington_mutual_wamu_collapse_the_lost_bank_by_kirsten_grind_reviewed_.html.

[2] Steven Pearlstein, review of *The Lost Bank: The Story of Washington Mutual* by Kirsten Grind, *Washington Post,* July 21, 2012, http://www.washingtonpost.com/opinions/the-lost-bank-the-story-of-washington-mutual-by-kirsten-grind/2012/07/20/gJQA-sPoQ0W_story.html.

[3] Ibid.

CHAPTER 17: Git-R-Dun

[1] Larry Bossidy and Ram Charan, *Execution: The Discipline of Getting Things Done.* Crown Publishing: New York, 2002, 125.

[2] Steve Lohr, Slowdown, Brave Multitasker, and Don't Read This in Traffic, *New York Times,* Sunday, March 25, 2007, http://www.nytimes.com/2007/03/25/business/25multi.html?_r=2&pagewanted=all&.

[3] Peter Drucker, *The Effective Executive.* Harper & Row: New York, 1966, 100.

[4] Lohr, Slowdown, Brave Multitasker.

[5] Scott Pelton and Jogi Rippel, *Sink, Float or Swim: Sustainable High-Performance Doesn't Happen by Chance—It Happens by Choice.* Redline Verlag: Munich, 2009.

[6] Cord Cooper, IBD's 10 Secrets to Success, *Investor's Business Daily,* May 9, 2000, A4.

[7] Napoleon Hill, *Think and Grow Rich.* Fawcett Crest Book: New York, 1937.

[8] Anthony deMello, *Awareness: The Perils and Opportunities or Reality.* Doubleday: New York, 1990, 28.

[9] Professor Fran Grace, "Why Meditate? A Summary of the Research," Department of Religious Studies, University of Redlands, 2007, http://www.redlands.edu/academics/meditation-room/5173.aspx.

[10] Patti Milligan,TIGNUM: Institute for Sustainable High Performance, Lack of Sleep Depletes Your Metabolic Function and Nutritional Status, August 7, 2010, http://tignum.com/blog/lack_of_sleep_depletes_your_metabolic_function_and_nutritional_status.

[11] Helton and Ripple, *Sink, Float or Swim.*

[12] American Management Association, *The Keys to Strategy Execution: A Global Study of Current Trends and Future Possibilities,* 2006-2016, http://www.enrollmentmarketing.org/research/AMA-keys-to-strategy-execution.pdf.

[13] Douglas Ready and Jay Conger, Enabling Bold Visions, *MIT Sloan Management Review,* Winter 2008, 70-76.

[14] Kathleen Reardon, Courage as a Skill, *Harvard Business Review,* January 2007, 58-64.

[15] David G. Jensen et al., Individual Variability of Radionuclide Ventriculography in Stable Coronary Artery Disease Patients Over One Year, *Cardiology* 71 (1984), 255-265.

[16] Edmund Morgan, *The Meaning of Independence*. University of Virginia Press: Charlottesville, 1976, 48.

[17] Leading by Feel, *Harvard Business Review,* January 2004, 27-37.

[18] Kathleen Eisenhardt et al., How Management Teams Can Have a Good Fight, *Harvard Business Review,* July-August, 1977, 77-85.

[19] Eisenhardt, How Management Teams Can Have a Good Fight.

[20] Ami Albernaz, He Who Laughs Lives Longest, *Science and Spirit Magazine,* May/June 2007, 9-10.

[21] David Hackett Fischer, *Washington's Crossing*. Oxford University Press: New York, 2004, 291.

CHAPTER 18: When the Future Is Foggy—Camp!

[1] Stephen Ambrose, *Undaunted Courage*. Simon & Schuster: New York, 1996, 231.

[2] L. Gonzalez, *Deep Survival: Who Lives, Who Dies, and Why*. W. W. Norton: New York, 2003.

[3] American Management Association Report, *Leading into the Future,* New York, 2005.

[4] Michael A. Roberto, Why making the decisions the right way is more important than making the right decisions, *IVEY Business Journal,* September/October 2005.

[5] Bart Becht, Building a Company Without Borders, *Harvard Business Review,* April 2010, 103-106.

[6] A. G. Lafley, I Think of My Failures as Gifts, *Harvard Business Review,* April 2011, 86.

[7] Carlin Flora, Foreign Flings, *Psychology Today,* November/December, 2006, 13.

[8] James Flexner, *Washington: The Indispensable Man,* Little, Brown: New York, 1974, 232.

[9] Jonathan Gosling and Henry Mintzberg, The Five Minds of the Manager, *Harvard Business Review,* November 2003, 54-63.

[10] Marianne Lewis, Exploring Paradox: Toward a More Comprehensive Guide, *Academy of Management Review* 35, no. 4 (2000), 760-776.

[11] Richard Lepsinger, How Top-Performing Companies Get Ahead of the Pack and Stay There, *MWorld: Journal of American Management Association,* Summer 2007, 3-4; see also, Melanie Kana and Ken Parry, Identifying Paradox: A Grounded Theory of Leadership in Overcoming Resistance to Change, *The Leadership Quarterly* 15 (2004), 467-491.

[12] Jim Collins and Jerry Porras, *Built to Last: Successful Habits of Visionary Companies.* Harper Business: New York, 1994.

[13] Joe Flower, Building a Visionary Organization Is a Do-It-Yourself Project: A Conversation with James C. Collins, *The Healthcare Forum Journal* 38, no. 5 (September/October 1995), http://www.well.com/~bbear/collins.html.

[14] Robert Quinn, *Beyond Rational Management: Mastering the Paradoxes in Competing Demands of High Performance.* Jossey-Bass: San Francisco, 1988, 91.

[15] Wendy Smith, Andy Binns, and Michael Tushman, Complex Business Models: Managing Strategic Paradoxes Simultaneously, *Long Range Planning* 34 (April-June 2010), 448-462.

[16] Nathan Washburn, Why Profit Shouldn't Be Your Top Goal, *Harvard Business Review,* December 2009, 23.

[17] Derm Barrett, *The Paradox Process: Creative Business Solutions... Where You Least Expect to Find Them.* AMACOM: New York, 1998, 18.

[18] D. Conlon, The Dynamics of Intense Work Groups: A Study of British String Quartets, *Administrative Science Quarterly,* June 1991.

[19] Nic Beech, Contrary Prescriptions: Recognizing Good Practice Tensions in Management, *Organization Studies,* January 2003, 1-28.

[20] Gautam Mukunda, Abraham Lincoln, Poster President for the Great Leadership Paradox, *Fast Company,* September 14, 2012, http://www.fastcompany.com/3001249/abraham-lincoln-poster-president-great-leadership-paradox.

[21] Roger Martin, *The Opposable Mind: How Successful Leaders Win Through Integrative Thinking.* Harvard Business School Press: Boston, 2007, 31.

[22] Smith, Binns, and Tushman, Complex Business Models.

[23] Interview with Ray Stata, *Silicon Genius,* June 28, 2006, http://silicongenesis.stanford.edu/transcripts/stata.htm.

[24] The Pivotal Moment, *The Economist,* December 4, 2010, 84.

[25] Smith, Binns, and Tushman, Complex Business Models.

[26] Javier Espinoza, CEOs Say: What's the Most Important Thing We Must Do Right Now? *Forbes.com,* June 11, 2009.

CHAPTER 19: Marry Head and Heart

[1] Daniel Goleman, Richard Boyatzis, and Annie McKee, Primal Leadership, *Harvard Business Review,* December 2001, 49.

[2] Travis Bradberry and Jean Greaves, Heartless Bosses? *Harvard Business Review,* December 2005.

[3] Daniel Goleman, What Makes a Leader? *Harvard Business Review,* January 2004, 82-91.

[4] G. A. Van Kleef et al., Searing sentiment or cold calculation? The effects of leader emotional displays on team performance depend on follower epistemic motivation, *Academy of Management Journal* 52, no. 3 (2009), 562-580.

[5] Mark C. Crowley, How Washington Mutual Lost Its Heart, *Lead from the Heart* (blog), September 26, 2011, http://markccrowley.com/2011/09/26/how-washington-mutual-lost-its-heart/.

CHAPTER 20: The Jungle Is Neutral

[1] Erica Foldy, Laurie Goldman, and Sonia Ospina, Sensegiving and the role of cognitive shifts in the work of leadership, *The Leadership Quarterly* 19 (2008), 514-529.

[2] Richard Farson and Ralph Keyes, The Failure-Tolerant Leader, *Harvard Business Review,* August 2002, 3-8.

[3] John Antioco, How I Did It, *Harvard Business Review,* April 2011, 39-44.

[4] MIT Inventor of the Week Archive, http://web.mit.edu/invent/iow/frysilver.html.

[5] Nobel Peace Prize 2002, Jimmy Carter, http://www.nobelprize.org/nobel_prizes/peace/laureates/2002/.

[6] Diane Coutu, How Resilience Works, *Harvard Business Review,* May 2002, 46-55.

[7] Jim Collins; *Good to Great.* HarperCollins: New York, 2001, 85.

[8] Dawn Eubanks et al., Criticism and outstanding leadership: An evaluation of leader reactions and critical outcomes, *The Leadership Quarterly* 21 (2010), 365-388.

[9] Kathleen Sutcliffe and Klaus Weber, The High Cost of Accurate Knowledge, *Harvard Business Review,* May 2003, 76.

CHAPTER 21: Quality Decision-Making and Problem-Solving

[1] John W. Payne, James R. Bettman, and Eric J. Johnson, *The Adaptive Decision Maker.* Cambridge University Press: New York, 1993, 2.

[2] John S. Hammond, Ralph L. Keeney, and Howard Raiffa, The Hidden Traps in Decision-Making, *Harvard Business Review,* January 2006, 118-126.

[3] Hammond, Keeney, and Raiffa, Hidden Traps in Decision-Making, 120.

[4] Itamar Simonson and Peter Nye, The Effect of Accountability on Susceptibility to Decision Errors, *Organizational Behavior and Human Decision Processes* 51 (1992), 416-446.

[5] Robert Cross and Susan Brodt, How Assumptions of Consensus Undermine Decision-Making, *MIT Sloan Management Review,* Winter 2001, 86-94.

[6] Information Failures and Organizational Disasters, *MIT Sloan Management Review,* Spring 2005, 8-10.

[7] D. Malhotra, G. Ku, and J. Murnighan, When Winning Is Everything, *Harvard Business Review,* May 2008, 78-86.

APPENDIX A: Desperately Seeking Someone

[1] Doris Kearns Goodwin, *Team of Rivals: The Political Genius of Abraham Lincoln.* Simon & Schuster, New York, 2005, 319.

[2] Patrick J. Kiger, When people practices damage market value, *Workforce Management,* June 3, 2006.

[3] Dan Heath and Chip Heath, Hold the Interview, *Fast Company,* June 2009, 51-52.

[4] George Hollenbeck and Robert Eichinger, *Interviewing Right: How Science Can Sharpen Your Interviewing Accuracy.* Lominger International: Minneapolis, 2006.

[5] Elaine D. Pulakos et al., Individual differences in interviewer ratings: The impact of standardization, consensus discussion, and sampling error on the validity of a structured interview, *Personnel Psychology* 4, no. 1, 1996.

[6] M. M. Lombardo and R. W. Eichinger, High potentials as high learners, *Human Resource Management* 39 (2000), 321-329.

[7] Timothy Tran and Melinda Blackman, The dynamics and validity of the group selection interview, *The Journal of Social Psychology* 4, no. 1, 2006.

APPENDIX B: How to Counsel Underperformers

[1] Avraham Kluger and Angelo DeNisi, Effects of feedback intervention on performance: A historical review, a meta-analysis, and a preliminary feedback intervention theory, *Psychological Bulletin* 119, no. 2 (1996), 254-284.

[2] Human Resource Institute, Nine Keys to Performance Management, *MWorld: Journal of the American Management Association,* Spring 2007, 3.

[3] B. Gaddis, S. Connelly, and M. Mumford, Failure feedback as an affective event: Influences of leader affect on subordinate attitudes and performance, *The Leadership Quarterly* 15 (2004), 663-686.

APPENDIX C: Executive Development: XLM Research at the Top

[1] Creating Sustainable Human Capital Investment, A Final Report of the 2012 APTA Workforce Development Task Force, September 2012, http://www.apta.com/resources/profdev/workforce/Documents/Creating-Sustainable-Human-Capital-Investment.pdf.

[2] Dominic Dodd and Ken Favaro, Managing the Right Tension, *Harvard Business Review,* December 2006, 62-74.

[3] Nic Beech, Contrary Prescriptions: Recognizing Good Practice Tensions in Management, *Organization Studies,* January 2003, 1-28.

Index

A

B

C

D

E

F

J

K

L

M

N

O

P

Q

R

S

T

U

V

W

X

Y

Z

About the Author

DAVE JENSEN is a recognized leadership consultant, coach and speaker. As president of his own management and organizational development firm, he helps executives stretch, instead of snap, when they're pulled by their numerous conflicting and contradictory goals.

Dave combines his past leadership experience (at Siemens and UCLA) with his academic expertise (at UCSD and Emory University) to educate executives and engage audiences. Clients who have benefited from his programs include: *American Public Transit Association, Boeing, The Center for Creative Leadership, Canadian Urban Transit Association, Federal Reserve Bank, Qualcomm, San Mateo County Transit District, TSYS, Wells Fargo Bank, Xerox, and Zig Ziglar.*

A few of Dave's most requested keynotes and presentations include:

- **MANAGING THE EXECUTIVE'S PARADOX**
  How to Stretch When You're Pulled by Opposing Demands
- **MAKING CHANGE STICK**
  How to Lead Change by Managing Stability
- **DEMOLISHING INTERNAL SILOS & TURF WARS**
  How to Increase Cross-Functional Collaboration
- **USE IT; DON'T LOSE IT**
  How to Implement the Best Ideas from ANY Meeting

Contact Information:

To discuss how Dave can customize these programs to suit your specific needs or help you operationalize any of the innovative ideas in this book, contact Dave:

http://DaveJensenOnLeadership.com/
3518 Barry Ave., Los Angeles, California 90066
(310)397-6686

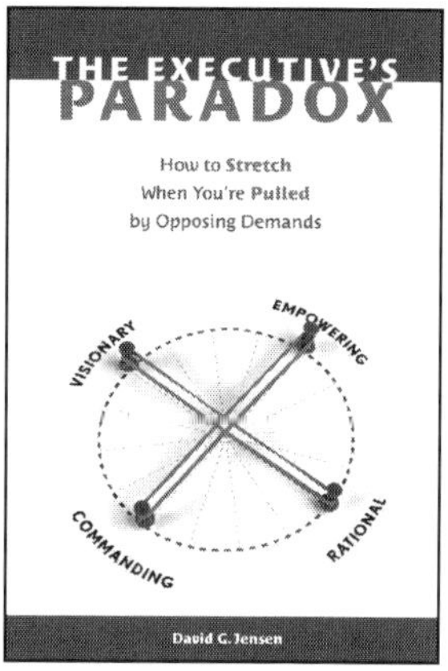

Quick Order Form

FAX ORDERS: (310) 397-6607
TELEPHONE ORDERS: (310) 397-6686
ONLINE ORDERS: http://www.createspace.com/4400459
OR http://www.amazon.com

	Quantity	Price	Total
The Executive's Paradox: How to Stretch When You're Pulled by Opposing Demands (Call for discount pricing if ordering more than 10 books)	______	x $24.95 =	______
Sales tax: Please add 9% sales tax for products shipped in California			______
Shipping: Add $4.00 for the first book, $2.00 for each additional book			______
Total (including shipping and sales tax)			______

I understand that I may return any book for a full refund—for any reason, no questions asked.

Name ____

Address ____

City ______________________ State __________ Zip __________

Telephone ______________________ Email address ______________________

PAYMENT:

☐ MasterCard ☐ Visa ☐ AMEX ☐ Check (Payable to David Jensen)

Mail completed form to: 3518 Barry Ave., Los Angeles, California 90066

Card Number ______________________________________

Names on Card ______________________ Exp. date __________

PLEASE SEND MORE FREE INFORMATION ON:

☐ Speaking/presentations ☐ Dave's Raves Newsletter ☐ Consulting

5819689R10195

Made in the USA
San Bernardino, CA
22 November 2013